The Hermit of Cat Island

The Hermit of Cat Island

The Life of Fra Jerome Hawes

BY PETER F. ANSON

P. J. KENEDY & SONS
New York

TO
CHARLES S. SELBY–HALL
A close friend of the Hermit of Cat Island
for more than a century

Foreword

MY FRIENDSHIP with the Hermit of Cat Island—Monsignor John C. Hawes—began in 1939 when he first wrote me to congratulate me on the publication of *The Benedictines of Caldey* which, he explained, had aroused many long-buried memories. I had been familiar with the career of Fra Jerome, as he now called himself, since I had first heard of him in 1911 as an Anglican Franciscan. I was aware of his successful architectural ventures, his conversion to Catholicism and subsequent work as a missionary in Australia. Now I learned that only a few weeks before his letter arrived he had become a Franciscan tertiary hermit in the Bahamas. From this time we corresponded regularly and frequently, Father Jerome enlivening his vivid and detailed impressions of people and places with amusing sketches or rough drawings of the churches he was designing.

When in 1945 he asked me to write his biography, explaining that his bishop in Australia had put him under obedience to tell the story of how, by a long series of strange events, he had received what he believed to be a clear call to end his days as a hermit in the Bahamas, I replied that I would be delighted to prepare his story for publication.

Three months later two large parcels, containing diaries, notebooks, chapters of an unfinished autobiography and much miscellaneous material, arrived, followed by a third parcel of drawings and photographs of his architectural work at all stages of his career. Finally came a bundle of letters which he had written to Mr. Charles S. Selby-Hall, some of them dating back to the days when they were both Church of England clergymen.

I immediately set to work fitting together the bits and pieces of his extraordinary career, and by the time the biography had been brought up to 1948 I felt that I knew intimately the Hermit of Cat Island, even though we had never met face to face. But then Father Jerome wrote me that the book must not be published before his death, so reluctantly I put aside the manuscript. It was not until eight years later, after receiving word from Bishop Leonard Hagarty, O.S.B., Vicar Apostolic of the Bahamas, of the death of Father Jerome at Miami Beach, Florida, on June 26, 1956, that I was able again to take up this work. Now, twelve years later, it has been revised and put into its final shape.

In the midst of a material civilization visibly crumbling away before us, the story of a man such as Father Jerome going apart into solitude bears a silent witness to the reality of the unseen, to the lordship of mind over matter, to the supremacy in man of the spirit. And, quite apart from the fascinating content of his life story, it has a real historical and spiritual importance.

Father Jerome was one of the very few Catholics in modern times who embraced the hermit's vocation. Like Charles de Foucauld, his French counterpart, he was inspired by the solitary ideal. And, like him, he was unable completely to achieve his object because circumstances presented active work for souls which could not be refused.

Just because of his God-given temperament, it would have been almost impossible for John Cyril Hawes to have become one of those solitaries who, valuing solitude as their most cherished possession, take good care that it is not discovered. Their one object is to efface themselves so that they are not recognized for what they are. They realize that the surest way to hide themselves is to live in the midst of the crowd where they are unknown, unthought of and unremarked. They are always trying to make themselves inconspicuous—to put people off the scent—so that their lives can be completely hidden with God.

Had Charles de Foucauld remained in his log hut in the garden of the Poor Clare Convent at Nazareth, where he worked as a servant, he might have been forgotten until after his death. But Abbé Huvelin, his spiritual director, felt that that was not De Foucauld's true vocation and so, having been ordained priest, he ended up as a hermit-missionary in the Sahara from where his fame spread throughout the world. The case of John Cyril Hawes is almost similar. Like De Foucauld, he really wanted to become an absolute solitary, but the ecclesiastical authorities were sure that his talents must not be wasted. As a result, the last years of his life were almost as active as those spent as a missionary in Australia.

But if Father Jerome did not entirely succeed in achieving complete solitude on his isolated island, if his eremitical life was constantly interrupted by demands on his architectural talents, by necessary ministrations to the native Bahamians, and by a steady stream of visitors, nevertheless the means which he chose to hide himself were in keeping with his basically artistic nature. A shrewder or more worldly-minded man might have guessed that to build a hermitage on the highest hill in an archipelago frequented by tourists would inevitably lead to his solitude being invaded. But who can deny that his vocation may have been to remind the modern world of the value of the solitary life—that the Hermit of Cat Island was meant to serve as a living sermon, stressing something so many of us have forgotten? For a Christian hermit is not running *away* from something; he is running *after* something. And that something is God.

PETER F. ANSON

Contents

The Hermit of Cat Island

1.

The Young Seeker [1876–1901]

"WELL! That's the funniest little baby I've ever seen—just like an old bishop."

This comment by the grandmother of John Cyril Hawes is all that he himself tells us of the circumstances of his birth on September 7, 1876, except for the fact of his baptism a few weeks later at St. John's Church.

John was the third son of a London attorney who lived in Richmond, Surrey, now a part of London, but then still a small town in the country. It was filled with stately Georgian and Queen Anne mansions, their private gardens and grounds enclosed by long stretches of high red-brick walls. Pair-horse carriages driven by gold-laced coachmen and attended by flunkies rolled along the quiet tree-shaded roads while beyond the town lay fields and market gardens.

The Hawes lived in a house in Paradise Road, where, in the Victorian tradition, the family formed a close-knit unit. As soon as John was old enough his two older brothers, Ted and Robert, accepted him as an equal and drew him into their games. The three boys sallied forth to sail their boats on a pond in Richmond Park, or maneuvered their indoor fleet across a table at home, naming their six-inch-long battleships after vessels in the Royal Navy. Once a year they were taken to a Christmas pantomime at the Drury Lane Theatre, and Mrs. Hawes annually entertained her sons' friends at a Christmas children's party with games, supper and dancing. John hated the dancing, for it made him giddy, but he submitted to it for the sake of being allowed to go to similar gatherings at the homes of other boys and girls.

In the summer holidays the family went boating on the Thames, and every August established themselves in a quiet resort on the coast of Sussex, such as Bognor or Littlehampton. Then there were musical evenings at home with Mrs. Hawes accompanying on the piano while Ted played the violin and Bob the flageolet or the cornet.

Like most middle-class English families of the period, the Hawes were devout Christians. Mr. Hawes, who belonged to the evangelical section of the Church of England, held strong "Protestant" views so uncompromising that he resigned his office of churchwarden after a pair of candlesticks had been placed on the communion table of St. John's. No excuse ever served, recalled John, to prevent his father from taking his children to church on Sunday morning. And on weekdays he read family prayers morning and evening while the household knelt at chairs turned to the walls around the dining room—a custom prevalent in most Victorian families.

Mrs. Hawes had her special devotions at midday, and during their holidays her sons joined her. Each of them read in turn from the *Book of Common Prayer* the verses of the psalms for the particular day of the month. Then their mother read the two appointed lessons from the Old and New Testament, followed by the *Te Deum* and the Collect for the preceding Sunday. John never found these devotions tiresome because his mother varied them with explanations and commentaries.

John's "Franciscanism" developed early, so he jokingly wrote, when he became attached to his cousin's sturdy bull terrier, Phiz, an affectionate dog who expressed his fondness for the small boy by licking his face all over and joining in the games. And it was on his fifth birthday, when a large box of toy bricks was given to him, that he found his vocation. "There were blocks and beams of various lengths, curved

"My Fifth Birthday"

arch pieces, round pillars and triangular spandrils; making it possible to build houses, bridges, harbors, forts or towers. Henceforth I was an architect, engineer and builder." He adds that he now became interested in drawing as well, and constantly bothered his father for paper and pencils.

At the age of six John's formal education began. He was sent to a small private day school, and three years later to a preparatory boarding school in Sussex Square, Brighton. There his clearest memory was of Sunday mornings when the eighteen little boys at the school settled themselves in the pews at St. George's Proprietary Chapel, where the minister preached in a black Geneva gown, and the service was terribly dreary. This no doubt served to set his inclinations in the direction of High Church rites, an enthusiasm that developed further when, at thirteen, he entered King's School, Canterbury.

There, he wrote, "I came under the influence of the past—the great medieval cathedral welcomed and sheltered me under its wings. I drank the cup of tradition. The very stones of the glorious old temple of God cried out in testimony of its Catholic past." Stirred as he was by Canterbury, young Hawes reveled in history, particularly in its architectural manifestations, and further solidified his professional leanings by capturing the first prize for drawing.

At King's School John did not confine himself altogether to his studies, but threw himself happily into sports, an important part of English public-school life. His choice was football and he soon found himself playing halfback in the third "Rugger" fifteen. "We played in wet and mud—even when it was snowing—but woe betide anybody who was discovered wearing a singlet or shirt under his football jersey. Everything would be torn to shreds off his back for being a 'molly-coddle.' I am thankful I was brought up in that school of hardness, but I was a very quiet and unaggressive boy."

One of John's favorite preoccupations was to wander around Canterbury Cathedral, and soon he became familiar with every nook and cranny of the great structure. He reinforced his firsthand knowledge with many hours spent in the library poring over related books, and here he discovered the Rule of St. Benedict. This so impressed him that he says, "Expressive of my admiration, I got a block of wood and carved with my penknife a small eight-inch statue of the Patriarch of western monasticism—my first idolatrous graven image!"

It was at about this time that John made friends with a group of boys who were High Church, among whom was H. J. Fynes-Clinton, later to become one of the leaders of the Papalist party in the Church of England. With them, for the first time, he attended the sung Eucharist at the ancient church of St. Peter.

The excitement of these new experiences was somewhat dampened by his instruction for the Anglican rite of Confirmation. " . . . Concerning the sacrament of the Holy Communion the nearest we got to an explanation of the Real Presence was the quotation of an ambiguous verse (attributed to Queen Elizabeth) : 'Christ was the Word and spake it; that I believe and take it.' I longed for something more Catholic, but had not the courage to ask: 'Please sir, *what* does the *Church* believe and teach that the Word makes it?' " The Bishop of Dover who confirmed the boys reminded them that "the Church of England accepts only two sacraments and that the other five . . . are nothing more than a corrupt following of the Apostles."

In spite of such evangelical warnings, John found himself more and more attracted by High Church services and began to dream of becoming an Anglo-Catholic clergyman, but when his father proposed that he take up architecture as a profession, he lacked the courage to confess his preference. John therefore found himself at sixteen articled to the firm of Edmerton and Gabriel, whose offices were situated in the very heart of London. He might have enjoyed the work except that it chiefly consisted of plans for banks and schools, whereas John's heart was in church design.

For five years he endured this drudgery, at the same time attending evening classes at the Royal Institute of British Architects and the Architectural Association schools. He also enrolled in handicrafts classes at the London Polytechnic and the London County Council Arts and Crafts School where he learned how to carve in stone and wood and acquired a practical knowledge of the use of building materials and the intricacies of plumbing.

John's very thorough grounding in architectural theory and practice was established by some of the best teachers of the time. Among them were William R. Lethaby, a former disciple of John Ruskin and a founder of the Art Workers' Guild and the Arts and Crafts Society, who was principal of the London County Council school; and E. S. Prior, well known for his writings on medieval architecture. John was further influenced by the work of John D. Sedding, an architect who by contemporary standards was almost revolutionary. He was particularly inspired by Sedding's design of Holy Trinity Church, Sloane Street, which blended Renaissance details with Gothic, and this architectural style had a lifelong influence on the young man whose taste was always eclectic.

But it was not only ecclesiastical architecture that fascinated John Hawes at this time; he became just as interested in the externals of worship. He recalled that "the then countless City churches were always open during London's busy midday luncheon hour. Through the zeal and energy of the High Church party, the Lenten season was made a real mission time, with daily services in many churches during the luncheon interval. Office clerks . . . gulped down a few sandwiches in order to get in early to services, and the little medieval Gothic Church of St. Ethelburga, Bishopgate, was the favorite place of pilgrimage for Anglo-Catholics. Here in Lent there was a daily midday Mass, and on saints' days a solemn *Te Deum* was sung after it, with the celebrant in a cope, and "enough incense to choke you!" John became more and more familiar with the Anglo-Catholic world of the eighteen nineties, although he does not seem to have penetrated into its underworld. He remained on the threshold, as it were, perhaps because he was too shy to indulge in any reckless adventures.

But he was bold enough to wander into several "Roman" churches, including the imposing Renaissance church of the Oratorian Fathers. Here—to quote his own words—"Light suddenly came to me that the Catholic and Roman Church must be the True Church. I knew I ought to become a Catholic. But what a blow this step would be to my dear parents —what a terrible separation. I trembled. Then I reflected in my ignorance that, if I became a Catholic, I would have to believe that my father and mother would be damned—impossible! To strengthen my resistance to God's grace, I fell back on the quibbling and sophisticated arguments of *The Church Times*."

It is difficult for the average person to understand the evolutionary process which takes place before an ordinary Anglican becomes a full-fledged Anglo-Catholic. Subconsciously the individual, especially in the case of a youth, feels the thrill of doing something wrong. In the case of John Hawes, who was essentially of an emotional temperament, his attraction to Catholicism was romantic rather than intellectual. It is permissible to wonder whether this "light" that he saw in the London Oratory was anything more than the quite-understandable glamor of the gorgeous baroque architecture, combined with the elusive smell of incense.

Shortly after this he summoned up his courage to make his first confession in the Church of St. Mary Magdalene, Munster Square, at that date one of the most popular Anglo-Catholic strongholds in London. For a few months he remained fervent. Then he became careless, and, apparently not yet considering that it was a mortal sin for him to miss Mass on Sundays, often went off cycling, never entering a church at all. His religious emotionalism is shown by the fact that after a few of these brief spells of paganism he grew pious again; so pious, that he wanted to abandon the architectural profession and become a clergyman. He saw himself as a young priest vested in cassock, lace-trimmed cotta and biretta, or as the celebrant at High Mass wearing a splendid embroidered chasuble. Then he thought of becoming a missionary, and developed a special interest in the Universities Mission to

Central Africa, whose services were reputed to be more "Catholic" than almost any of those in England. But how could he leave his home and relations, not to mention all the ecclesiastical attractions of England—its beautiful churches and cathedrals, and the increasing fascination of the ritualistic movement in the Anglican Church?

An Easter vacation tour in Normandy with one of his brothers, then an undergraduate at Trinity College, Oxford, helped to make John even more enthusiastic about the externals of the Catholic religion. Among the towns they visited was Caen, where, so he tells us, he "felt raised to Heaven. It was all so different from England. I went into several churches, richly dim and mysterious, with twinkling lights of candles glimmering here and there where priests were offering the Holy Sacrifice in little side chapels—no glare of daylight, no stiff rows of long pews, but *prie-dieus* and chairs, higgledy-piggledy anyhow. Worshipers knelt at prayer in reverent silence, nor was there any loud mouthing at them by the minister, of long prayers. Only the quiet 'blessed mutter of the Mass.' The very atmosphere moved to worship, to bring one to one's knees. And all the churches were the same. You did not have to worry about exercising care to choose one that was 'Low' or 'High.' "

Two years later John and his brother made a longer tour in France on a tandem bicycle. Starting at Le Havre, they visited Jumièges, Caudebec, Rouen, Chartres, Bourges, and so on into the mountainous country of Auvergne, reaching Le Puy, which John described as "the most marvelous and fairy-like of old cities." The tour ended with Paris, Beauvais and Amiens. The effect on him of the glories of French ecclesiastical architecture seems to have been overwhelming; not so much because of the buildings themselves, but because of their Catholic atmosphere.

On September 7, 1897, John kept his twenty-first birthday,

and became his own master. Immediately he started to work on his own at Bognor in Sussex. He designed several houses and cottages, as well as a curious-looking building named "The White Tower," which was commented on favorably and illustrated by a drawing in *The British Architect*. It seems that his enthusiasm for Anglo-Catholicism suffered a partial eclipse, and for the whole of one summer all his spare time, including Sundays, was spent in sailing his first boat, in which he sometimes ventured as far as the Isle of Wight.

In February 1898 he started work on a model intended for the Royal Academy Exhibition. It took the form of an imaginary church set among the mountainous Cumberland Fells. He tells us that every little detail, inside and out, was made to scale with meticulous care, including the pulpit, rails, and altar, with its six candlesticks, backed by a painted triptych of the Crucifixion. The model was accepted and— to quote his own words—"it brought me recognition, publicity and praise, also my first commission to build a church, at Gunnerton in Northumberland."

It was shortly after this that he experienced what he always regarded as a genuine religious conversion. It followed a brief but harmless flirtation with a beautiful girl of about his own age, during which he records he "walked on air, intoxicated with dreams and visions."

One evening he happened to be in London, about to take the train back to Bognor. He was walking down Regent Street, and turned into the Church of St. Thomas, where a festival service of some sort was going on. His own words reveal his emotional reaction clearly.

"I recollect standing at the back of the crowded church, and the stirring roll of the Gregorian chants as the whole congregation joined in the psalms of Evensong to the thunder of the organ. Then came the Magnificat, with copes and much incense. And now a white-haired clergyman with a strong square face entered the pulpit—Canon Rhodes-Bristow of Lewisham—never shall I forget his name! God bless him! In earnest, convincing tones he spoke of Vocation—of the world and its allurements and of the purpose of Life. The Lord said to Abraham, get thee forth out of thy country, and from thy kindred and out of thy father's house and go into the land that I shall show thee. And how Elijah the Prophet called Elisha when he was in the midst of plowing and Elisha left his plow and oxen in the field and followed Elijah. And how St. Francis Xavier heard and pondered the words: 'What shall it profit a man if he gain the whole world and lose his own soul?'

"I had that night seen the veil lifted back. I had seen *The Vision*. I went home in deep thought. Something *terrible* had crossed my path. 'It is hard for thee to kick against the pricks,' and to whom it applies it is absolute—it must be responded to without any conditions. . . . 'If thou wilt be perfect, go sell all that thou hast and give to the poor and come, follow Me.' I couldn't! I couldn't! I was troubled. It became impossible for me to apply myself to my work—the work that I loved so much.

"And then suddenly Our Lord touched me with His grace —He called me literally from the instruments of my work. I remember I rose up from my stool before the drawing board with the T square in my hand, and I laid it down in happy surrender. Unspeakable joy flooded my soul. Lord, I will follow Thee, whithersoever Thou goest. The flood of that joy carried me on so that I thought sacrifice is no sacrifice at all because it is such a joy to offer it. Ignorant of the spiritual life, I did not understand that we cannot build everlasting tabernacles on the holy mountain—that the joy of Tabor is only to fortify us against the going up to Jerusalem. I did not realize what dark days were to follow, and that when the Master says, 'Follow Me,' it will be through the Garden of Gethsemane."

John wasted no time. The following morning he took the train from Bognor to London, went straight to the office of the Universities Mission to Central Africa, and demanded an immediate interview with the secretary. It was a bitter blow to be told that what the Mission wanted most was lay workers, but he accepted this as the will of God, even if he now longed to become an Anglo-Catholic priest. The secretary said he would arrange for an examination by the medical board as soon as possible, and inform John of the date fixed.

His parents, naturally, were horrified when he told them that he was making plans to go to Central Africa. They could not understand his sudden religious conversion, and pointed out that it was ridiculous for him to throw over the career for which he had been trained without serious reflection on the consequences. To their intense relief the doctors refused to pass their son, saying that his heart would not stand up to the tropical climate. From the parents' point of view a major crisis had been averted, but to John it was a bitter disappointment. All he could do was to wait and pray for further guidance.

Three years before John's religious conversion the intellectual world had been taken by storm by the publication of Paul Sabatier's *Vie de S. François d'Assise* which almost simultaneously was placed on the Index and crowned by the French Academy. This remarkable biography was soon translated into most European languages, including English. As Dr. John R. H. Moorman remarks: "Immediately the printing presses of Europe began to hum with Franciscan literature of all kinds and of widely different value. Works appeared with bewildering rapidity." [1] This book, written by a French Protestant theologian, certainly gave the greatest impulse to the modern study of Franciscan history as has been ad-

[1] John R. H. Moorman, *The Sources for the Life of St. Francis of Assisi* (Manchester, 1930), p. 9.

mitted by the late Archbishop Paschal Robinson, O.F.M.

In England this sudden "rediscovery" of St. Francis was closely associated with the Christian Socialist movement, one of whose leaders was an Anglo-Catholic clergyman, the Reverend James G. Adderley, a son of Lord Norton. In 1893 he had published a little book with a strongly Franciscan flavor entitled *Stephen Remarx—The Story of a Venture in Ethics,* an effort in fictional form to popularize Christian Socialist principles.

The following year Adderley with a few like-minded young clergymen inaugurated a brotherhood, the Society of Divine Compassion, whose members sought to live a mortified life, sharing the privation and discomfort of those who have no choice but to be poor. Adderley, however, left the Society within three years and it was while he was trying to convert a Mayfair congregation to Christian Socialism that John Hawes's path crossed his. It was Adderley who pressed upon John Sabatier's *St. Francis of Assisi,* which he devoured from cover to cover in one evening. Thus occurred John's first meeting with the Little Poor Man who from that moment became his spiritual inspiration, the saint whom he longed to imitate in the most literal manner possible.

Fired by his new enthusiasm, John scoured the bookshops for Franciscan publications. His first find was Canon Knox Little's biography of the saint written from an Anglican point of view. Then how could he resist the olive-green, leather-bound *Little Flowers of St. Francis*—it fit into his coat pocket! Equally tempting was the newly-published translation of *The Mirror of Perfection,* and in a short time he would have Lina Duff Gordon's *The Story of Assisi,* which must have sparked his interest in Franciscan architecture. It is a foregone conclusion that John read *The Commonwealth,* the monthly magazine of the Christian Social Union, whose articles based on Franciscan ideals pointed out how the working classes could be saved from sweated labor and exploitation.

Little by little the new discoveries that John was making drew him close to the Roman Catholic Church. Then one day came a letter signed ✠Wilfred, Bishop Hornby. The unknown writer explained that he had greatly admired the model church exhibited at the Royal Academy and wanted John Hawes to design for him a country church in Northumberland. Would the young architect meet him at his London club and talk over the matter?

The invitation threw John into a quandary. He felt that it was a subtle form of temptation and, as he confesses, that the Bishop was the devil in disguise! His first impulse was not to reply, but after waiting a week he consulted his father, who told him not to be stupid. The next morning he went up to London to lunch with Bishop Hornby, who, he discovered, was the former bishop of Nyasaland. When John said goodby to him a short time later he had committed himself to prepare plans for the Bishop's north-country church.

For the rest of his life John was to suffer from scruples at the wisdom of accepting this commission. Looking back long afterward he said that it is probable that he might have become a Catholic there and then had he not fallen into temptation. He felt that if he had entered the Friars Minor or the Capuchins his spiritual life would have been developed in submission of his will to authority and wise guidance, although his intimates, knowing his strong individualistic temperament, were inclined to doubt his ability to endure the novitiate. Nevertheless, John remained convinced that had he been faithful to the resolution made after his spiritual awakening, not only he but his parents would have found their way into the Catholic Church. In his own words, "I fell into the lower place, and tried to serve God there by putting all my heart and soul into the designing of that little church in Northumberland. But alas! Once he who has put his hand to God's plow looks back he falls, not once but many times. These forty years past how have I fallen from ideals. From one lower place to another still lower. . . . "

But in spite of his scruples, like St. Francis answering Christ's call to " . . . repair my church which is wholly a ruin," John set out not to rebuild a ruined church but to design a new one. He said good-by to his parents and moved to the pleasant Upper Tyneside village of Chollerton. There in Bishop Hornby's comfortable vicarage John settled down to work. On Sundays he acted as a "lay reader," and conducted evening services in the neighboring village of Colwell. He visited the scattered farms and cottages, and taught the catechism in the village school at Chollerton. To all intents and purposes he acted as the Bishop's unordained curate.

Once again he began to dream of becoming a Franciscan, but for the moment all he could achieve in this direction was to wear a homespun brown suit as an outward sign of his spiritual ideals. At first he was satisfied to make his long expeditions on foot, but later he was unable to resist the temptation to borrow a horse and ride over the countryside. He refused, however, to join in the killing of "Brother Fox" for sport—this was absolutely vetoed by his natural and Franciscan love of animals.

It was while he was living with Bishop Hornby at Chollerton that John had his first real contact with Catholics. Within a mile or two of the village was Swinburn Castle, the seat of the ancient Catholic family of Riddell, with its own chapel and resident priest. Many of the farmers and cottagers in this remote northern part of England had clung to the "Old Religion" after the Reformation, and it was a shock to John to find "Romanism" so very much alive in rural England.

Although like most Anglo-Catholics of his generation John no doubt would have argued that the Catholics were "dissenters" and not part of the *true* Church of the country, he was dangerously attracted both to the worship and the chapel of the "schismatics." With his customary enthusiasm he set about designing his church at Gunnerton with the idea of making it approximate as closely as possible a Catholic place of worship. This first church of John Hawes achieved a charm and originality equal to any other design of the period, and established him firmly in one of his two parallel careers. And slowly but insistently Bishop Hornby was urging him toward the second.

2.

The Poor Man's Follower [1901–1908]

By this time John had determined to model his life on that of St. Francis of Assisi, and in imitation of Francis, who out of humility had refused to become a priest, had set his will against taking holy orders. Bishop Hornby, however, was sure that John had a vocation to the priesthood and used all his powers of persuasion to induce the younger man to study for Anglican orders. Finally John gave way and entered the Lincoln Theological College in 1901.

At this time advanced liberal views were being expressed in some English theological circles, and although these filtered through to the Lincoln students by way of commentaries by nonconformist divines, the spiritual atmosphere of the college was not entirely congenial to a student who regarded himself a "Catholic." The head of the diocese, Bishop King, was "High" in his opinions, but Dean Wickham, who ruled over the cathedral, was "Broad," and he and his canons formed a compact and uniform social set that governed the thinking of the school.

This, together with his discovery that the college buildings were of a nonecclesiastical cast, caused some dissatisfaction to John, but he set about remedying the latter by securing the permission of the Warden to affix a six-foot wooden

18

cross in the central pediment at roof level. His fellow students helped him adorn the cross with gold leaf so that it could be seen glittering in the sunlight above the lower parts of the city.

Then he discovered a beautiful old church in the village of Nettleton five miles north of Lincoln where, on a Sunday morning, he and his friend Charles Selby-Hall used sometimes to attend the sung Eucharist which was more to their taste than the choral matins in the cathedral. This and his friendship with Selby-Hall helped to make up for the lack of Anglo-Catholicism at Lincoln.

John's dreams of entering a religious community began to crystallize during his early months at Lincoln, and he not only explored the possibilities of existing Anglican groups, but designed a Gothic gatehouse for Alton Abbey, Hampshire, and drew up plans for a stately abbey church. In addition he came upon an article in *The Church Review* which described the establishment of the Anglican Benedictine community in Yorkshire, a community founded in 1896 by a twenty-year-old medical student, Benjamin Fearnley Carlyle, who took the religious name Aelred. Dynamic, imaginative and irrepressibly optimistic, Carlyle visualized Anglican Benedictine abbeys scattered up and down the length of England. But things had not turned out exactly as he had expected. After six years his only community numbered but a dozen monks, and although he himself had managed to obtain the approval of Dr. Frederick Temple, the Archbishop of Canterbury, for his election as abbot, neither Aelred nor any of his monks had found an Anglican bishop willing to ordain them.

In spite of these drawbacks Painsthorpe Abbey represented a monastic asceticism that quite swept John Hawes off his feet. He wrote at once to the Abbot and having received permission from the warden to spend a weekend at the monas-

tery he set off to visit Painsthorpe. "Everything surpassed my
expectations," he wrote. " . . . I longed to join the community
then and there for the sake of the monastic life, but felt I
could not because for me the religious life meant definitely
the Franciscan form of it and nothing else."

Nevertheless, the outwardly Catholic ethos of Painsthorpe
delighted John. Here, for the first time, he assisted at the
Divine Office chanted in Latin. The sight of tonsured monks
in choir dressed in white habits and black scapulars, with
black cowls or cloaks, raised him to the seventh heaven. Abbot
Aelred was equally delighted with John and tried to divert
him from what he considered his quixotic idea of founding
a Franciscan brotherhood in the Church of England. He
proposed that John enter the Benedictine novitiate as soon
as he received Anglican orders, thereby assuring the abbey of
the services of an ordained clergyman.

In spite of Abbot Aelred's dominant personality and evident fascination, Hawes managed to withstand his persuasive
powers. Of this encounter he says, "He saw that I was of a
yielding, subjective nature, easily influenced and handled.
But . . . the Abbot did not reckon how absolutely unyielding
and uncompromising I could be on a matter of real principle,
so we never got down to definite conclusions."

There was one immediate result achieved, however. The
Abbot persuaded his architect guest to draw up plans for a
chapel for which the foundation stone was laid in June 1902,
and which was opened on November 11 of the same year.

In the meantime John returned to Lincoln to continue
his studies, but even though he had not taken the risk of com-
mitting himself to the Abbot of Painsthorpe, his contact with
the Benedictines had aroused new discontent with typical
Anglicanism. As the time drew near for his ordination to the
diaconate he began to wonder if he would find a church with
services sufficiently "Catholic." Bishop Hornby came to his

rescue by giving him a letter to the Reverend Vincent Eyre, vicar of the Church of the Holy Redeemer, Clerkenwell— the stronghold of "extreme" Anglo-Catholicism in London. Father Eyre agreed to take on John as his junior curate as soon as he was raised to the diaconate, and Dr. Winnington Ingram, the Bishop of London, accepted him for his diocese.

John with sixty other young men who were to be ordained retired to Fulham Palace for the short retreat that followed their two years at Lincoln. There the Thirty-Nine Articles were "administered to the ordinands like a dose of castor oil." Poor John, who at no time in his life was a casuist and never was given to equivocation, hardly knew what to do when it came to giving his assent to the Articles. He tells us that "when we raised our hands in Fulham Palace Library and solemnly swore before the bishop our assent to the Thirty-Nine Articles of religion, I felt a sudden trembling— it was the worst thing I had ever done in my life. At Lincoln I had read privately many books on Catholic doctrine adopted by the extreme Anglo-Catholic theologians, which argued how the blunt and obvious Protestant statements of the Articles and 'black rubrics' could be interpreted in a Catholic sense. It seemed that it was not really the sacrifice of the Mass that one of the Articles condemned in plain words as a blasphemous fable and dangerous deceit, but the sacrifices of Masses offered as fresh and numerical sacrifices independent of Calvary. It struck me then as a most lamentable and dishonest piece of special pleading. The *real* meaning seemed to be proved by the destruction of altars at the Reformation, and the rivers of blood poured out by 'seminary priests.' My dear Mother, in her simple evangelical faith, had inculcated me with a deep and sacred reverence for *literal* truth, and here I was being unfaithful to her teaching."

Once the Reverend John Hawes found himself the junior curate of the Holy Redeemer, Clerkenwell, however, it was easy for him to forget the more Protestant aspects of Anglicanism. This church was something quite unique when opened in 1888. John D. Sedding had designed a gorgeous Renaissance interior, with the high altar standing beneath an imposing baldachino, which was a fairly close replica of that in Brunelleschi's Church of Santo Spirito at Florence. So Italian was the interior that Walter Pater said that it made him think of how some of the Renaissance churches in Venice must have looked when they were fresh and clean. The setting and *décor* were completely "ultramontane." A visitor would have found it hard to believe that he was in a place of worship belonging to the Church of England, what with the three altars, businesslike confessionals, stations of the cross, statues, vestments and incense. The new curate must have been thankful to Bishop Hornby for having found him an environment which was so utterly and uncompromisingly "Catholic" in externals. Moreover, the immediate surroundings of the church provided exactly the outlet he sought for the fulfillment of his Franciscan ideals.

Fifty years ago the slums of Clerkenwell were as bad as any in London. Squalor, disease, unemployment and destitution were commonplaces. At times, in desperation, the tenants would smash up the doors of the rooms for firewood and then disappear the night before the rent collector was due. John found it easy to share the poverty of the third of the parish allotted to him. He did not live in the clergy house, but in a little room, high up the stone stairs of a gloomy so-called "model dwelling" off Farringdon Street. From there he went out to work among the poor families of the district, more than once, so he recalls, sitting up all night by a sickbed. He gave away everything he could spare, and that was not much, for he had refused to accept the salary of one hundred fifty pounds offered him by Father Eyre, saying that he could manage quite well on ninety pounds a year. During

Lent he made his breakfast off black coffee and hard ship's biscuit, often suffering acute indigestion from hungrily devouring a surfeit of lentils at the one full meal of the day. He ate no meat from Ash Wednesday through Holy Saturday.

The spiritual atmosphere of the clergy house would have struck any Catholic visitor as being very peculiar. The vicar belonged to one of the old English Catholic families which had held on to the Faith for nearly two centuries, and then lapsed into Anglicanism. Nevertheless, he had an intense love and veneration for the Pope and everything Roman, and longed to be in communion with the Holy See. John always maintained in after years that it was his vicar who taught him the foundation principles of Catholicism, above all the necessity of submission to authority. It was in this respect that Father Eyre differed from some of his fellow Anglo-Catholic clergy, who demonstrated their "Catholicism" by defying the orders of their bishop on every possible occasion; maintaining that he had no binding power because Anglican bishops were merely state-appointed officials!

Father Eyre, in deference to the Bishop of London, had already removed the sixth station of the cross, because St. Veronica does not appear in the Gospels, given up processional lights and the ceremonial use of incense, and finally removed the confessionals and substituted curtained prayer desks. When his new curate expostulated with him about pandering to Protestant prejudices, he remarked that no amount of external ritual and ceremonial could make the Church of England Catholic! Indeed, the vicar of the Holy Redeemer was looked upon as not being quite sound by some of his more aggressive clerical brethren. All the same, the Protestant Truth Society and the Church Association kept a close watch on the "goings on" in Clerkenwell, and from time to time reported illegalities to the Bishop of London.

At the end of his first year at Holy Redeemer, John was

raised to the Anglican priesthood. Apparently he had no doubts about the validity of his Orders, and derived intense spiritual satisfaction from "saying Mass." Then in 1904 Father Eyre had to resign his living for reasons of health, and Bishop Hornby persuaded him to take over the parish of Chollerton in Northumberland. John Hawes's new vicar was the Reverend Herbert Frith, who came to the Holy Redeemer from St. Mary Magdalen's, Munster Square. He was another extreme Anglo-Catholic, so there was no alteration in the services.

Within the parish was situated the motherhouse of the Sisters of Bethany, a community founded in 1866. One of the sisters—Sister Rosina—was especially loved and respected by the poor because of her detachment and humility. A mutual devotion to St. Francis of Assisi led to the development of a close friendship between her and Father Hawes. Largely through his influence Sister Rosina severed her connection with the Sisters of Bethany, and together with three members of the Society left her convent in Lloyd Square resolved to establish a new community whose manner of life would conform to the most strict interpretation of holy poverty. Father Hawes found them a temporary refuge with the Sisterhood of the Holy Comforter at Edmonton, north of London, a small community which was in the process of becoming Benedictine, and was in close touch with Dom Aelred Carlyle. The latter arranged for Mother Rosina and her three companions to move to Hull, where the vicar of St. Mary's, Sculcoates, offered them a small house, which they named "St. Damian's" after the first convent of the Poor Clares outside Assisi. The new community adopted a brown Franciscan habit, knotted white cord and sandals. Mother Rosina, in her intense zeal for holy poverty, was trying to imitate the first Poor Clare nuns, but dispensed with their strict enclosure. Several young women joined her at Hull, and it was not long before they won the hearts of the poor working-class families around them.

The success of Mother Rosina's venture aroused Father Hawes's desire to establish a similar community for men. The obvious thing to do was to seek admission to the Society of Divine Compassion whose Rule and manner of life approximated fairly closely to that of the first companions of St. Francis of Assisi. It seems, however, that Father Hawes had serious doubts as to whether these quasi-Franciscans were really "Catholic!" Moreover, the Brothers wore a black habit, like that of the Friars Minor Conventual. He could not conceive of any true son of St. Francis wearing anything but brown or gray. So he felt he could not throw in his lot with the "black friars" who were working among the poor in the East London suburb of Plaistow. Their spirit struck him as too parochial, and the thought of having to recite the day hours in English instead of the Breviary in Latin was more than he could face.

In his own words: "With the ignorance of youth and the presumptuous folly of a spiritual dilettante, I was determined to found a new community myself. Just as Aelred Carlyle had revived or re-established the Order of St. Benedict in the Church of England, so would I revive the Order of Friars Minor in communion with Canterbury. Before my imagination rose up all the glamor of the coarse brown tunic, white knotted rope, and sandals, and poor brethren living in a humble friary." It would appear that Father Hawes's knowledge of Franciscan life was derived mainly from his reading. There is no evidence that he ever took the trouble to visit any of the then fairly numerous communities in England of the Observant Friars Minor or the Capuchins or that he ever studied their constitutions.

In the summer of 1906 Abbot Aelred wrote to Father Hawes the astonishing news that he was about to become the owner of the Isle of Caldey, off the coast of South Wales, thanks to the generosity of a young man who had offered to lend him six thousand pounds and take a mortgage of eight thousand pounds on the property. The Abbot asked Father Hawes if he would be prepared to resign his curacy in London and take on the job of architect at Caldey. At the same time Father Hawes could combine architectural work with the novitiate which it had been understood he would make under Abbot Aelred as a probation for the Franciscan life. Such an offer could not be turned down, so in June Father Hawes slipped away from the slums of Clerkenwell without any farewell sermon or demonstrative sendoffs.

After a brief holiday with his parents in Sussex, Father Hawes, described at this time as "very Roman in appearance, with his little cape and many buttons on his soutane, and a jaw which essayed to meet his nose," traveled to South Wales with Abbot Aelred toward the end of July 1906. The latter, with even more than his usual optimism, was hopeful of raising at least seven thousand pounds to cover the cost of the really essential buildings which he pictured. The first thing he wanted were plans for a guesthouse. Then would follow a temporary monastery, referred to as "The Gatehouse," to accommodate between thirty and forty monks. Although the community numbered no more than twenty, Abbot Aelred believed firmly that within a few years it would increase to more than a hundred. So Father Hawes was told that he must also plan a future abbey which would be a worthy successor to the great Benedictine masterpieces of medieval England. In addition to these new buildings, the Abbot wanted the church of the medieval priory restored; stalls for the brethren must be made at once and a new stone altar erected. Then the even more ancient village church must be restored and beautified. A round tower on the cliffs must be converted into an oratory.

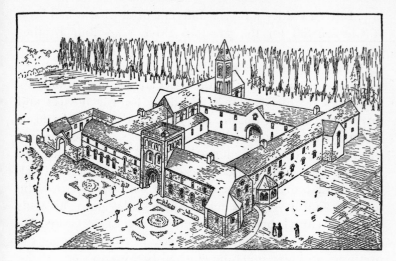

Abbey Gatehouse, Caldey Island

Never before had the priest-architect been given so much work to do in so little time. Bryan Burstall, the wealthy benefactor who had lent the money to buy the island, had offered to take on the job of clerk-of-works. He and Father Hawes settled down in a vacant cottage, where they lived in the utmost simplicity, and worked from dawn till dusk to get everything ready for the arrival of the community.

"The Homecoming," as it was called in after years, took place on October 18, 1906. For the first six months the brethren occupied the somewhat inconvenient quarters of the medieval priory. It was within its stone-vaulted church that Father Hawes was clothed with the novice's habit and given the religious name of Jerome. He and Burstall, who was made an oblate and known as Brother Illtud, were kept busy. Everything had to be assembled—lime to be burned, workmen engaged; bricks, tiles and timber to be brought over from the mainland and unloaded on the beach at low tide. Life on Caldey was very different from what it had been at Clerkenwell for the previous three years, but Brother Jerome seems to have enjoyed himself, up to a point.

In his reminiscences he tells us of rising at midnight to recite Matins and Lauds, of the strict silence broken only by an hour's recreation which was daily for the novices and three times a week for the seniors, and the meatless meals unappetizingly prepared by amateur cooks. Brother Jerome was introduced here to monastic manual labor, and learned to wash clothes and to bake bread in an old-fashioned brick oven. He admits that when occupied with ax or trowel he used "to find it very irksome" to have to lay down his tools when the church bell rang for one of the Little Hours. He speaks highly of the spirit of fervor and charity among the brethren, and how much he enjoyed bathing in some of the lovely sandy coves. He reveals that "the even course of life was sometimes agitated," especially when two of the Brothers left the island without warning, to be received into the Catholic and Roman Church. It was about this time that Abbot Aelred had to contradict the widely circulated reports that he had "sought recognition of his community from the Abbot Primate of the Roman Obedience." As Brother Jerome remarks: "A tremor from Rome had shaken the foundations of this Benedictine house built on the shifting sands of Anglo-Catholicism—portent of the earthquake which would occur six years later with the conversion of the majority of these Anglican monks."

Reading between the lines of these memoirs of a year on Caldey Island, one forms the impression that relations between the novice and his dynamic Abbot were often somewhat strained, chiefly because of the latter's utter indifference to monastic poverty when it concerned buildings. Brother Jerome confesses that it was annoying, when he had been working on plans and elevations, to have the Abbot scrap the drawings and insist on something more ambitious. The abbatial imagination ran riot and costs were never counted. Nothing but the biggest and the most ornate would satisfy him. Brother Jerome, on the other hand, was more interested in humble little hermitages like those of the first Capuchins. "I myself," he wrote, "longed to rebuild the ruins of the hermitage on St. Margaret's Island, adjoining Caldey." The basically more practical-minded novice could not work up any real enthusiasm for a dream abbey planned on a scale greater than that of any medieval Cluniac monastery.

By the summer of 1907 it became quite clear to Abbot Aelred that he had lost all hope of turning Brother Jerome into a Benedictine, or of making permanent use of him on Caldey. So he called in another architect, and all those plans, sections and elevations which the novice had drawn under holy obedience were laid aside and forgotten. The cardboard model of the dream abbey on which he had worked so hard was destroyed.

Now, to his joy, Brother Jerome was given more freedom. He started to grow a beard, and was allowed to retire to a cave in the limestone cliffs, where for a few weeks he lived as a hermit. Every morning, after a dip in the sea, he walked to the village church where he said Mass. His austerity and fervor filled one of the novices with such wonder and admiration that he confided to the hermit that he would throw in his lot with him, once the Franciscan brotherhood had been established. Abbot Aelred must have felt that Brother Jerome was a dangerous influence, and that the sooner he left the island, the better it would be, otherwise more novices—even professed monks—might be tempted to desert St. Benedict for St. Francis.

At the end of the year of his novitiate, therefore, Brother Jerome left Caldey to begin his Franciscan adventure. He had not, however, been professed, for he was told that he needed further probation. This was a blow to the eager would-be friar and he decided to go to Essex to the novitiate of the Society of the Divine Compassion. Here again he was disappointed. The superior of the community, Father William Sirr, refused to accept the validity of the Caldey probation, and regretted that he felt unable to profess Brother Jerome. If the latter felt called to be a Franciscan, why could he not join the Society of the Divine Compassion instead of wanting to found a rival brotherhood?

Brother Jerome did not know what to do. Perhaps a further test was needed. He resolved to follow the example of St. Francis by undertaking a pilgrimage in the medieval manner—he would go on a tramp through England.

One of the Caldey Benedictines—Dom George Chambers — who was spending the year of his diaconate as curate of St. Philip's, Dalston, put him up for a week or two.

Having made his confession and said Mass in St. Philip's Church on the feast of St. Francis, October 4, 1907, Brother Jerome changed into the "beggar's clothes" which he had brought with him—a shabby jacket, flannel shirt, patched trousers and an old cap. Without a penny in his pocket, with nothing but a breviary and a crucifix, he stepped barefooted into the street at midnight. With his face smeared with mud, and with his ragged, unkempt beard, nobody he met was likely to recognize him as a priest of the Church of England.

"It was my strict rule never to beg," he recorded, "but take anything offered me, and to do any work when I could. God and St. Francis provided for all my wants. As I walked along the road, a man would call to me and throw me a penny. Or some shy-looking fellow would come up and press a sixpence into my hand. After four days' tramping my feet were cut and bleeding, then a woman leaning on the fence of a poor little cottage called me to stop. I went in and she brought out an old pair of boots of her husband. I learned much. I consorted with other tramps and outcasts; no man could say that he was poorer than I was. I slept (or shivered) under hedges, haystacks, railway trucks, in church porches, in the casual wards of workhouses, and once was taken up by a policeman, very nearly being lodged in prison. I learned the value of a penny. I would buy a farthing's worth of tea in a screw of paper, another of sugar and a ha'penth of bread. When rich I could pay twopence for a good night's rest in a bed of a common lodginghouse. In a town I picked up and ate the bread that school children had thrown away on the street. On one occasion, after such a meal, I was forty hours without another bite of anything—only drinks of water—and walked some thirty miles on it.

"I walked with the praises of God on my lips, and joy and liberty in my soul. I would find some quiet, deserted place where I could stop and rest under a tree, and read my Office. Whenever possible I would hear Mass in the morning at some Catholic church lying on my way; or at the daily celebration of the Eucharist in an Anglican church, but in these latter the verger kept a very suspicious eye on me.

"After tramping through Surrey and Sussex, I arrived one evening at Crawley, where I camped in a ditch under a scanty hedge of thorn. It came on to rain, and the night seemed very long. In the morning I was glad to hear the bells of St. Francis' Church ringing. I went to Mass. It was Sunday, but nobody looked askance or stared at me as people would have done in an Anglican church. After Mass I went round to the friary and rang the bell. A kind bearded Capuchin lay Brother gave me a huge cup of tea and two big slices of bread, and let me sit down in the entrance hall to eat my breakfast.

"I decided that I would call at St. Hugh's Charterhouse, about ten miles from Crawley. Late that evening I arrived at this great Carthusian monastery, quite dead beat. The lay Brother who opened the door said: 'We don't give anything away now; we used to do, but so many came that the police objected. If you go on to West Grinstead and call at the presbytery, they will give you some food there.'

" 'How far is it?' I asked. 'About two miles,' the Brother replied, as he closed the great door. So all I could do was to lie down with my head against the door. I was much too weary to tramp any farther. It was raining hard. I dozed and shivered through the long night, soaked to the skin. I heard the bell toll for Matins as I lay on the hard stone pavement. Morning dawned at last, and another lay Brother opened the door. I asked him if I could hear Mass. 'No!' he said. So, refreshed with the rest to my feet, if not to other parts of my body, I went off down the drive.

"I tramped on day after day in a westward direction, passing through Reading, until I reached Oxford. Here I called at the Mission House of the Society of St. John the Evangelist, better known as 'The Cowley Fathers.' I asked if there was any wood I could chop, or odd jobs I could do about the yard. 'Never mind about that, God bless you,' said the kindly Anglican lay Brother, who gave me a grand feed of meat. After leaving Oxford I made my way north to Warwick, and so through Lincoln until at last I landed up at Hull. With some difficulty I discovered St. Damian's Convent, where I knocked at the door and asked the Sister if she could spare a bit of something to eat. I laughed when she did not recognize me. Needless to add that Mother Rosina and her little community then gave me a real Franciscan welcome."

The "tramp" returned to London on a small coastal steamer. While he was hanging around the streets of Dalston, awaiting his friend, Dom George Chambers, the police watched him suspiciously, and warned the vicarage staff about this disreputable character they had noticed going into St. Philip's Church. But after Brother Jerome had taken off his dirty old clothes and resumed his clerical suit, there was no more trouble.

Things then began to move quickly. Abbot Aelred, who was on one of his fairly frequent begging tours around Britain, wrote from the Isle of Man that his host, Goldie Taubman, a wealthy Anglo-Catholic bachelor squire, needed a domestic chaplain. Mr. Taubman had hoped that one of the Caldey monks would be at his disposal, but the Abbot explained that only one of them was in holy orders and that he could not leave his curacy in London. So he suggested that Brother Jerome should take on the duties, and pointed out that the almost complete seclusion of the large property would be ideal for a further testing of his Franciscan vocation. This really looked like a direct answer to prayer. Within a few days Brother Jerome and Brother Cuthbert—the ex-Caldey novice—were in Liverpool. Here they met Abbot Aelred, who was on his way back from the Isle of Man. The Abbot, so one gathers from Brother Jerome's reminiscences, was not exactly sympathetic. He warned him not to cross his path, or to try to steal away any more of his community, otherwise there would be trouble!

It was in the last week of November 1907 that the two would-be Franciscans reached the Isle of Man by steamer from Liverpool. No more romantic spot could have been chosen as the setting for "reviving" the First Order of St. Francis in communion with Canterbury than this large island halfway between England and Ireland. Mr. Taubman's private chapel, dedicated to St. Bridget of Ireland, was a restored medieval building, dating from the fourteenth century. It stood at the far end of the park, well away from the big house, which was known as "The Nunnery."

Having taken possession of the chaplain's comfortable little house, Brother Jerome wasted no time in trying to make it as uncomfortable as possible. He had clear and definite ideas as to what a Franciscan friary ought to resemble, and this one must be as poverty-stricken as the derelict shelter at Rivo Torto, where St. Francis lodged with his first disciples. Mr. Taubman was both surprised and shocked to discover that all the easy chairs, curtains, cushions, ornaments and tablecloths had disappeared. He noticed that the many pictures had been removed from the walls, and the carpets lifted. When he asked what had been done with his furniture, he was told that it was safely stored away in a lumber room. The iron bedsteads with their spring mattresses were dismantled, and the two friars slept on the bare, hard floor boards. Mice ran over them at night. Brother Cuthbert set traps, and when the "Father Guardian," in true Franciscan spirit, released the captive mice, the Brother protested. The observance instituted by Brother Jerome seems to have been based upon what he had read about the manner of life of the first followers of the Little Poor Man, or that of the early Capuchin hermits. The two young men rose at midnight to recite Matins and Lauds in Latin. Their diet was nothing if not penitential.

For the first few weeks Mr. Taubman was delighted to have found a chaplain of such uncompromising "Catholic" opinions. But this quixotic Franciscan adventure came to an end after little more than four months. Mr. Taubman warned his domestic chaplain that the Isle of Man was a stronghold of old-fashioned Protestantism, which had remained impervious to Anglo-Catholic influences. Hence it was most unwise for Brother Jerome and his companion to walk in their brown habits and sandals along the country lanes and over the hills. The people would be scared out of their lives, because the only Religious they had ever set eyes on were the few Roman Catholic Sisters of Mercy who conducted a small school in Douglas.

Tension increased when Mr. Taubman insisted that all the furnishings of the chapel must be exactly as *he* chose to have them. If Brother Jerome moved flower vases or candlesticks, they were put back again immediately. The situation became impossible. One day the two friars packed up their few personal belongings and bolted from the Isle of Man. Uncertain as this left them as to their future, it turned out to be providential for Brother Jerome for he received an invitation from Father Adderley to become one of his curates at Saltley, Birmingham. With the blessing and permission of Dr. Gore, the Bishop of Birmingham, Brother Jerome was professed as a Franciscan by Father Adderley, and given charge of the newly opened mission church of St. Francis of Assisi. The so-called "friary" consisted of two slum cottages knocked into one.

Shortly after Easter, 1908, Brother Jerome and Brother Cuthbert resumed very much the same sort of life they had attempted in the Isle of Man, and with an equal indifference to the fact that conditions which were endurable in Italy in the thirteenth century were more than the average young Englishman of the early twentieth century could put up with. But after a month or two Brother Cuthbert departed, to find his vocation eventually as a clergyman of the Episcopal Church in the United States, where he married a rich widow. Then another young man, but this time not from Caldey, came to join Brother Jerome. This was his only postulant, and he did not manage to endure the austere life for more than a few weeks. The Founder found himself a hermit-missionary in the slums of Saltley.

It must have been a consolation to him that Mother Rosina's Community of St. Francis was adding to its numbers. By the summer of 1908 the Sisters had moved from Hull to London, and found a house in Dalston for their convent where several novices were professed by Dr. Cosmo Gordon Lang, then Bishop of Stepney, who in after years became Archbishop of York and then of Canterbury.

But for Brother Jerome a year had gone by and he was still without a community. He was frustrated, and "very disgusted with the ritualistic, socialistic and incipient modernism of most of the clergy at Saltley." Furthermore, his faith in Anglicanism had been shaken by the news received in the early summer of 1908 that the Reverend William McGarvey and six other American Episcopalian clergymen had been received into the Roman Church, and the Community of the Companions of the Holy Savior disbanded. By autumn of 1908 it was reported that twenty-one clergymen and about fifty laymen across the Atlantic had followed Father McGarvey and his companions on the road to Rome. Never before had there been such terrible losses to Anglo-Catholicism.

One day he could stand the environment no longer. The urge came to go on the tramp again, for "a breath of real Franciscan freedom, rags and rain." So early one Monday morning he took off his friar's habit and donned the old clothes of the tramp, which had been carefully preserved, and set off on the roads. This time he intended to try street preaching.

He traveled all day northward from Birmingham through the squalid streets of coal-mining villages—the depressing poverty-stricken "Black Country." That evening he stopped in the midst of one of these straggling villages, and with a conscious effort, screwed up his courage to begin. Having sung a verse or two of one of the sentimental Llanthony mission hymns, the "tramp" mounted a doorstep to begin his sermon. He spoke to the people as simply as possible of God our Creator, His love for mankind, of sin, hell, repentance and heaven. A crowd soon collected around the queer-looking bearded lay preacher. When he finished, they pressed forward with pennies. Brother Jerome raised his voice and said: "Dear brothers and sisters, I don't want your money: I am bound by a vow not to take any, but if you can give me some food I will take what is enough for my need." Some went back to their cottages and brought out bread and slices of meat, tea, sugar and other food. They pressed their gifts upon the preacher, saying, "God bless you."

Brother Jerome bade them good-by and climbed up on to a slag heap beside a coal mine, where he found an overturned railway wagon. Beneath it he spent the night. His sleep was disturbed by a fierce dog that prowled around and barked at him. After preaching in a few more villages he made his way back to Saltley, feeling that he had achieved at least a modicum of Franciscan release.

In those reminiscences which he jotted down many years later Brother Jerome recalls that Father Adderley's large vicarage was "a rendezvous for all sorts of social reformers —some wise, some cranks, some worse than cranks." Among the men whom he mentions having met there was George Lansbury, Cecil Chesterton and Philip Snowden—all later to become famous as social reformers and politicians. Hardly knowing what to do with his zealous but eccentric curate, Father Adderley suggested that he might consider joining another Anglican clergyman who had recently launched out into the depths of Franciscanism. This was the Reverend George Martin, formerly the rector of a parish in Devonshire, and very wealthy. One day he had astonished and shocked his friends and relations by giving away all his money and ridding himself of all other possessions. Now he was living from hand to mouth in the slums of South London, supporting himself by working as a common porter in the Southwark Market.

"It seemed just the right sort of Franciscanism," Brother Jerome writes, "but I could not bring myself to make such an utter surrender, involving having no church and not being able to celebrate Mass daily. It would also have meant abandoning the ideal of founding an order with a regular religious observance, and I just could not face giving up wearing my brown habit.

"I think that here again I missed something higher and of greater reality that God was then calling me to. Had I gone to join George Martin, as Father Adderley advised, the Light to see and enter the one true Church might have come to me sooner; and perhaps George Martin might have come with me."

Then while Brother Jerome was alternately toying with the idea of finding his true vocation in life of complete poverty in the slums of South London and simultaneously discarding it, he got word that an unexpected field of work awaited him in a place where he would be quite free to practice all his Catholic ideals, and to continue as a Franciscan.

3.

"Roman Fever" [1908–1911]

ONCE again it was Bishop Hornby who came to Brother Jerome's aid. In a letter written in the late autumn of 1908 he told the younger man of the devastation that had been caused by a hurricane that had recently swept the Bahamas, and appealed for both his architectural and priestly help. The Bishop offered Brother Jerome the charge of Long Island, saying, "Surely this is a *God-sent* opportunity for a work that only *you* can do."

No sooner had he finished reading the letter than Brother Jerome felt that here was a sign. Jumping up, exultant, he dashed straight to Father Adderley to beg his permission to resign his curacy so that he could be off at once to the Bahamas. The good vicar gave his impetuous curate his blessing, the "friary" was dissolved, and Brother Jerome immediately cabled Bishop Hornby that he would be with him at the first possible moment.

In a fit of prudence, however, he decided that it would be wise to inoculate himself against possible future attacks of "Roman fever," so having said farewell to his parents he rushed off to South Wales to spend a week on Caldey Island. There he was both soothed and stimulated by the glamor and romance of this "Church within the Church." In the little chapel with its curtained tabernacle and its bitter-sweet odor of incense, from where the black-cowled figures slipped away into the blackness of night after a final chanting of the *Adoremus in aeternum,* how could the guest have further doubts about being truly a Catholic? Every morning he went to the altar and celebrated Mass—to have questioned his priesthood would have been almost blasphemy. His recurring doubts about Anglicanism were quieted by his week on Caldey. All the old fires were rekindled and he returned to the mainland convinced that the Church of his baptism would also be the Church of his death.

But emotional ups and downs seemed to be the core and fabric of Brother Jerome's character at this period. His renewed faith in Anglo-Catholicism again was shaken when he heard that his cousin, whom he had started on the High Church path, had been received into the Roman Church. Nevertheless, he shook off his doubts and boarded the New York-bound *Mauretania.*

Off the coast of Ireland the ship began to pitch and toss in the mountainous seas of a winter gale. Brother Jerome, groaning in his berth, began to fear drowning and to wonder if after all he would not have been safer in the barque of Peter. However, he landed safely in a snowbound New York from where he took the next steamer for Nassau. When he arrived at the island about the middle of January 1909, Bishop Hornby welcomed him with open arms, and the intensely sensitive young man found himself spellbound by the strong sun, blue skies and seas, and the strangely attractive tropical world of New Providence Island. Everything surpassed his wildest expectations.

At once he resumed his Franciscan garb and set off with the Bishop on a visitation tour of the northern islands. They traveled in a converted North Sea smack, brought out from England, which belonged to the Episcopalian mission and which was manned by a native crew of captain, cook and four seamen. Brother Jerome wrote enthusiastically of the voyage, "It was genuine sailing and seamanship as there were no auxiliary motors in those days to help a boat get out of a scrape. Even the mail boats at that date were sailing schooners, and some of them were very fast."

After his initial tour of the islands, Brother Jerome settled in on Long Island. Clarence Town, the center of his parish, had suffered badly from the hurricane, and its church had been razed to the ground, so that Sunday services had to be held in the rectory, which was relatively untouched. Brother Jerome established himself at Deadman's Cay, ten miles north of Clarence Town, where the nave of the church was still intact, with the chancel open to the weather. From the debris around he built himself a little eight-foot shack, filling the superstitious natives with horror. "An' you sleep right here in the churchyard among the graves? Aren't you afraid of the speerits?" they asked him. To which their pastor made answer that it was "right handy here, and that there was plenty of room for both him and the dead people." When he lay down at night in his little hut, big land crabs walked over him and scrambled over the roof of the shack. Sometimes he would hear a night bird let forth a weird screech. Had he been of a nervous temperament, the loneliness would indeed have been eerie.

But Brother Jerome looked around at his parish and felt that his earlier missionary yearnings were about to be satisfied. Although the population of Long Island was largely white, made up of poor farmers or fishermen, there was no color bar and nothing like the Jim Crow segregation of Nassau. The first task that faced him was to raise a new church to take care of these people, and this would obviously require all his ingenuity and architectural experience, for to make any building hurricane proof in these storm-swept islands was a herculean endeavor. There was nothing for it, he decided, but to discard any ideas of using concrete roofs, which would eventually crack from the salt-laden air, and get back to the simplicity of primitive building.

His first experiment with rock roofs was on the big Lady chapel of the ruined church at Deadman's Cay. He gathered a crowd of willing workers, each volunteering two or three days of labor. If a man possessed a trowel, it made him a mason; the ownership of a rusty old saw, a carpenter. Women and girls toted rocks on their heads, or pails of sand and water, and some of them lighted fires over which galley pots bubbled and boiled the hominy for a ten-o'clock breakfast. Half-naked children played underfoot with the dogs, or slept under the palm trees. In this gay and uninhibited atmosphere the eastern walls of the church of Deadman's Cay rose once again.

The moment came to remove the wooden centering. Brother Jerome called out, "Now come along there, you're a strong fellow—lend a hand." The man addressed drew back reluctantly and replied, "Not me, Farder, not for all the bank of Nassau would I take away one of them props from under the rocks!" Brother Jerome laughed heartily at this and told the men to watch. He demonstrated just how the wooden centering under the arch was to be dismantled and removed; then after some persuasion six men volunteered to help. Carefully they lowered the centering, leaving the stones apparently unsupported. Then Brother Jerome put a ladder against the wall, mounted it agilely, and danced on the crown of the arch to the great amazement of the onlookers, who expected it to fall in promptly.

With his church repaired, Brother Jerome felt it was time to visit the villages and church north of Deadman's Cay. Since this could be done most easily by sea he bought a small, decked cutter, the *Hispaniola,* so seaworthy a vessel that he once sailed her two hundred miles to Nassau to attend the

Diocesan Synod, taking three days for the voyage. He could sleep in the *Hispaniola,* and carry barrels of cement and other building materials, and for his crew he engaged a twelve-year-old Negro boy. Unfortunately the boat was not usable for visiting southern Long Island, which could be reached only by road, so he bought a sturdy pony to carry him to the southerly villages. And there were plenty of these visitations to be made since all except three of the dozen churches on the island had been destroyed.

For the most part Brother Jerome was able to indulge himself to his heart's content in "Catholic" services and externals, for the Church of England Bahamians were considered to be among the most advanced in the Anglican communion. But at one of his mission stations, Simms, the overwhelmingly white congregation was strongly opposed to High Church ways. They informed their Franciscan pastor that they did not want the Mass, but merely the "Lord's Supper." They would have nothing to do with confession, images, candles, incense, wafers or holy water. They strongly disapproved of the Virgin Mary.

Poor Brother Jerome was terribly upset at being confronted by this manifestation of militant Protestantism among his flock. He wrote, "I found the people assembled to meet me. . . . After polite and friendly greetings we got right down at once to brass tacks. What were my plans as to the ordering of faith and worship in their church? The storekeeper said, 'When my grandfather came here we were Church of England, and they tell us we were Protestants. When Father Wilkinson came along, he tell us it's Catholic, and he try and force all these strange things on us.' "

What could he tell them? Used as he was to diversities of opinion and "glorious comprehensiveness"—anything you fancy, high or low, short of popery, its meaning had never been brought home to Brother Jerome so clearly as at that moment. Here were people on a lonely island in the Atlantic, faithful to such tradition as they had received, who were impatient of novelties, and to whom religion was their only solace—in fact, their only diversion. Brother Jerome had always admitted that in the Church of England there were two rival and conflicting interpretations of its basic character. It struck him, then and there, that these people had just as much *right* to hold their point of view as he had to hold his. In a flash he saw his vision of a totally Anglo-Catholic Long Island parish crumble to ashes. His picture of Nassau as a united diocese was shattered to atoms. It dawned on him how futile it was to go on imagining that the Church of England would ever be "Catholicized" as a united body.

To quote his own words: "So I gave my reply (ignominiously 'climbing down' before the eyes of zealous men like 'Father' Wilkinson). I assured the people of Simms I would force nothing on them or in their church against their will. I only wanted to help them love and serve God better. My subsequent visits to their settlement were always peaceful and pleasant ones. At the Communion service I gave them ordinary bread instead of the small unleavened round wafers used elsewhere. They remained faithful and loyal to the Church of England until some later clergyman walked again in the steps of Father Wilkinson, when they all left the Anglican Church and joined one or other of some new American Protestant sects that happened to be proselytizing in the Bahamas. Thirty years later, when I revisited Long Island as a Catholic priest, the old people left at Simms who remembered me gave me the heartiest welcome of all."

The church at Deadman's Cay was entirely rebuilt within the next year. Abbot Aelred Carlyle of Caldey presented the cast of the statue of *"Notre-Dame sous Terre"* in Chartres Cathedral, similar to the small statue designed by Brother Jerome which used to stand in the monastery chapel at Painsthorpe. Two other altars, dedicated to the Sacred Heart and St. Francis, were erected, also a rood screen with a large crucifix. Over the high altar was a baldachino with four Greek Doric columns, carrying semicircular arches. Brother Jerome was determined that this church should look as "Catholic" as he could make it. An old Negro lady, when she first saw it, held up her apron and curtsied, exclaiming, "Ain' dat beautiful, dat de Hebenly Jerusalem!"

The following reminiscences give us an idea of Brother Jerome's state of mind at this time, "Never in my life, and especially since I became a clergyman of the Church of England, had I ever spoken a word against the Roman Catholic Church or the Pope. Bound up with my large altar edition of the *Book of Common Prayer* was the Latin canon of the *Missale Romanum*. Every time, and that was daily, I celebrated the Communion service I added secretly the Latin canon, and prayed that the holy Catholic Church might be granted peace, protected, united, and governed throughout the world '*cum famulo tuo Papa nostro Pio.*' In all good faith I believed I had valid Orders and was a real Catholic priest. I always taught the people that as we said the Creed, and recited the words 'I believe in the Holy Catholic Church,' that the Church was governed by bishops and that the chief bishop and head of the whole Church was the successor of St. Peter—the Pope.

"How fervent and responsive were those dear people on Long Island! What a crowded church we had on Sunday mornings! They traveled the roads barefooted, carrying their shoes and socks, putting these on by the churchyard before entering the building. A couple of men with violins, under the rood screen, led the singing, and if there had been any organ, I don't think you could have heard it!"

The biggest church to be rebuilt was St. Paul's, Clarence Town. Brother Jerome and his workers labored over this

large structure; then, just after the centering of the chancel
arches had been removed, a terrible storm arose. About midnight the whole roof collapsed and fell in. The work had to
be started all over again, this time with the walls a foot
thicker. Since then many hurricanes have swept over Long
Island, but the church at Clarence Town, with its twin
towers, has stood secure.

More than the physical collapse of a church was in store
for Brother Jerome, however. In spite of his contentment
with his Bahamian existence and the apparent fulfillment of
his vocation, a new series of shocks began to undermine the
last of his wavering Anglican convictions. For a number of
years he had taken a keen interest in the Society of the Atonement, an American religious order founded by the Reverend
Lewis T. Wattson, known in religion as Father Paul James
Francis, and Mother Lurana, a former member of the Anglican Sisterhood of the Holy Child Jesus. The Society, Franciscan in spirit, had as its purpose to pray for Church unity
and reunion with the Holy See. The Church Unity Octave,
first observed in 1908, had met a sympathetic response from
Brother Jerome, and *The Prince of the Apostles,* written
jointly by Father Paul and the Reverend Spencer Jones, had
had a pronounced influence on his thinking.

When the news reached him that the Graymoor community had "abandoned the sinking ship" to board the Barque
of Peter, he felt that the ground had been cut from under his
feet. He immediately wrote to Mother Rosina, whose views
were so similar to his own, only to discover after an exchange
of letters that she had come to the conclusion that she had
no alternative but to be received into the Roman Catholic
Church. Mother Rosina wrote that she and a few companions
were leaving their convent in North London and embark-
ing for North America. A short time thereafter Brother Jerome heard that she and her companions had been reconciled

to the Mother Church at Graymoor and had applied for admission to the novitiate of the Society of the Atonement.

Added to this news, which then and there almost catapulted Brother Jerome into the Catholic Church, came word that several leading Anglo-Catholic clergymen in Brighton, along with many of their parishioners, had made their submission to Rome. His sole hope lay in Abbot Aelred, who wrote that Anglicans must make an even more militant stand for the faith and fight all symptoms of "Roman fever," and who enlarged optimistically on the foundations he hoped to make at Pershore, Prinknash and Llanthony. The Abbot almost managed to rekindle Brother Jerome's waning enthusiasm for Anglican Franciscanism by describing his plan for purchasing a property at Assisi to serve as an Anglo-Catholic guesthouse. It was almost enough to send Brother Jerome posthaste to Umbria where he could see himself saying Mass daily in the world of St. Francis.

Nevertheless, his blissful isolation on his Caribbean island had cracked. Hard as he tried to follow Abbot Aelred's advice and to console himself with church building and the "Catholicization" of his warm-hearted flock, he found himself in a continuous state of spiritual depression. When he read in *The Church Times* that the Bishop of Salisbury had preached in a Lutheran church in Germany, that the Bishop of Manchester had refused to allow his clergy to wear vestments, that the Bishop of Hereford had invited dissenters to receive Holy Communion, and that the Bishop of Liverpool had asked nonconformist ministers to take part in interdenominational missions in his diocese, it was difficult for him not to despair of Anglo-Catholicism.

So Brother Jerome drifted on from week to week, from month to month. Then one morning in the late autumn of 1910 he opened a copy of the Graymoor publication, *The Lamp,* which had just come in the mail. An article on "The

Necessity for Certitude" caught his attention. Its clear reasoning and biting logic were so compelling that he read it through twice, then threw the magazine to the floor, exclaiming, "That finishes me!"

"From that hour," he wrote, "I began to set my house in order and to pack up. My *heart* had long been in Rome, but now my *head* was bringing me over boldly. . . ."

On the Sunday after the Feast of the Conversion of St. Paul, January 25, 1911, the first service was held in the restored church at Clarence Town. Standing before the baroque stone altar, dressed in his vestments, Brother Jerome told his congregation that he was going to Nassau for a visit, but he did not tell his people how long he would be gone. He did not return for thirty years. When he left the church after Mass he saw the mail boat in the harbor, three or four days before she was expected. In order to get on board he had to rush so much that most of his possessions, including his books, were left behind.

The moment the boat docked at Nassau, Brother Jerome went straight to Bishop Hornby to tell him that he had decided to "go over to Rome."

"I see it's no good arguing with you any more," said the kindly Bishop, after a half-hour's discussion. "Let's drop the subject and go for a walk."

The Bishop asked Brother Jerome as a final favor to discuss the Roman claims with Dr. Mortimer—a well-known Episcopalian theologian of High Church opinions—when he arrived in New York. He also informed Brother Jerome that he would continue to regard him as one of his clergy and pay his salary until such time (if it came) that he had actually been received into the Roman Church.

"Dear Bishop Hornby, so long my faithful friend—how it saddened me to give him this pain," wrote Brother Jerome. "We always corresponded up to the time of his death, and I met him again in England.

"The following Sunday I declined to 'say Mass,' but preached at St. Mary's—my final ministration as an Anglican clergyman."

The fortnightly mail steamer from Jamaica called at Nassau on its way to New York. There were few passengers on that trip, but among them was Brother Jerome who had a three-berth cabin to himself, and "was soon pretty seasick." He had discarded his Franciscan habit before leaving Nassau and assumed clerical garb, which somewhat confused the steward who came to his cabin to attend to him. "Catholic priest, Father?" he inquired. "No," answered Brother Jerome, "Episcopalian, but I hope to become a Catholic very soon." The steward remarked: "Now that's grand!" and from that moment did all he could for his seasick passenger, telling him about his home, his wife and children in New York, describing St. Patrick's Cathedral and many other churches in that city, and also the religious orders, saying that all would come easy in no time. "It was a cheering introduction at the start of my setting out to follow the Star," writes Brother Jerome, who adds that "the spontaneous brotherly welcome of this kindly Irish layman was far more sympathetic and encouraging than anything I got from any of the priests I first met with."

In deference to Bishop Hornby, Brother Jerome, as soon as he arrived in New York, immediately called on Dr. Mortimer at the Church of St. Mary the Virgin. But the two found little to talk about, and Brother Jerome soon departed to find a tailor's shop, where he removed his clerical collar and bought a gray ready-made suit.

Wandering around New York, the self-unfrocked Anglican priest discovered the Church of St. Paul the Apostle on Columbus Avenue, between West Fifty-ninth and West Sixtieth streets. The front was decorated with a huge placard announcing, "Mission to Non-Catholics: Subject Tonight: The Everlasting Catholic Church." As he remarked in his diary:

"How the good God had got everything just nicely ready for me! Next morning I heard Mass in this big church of the Paulist Fathers, and what balm to my soul that was: the *real* thing this time without doubt. As soon as I had made up my mind to accept unconditionally all that the Holy Roman Church holds and teaches, I thought I would have trouble in dispossessing my scruples and inner feeling that I was already a validly ordained priest. But as I knelt in the great church, in such restful peace and absolute certainty, all these notions drifted away: I was just a layman and Anglican Orders were absolutely, without a reservation, null and void from the Catholic point of view."

That same day Hawes boarded the train for Peekskill, and climbed the steep road that led up the hill to the then very simple buildings of the Convent of the Society of the Atonement. Here he met Mother Lurana and Father Paul James Francis. He recorded in after years that "their welcome seemed rather stiff and formal, with no cheering warmth. There was an air of constraint in the atmosphere, not at all what I expected to find among Franciscans. I inquired after Mother Rosina and the other Sisters from Dalston, and, of course, was anxious to see them. I was informed that they were here no longer. Next day came another disappointment. I was impatient to be received into the Church, but Father Paul told me I must wait and have at least two months' instruction. The Archbishop of New York had forbidden him to receive any more converts straightway off. Since I had come to Graymoor, I made up my mind to stay on and see things through."

It is not difficult to understand that the neophyte found Graymoor somewhat depressing, if only climatically. It was midwinter, and the contrast between the gray skies, the snow and those dark woods above the Hudson River, with the sunshine and bright colors of the Bahamas may have added to his sense of frustration. Forty years later he wrote: "The time passed wearily. The slow, drawn-out Offices in the chapel, with lots of extra-long prayers and devotions tacked on, bored me. The food was almost uneatable, the staple diet being stale salt herring and half-boiled potatoes, after Lent started. An Anglican 'nonceremonial' use of incense would have been welcome to counteract the knock-me-down fishy smell. I have hated fish ever since. Usually it was bitterly cold in the dormitory cubicles. I used to get up two or three times a night to replenish the anthracite stove."

Thirty-two years after that visit to Graymoor he still remembered "the horrible shock on the first Sunday there. The Mass was celebrated in the little wooden church of St. John's-in-the-Wilderness, originally an Episcopalian place of worship. Father Paul said the Mass in Latin, of course, and he was vested in an old Anglican chasuble of that 'arty' dull sage-green color with an art-russet Y shaped across. My heart sank. To make matters worse there were even the 'correct' brass flower vases and candlesticks. Mother Lurana and the half-a-dozen Sisters sang everything in English (by permission of the Apostolic Delegate, Monsignor Falconio), starting off with 'Lord have mercy on us,' but decently omitting their late former petition to 'incline our hearts to keep this law!' Then followed, 'Glory be to God on high,' and 'I believe,' all to the ill-fitting music of the *Missa de Angelis*. My heart sank. I had reveled in the consolation of hearing Mass at the Paulist Father's Church in New York City, but now I seemed to have dropped back into an environment of Anglicanism. I was hungry and thirsty for Catholic worship, but here I was with everything I thought I had done with forever.

"After a couple of weeks along came a 'Visitor' deputed by the Archbishop of New York—a grand old Friar Minor, a great missionary amongst non-Catholics. In the dormitory his cubicle was next to mine. I could hear him not only groan-

ing (because of his infirmities) but praying aloud nearly the
whole night through. He altered a lot of things and told
Father Paul that when he had sung Mass, the choir, i.e., the
Sisters, must sing all their part in Latin, in spite of what the
Apostolic Delegate had granted. 'I don't care,' roared the old
friar, 'I tell you it's got to stop and right away. It's confusing
and disedifying the laity."

In spite of his distaste for the Graymoor services, John was
not completely unhappy during his stay. For one thing, his
friend Mother Rosina had entered the novitiate of the Franciscan Missionary Sisters of the Sacred Heart at Peekskill,
New York, and he often made the six-mile walk to see her.
Another project that kept him occupied was the design for
St. Francis' Chapel at Graymoor. Although certain modifications were made to the original plan by Ralph Adams Cram
and Carlton Strong, essentially the design was John's. The
first stone was laid on March 17, 1911, two days before John's
reception into the Church, and the dedication took place on
January 18, 1912.

St. Francis Chapel, Graymoor

About a month after his first visit Father Francis, whose views on liturgical practice John found so sympathetic, returned to Graymoor and John made his confession to him.

"For three days previously," he wrote, "I had been full of scruples. I became more and more anxious and miserable. I felt sure that this general confession would take me at least an hour, but in a businesslike way the holy friar rushed me over all the hurdles in five minutes; and then at the act of contrition he just lifted my soul right up to God."

Everything was ready for the final step, and on St. Joseph's Day, March 19, 1911, Father Paul administered conditional baptism to John Hawes and received him into the Roman Catholic Church.

4.

From the Rockies to the Beda   [1911–1915]

Now that the great decision was behind him John was faced with an uncertain future. Father Paul seems to have been disappointed that his convert showed no desire to enter the Society of the Atonement, but John told him that if he chose to test his Franciscan vocation it would be with the Capuchins or the Friars Minor of the Leonine Union. Although in later years Hawes was willing to admit that his first impressions of Graymoor may have been prejudiced, he was by nature drawn toward the more baroque and rococo externals of Catholicism, and it is understandable that he should have found the ethos of Graymoor uncongenial.

Since returning to the Bahamas was out of the question, he took ship for England, dreading his first meeting with his parents. To his surprise his reception in the Catholic Church had not been the blow to them that he had expected. His father merely remarked, "I thought our Church is wide enough for anything and that you could have found all you wanted without leaving it." His mother expressed herself somewhat more warmly. "Dear John, I feel that you have done the right and straightforward thing. I never could feel happy while you took up with all those imitations of Catholicism in our Protestant Church, and now God's blessing be with you."

Relieved and happy, John went off to South London for a long talk with the Father Guardian of the Capuchin Friary at Peckham. This wise friar explained to John that since his previous life had been so varied and independent, and since he was no longer so young, he would undoubtedly find the discipline of the novitiate too difficult. He advised him to become a secular priest.

Immediately offers to Hawes were forthcoming. Bishop Amigo of the diocese of Southwark was eager to have him; Father Filmer suggested that he join the Guild of Ransom and devote himself to preaching for the conversion of England; the resident priest of Bermuda offered to send him to the seminary at Halifax. John's old friend Charles Selby-Hall, who together with his wife had been received into the Catholic Church at almost the same time as had John, begged him to let them pay his expenses at the Beda College, Rome, pointing out that this would leave him free to make a final choice of a diocese later on.

After the protracted nervous tension, mental struggle and external upheaval of a past life and relationships, many a new convert is apt to relax and sink down spiritually exhausted. When John delayed taking steps to receive "Roman Orders" some of his friends began to wonder if he had become a Roman Catholic layman in order to put off the burden of pastoral labors and to escape from spiritual responsibilities. But the truth was that he now wanted to look around and take his bearings. If there were real difficulties in the way of his becoming a Franciscan, the same reasons held good for not rushing into the other openings that presented themselves.

"No! I was too independent. I would go to work and earn enough to pay my own way," John wrote. "I decided to cross the Atlantic again, this time to Canada. Right away I booked my passage on an emigrant ship, the *Lake Champlain*. I was one in a six-berth cabin without a porthole. We had to keep the electric light on all night because of the swarms of rats that ran over us. One man, putting on his boots, found a nest of seven baby rats in one of them. The food was even worse than what I had tried to eat at Graymoor. The stewards swept most of it off the plates and threw it overboard. Then off Newfoundland we ran into a field of huge icebergs, next into a dense fog, and for three days lay to with continuous dismal blowing of the foghorn. My only solace was to repeat again and again *Ave Maris Stella*. It was the same year the *Titanic* rushed to her doom, but the old emigrant ship was not out to make records."

The ship berthed at Quebec, where John first made a pilgrimage to the shrine of St. Anne de Beaupré. Then he set out for Montreal and Toronto where he made a fruitless tour of architects' offices, but failed to find a job. It was a slack time and no new buildings were being put up. He lodged in Salvation Army shelters, having no dollars to waste on hotels. Perhaps he would have better luck farther west, he thought, so he boarded an emigrant train which took him to Calgary. As he wandered through the streets of Calgary he noticed an advertisement: "C.P.R. Crow's Nest Pass Construction Camp. Twelve teamsters wanted." As he knew something about horses, he went into the office of the Canadian Pacific, paid a couple of dollars over the counter, and signed on, receiving a railroad pass to MacLeod. He jolted into this small ranching town at midnight and dossed in a railroad shed. It was bitterly cold, and he had only five cents left, so the following morning, after a cup of hot coffee, he set off to walk the twelve miles to Pincher's Creek near where the camp was set up. Before long the sun came out, and the prospective teamster began to feel very weary. At last he arrived at the busy construction camp and presented himself to the boss, who told John that he could start the next day. The scenery, so he tells us, was "a glorious picture of pine and fir-covered hills, just at the foot of the snowcapped Rocky Mountains. The camp lay beside a rushing mountain river in a narrow ravine, over which a great trestle bridge, 140 feet high, was being built."

The railroad company gave their employees splendid food and plenty of everything. The ex-Anglican Franciscan slept in a tent with three other men. It was very damp, and since the mattresses were on the ground he used to wake up so stiff with rheumatism he could hardly move. When the sun rose, the heat was scorching, but it was very cold at night, and there were frequent hail- or snow- storms.

At first John worked with pick and shovel breaking up into small pieces rocks which had been dynamited to clear a way for tractors and horses. After a few days of this backbreaking labor he was thankful to be put on to driving a "dump wagon" and team of mules. Three days of one week he and another man were sent with their wagons to fetch lumber from the sawmills higher up in the mountains. "That was very jolly, driving through the pine forests," he recalls. "On the second day, owing to the other man's wagon sticking in a bad place, we had to sleep at the sawmills, a most delightful lonely spot right in the woods. Of course the wagons had no springs and bumped you all to bits. This I should not have minded if only my mate had not sworn and blasphemed the moment anything went wrong with his wagon. I found all the men very friendly, but alas! their swearing and filthy talk made their company almost unendurable. It was hard work loading and unloading the wagons—just the two of us to lift beams 8 by 8 feet square and 25 feet long! There were a dozen or so on each wagon, and sometimes we had to unload and reload a wagon in the track."

If nothing else, the former clergyman was getting a look

at a different side of life, and gaining experience of common humanity which would be most valuable in the not very distant future. To get to Mass on Sunday he had to walk ten miles from the camp to Pincher's Creek. After the blasphemy and foulness of the camp, which "made it just like hell to be in," it was a joy to see the spire of the church in the distance, and to hear the welcome and restful sound of its bell.

"When the harmonium played and the singers in the west gallery sang *Asperges me hyssopo et mundabor*—it brought the tears to my eyes—it was like a bath after wading through the mire." John wrote, "How wonderful is the Catholic Church all over the wide world—everywhere you find it, and just the same familiar worship; the same familiar images of the saints—how homely and companionable they feel, especially when you happen to feel lost and lonely. When I was wandering about the streets of a big city such as Winnipeg, one couldn't help feeling utterly lonesome as the shades of evening came on, but to turn in to one of the ever-open Catholic churches and see the glimmering lamps and flickering tapers, also the silent kneeling worshipers, gave one a sense of home and companionship at once. It brought renewed courage and hope. There is a wonderful fellowship in the Catholic and Roman Church."

It seems to have delighted John that all across Canada the priests wore their soutanes in the cities, villages and on the railroads. It pleased him also that so many of the priests had beards, presumably because he always seems to have associated a bearded face with St. Francis of Assisi.

Work at the railroad construction camp closed down in the fall of 1911. For two or three weeks John added to his experiences by becoming a farm laborer: driving a wagon to fetch in hay cut on the prairies, cleaning out the stables daily, milking cows, and running a cream separator. Then, feeling that being so near the Rocky Mountains it would be a pity to leave without seeing them a bit closer, he made a three days' tour and walked right through the Crowsnest Pass as far as the border of British Columbia, and back again. He slept free of charge in the little log cabins, already snow-covered, which were spaced at regular intervals of about ten miles at the side of the railroad track.

He made his way back east in charge of a van of cattle on a freight train, his chief duty being to let out the beasts and water them in the stockyards at the main depots. He traveled in the "caboose" with the guard, and often sat in a swivel armchair up in the lookout trunk on the roof, enjoying the glorious panorama of mountains, forests and lakes.

At every hundred-mile section the train was shunted, and the caboose and guard changed for new ones. To avoid losing his cattle van, John got in and slept in the hayrack over the beasts' heads. Among the cows was a large bull, which he had been instructed to leave tethered and to fetch its water. However, at Three Rivers this bull broke loose and stamped out with the rest. "It was plenty of trouble to catch him," John said. "I remember one tense moment when I was left alone on the floor of the arena, like a matador in a Spanish bull ring; with the bull advancing on me with angry eyes, fed up with railroad travel! 'Now's your chance, seize him by the ring in his nose,' yelled the stockman on the fence. The bull lowered his nose to the ground just in time, and I hopped up the fence pretty smartly to join the other men."

At the end of his journey John received word that his mother was dangerously ill. He immediately booked passage for England and a few weeks later arrived in Surrey, where he stayed with his parents at Sutton. There the Catholic priest, finding that the new member of his congregation had practiced as an architect, asked him to make designs for the enlargement of the church, a project which was begun in the spring of 1912.

Then John was offered the very attractive post of tutor to the son of the United States ambassador to Mexico. He toyed with the idea for a time, stimulated by the thought of seeing Mexico, but just when he had almost made up his mind to accept the offer, Bishop Amigo turned up at Sutton to make a canonical visitation of the parish. When John told the Bishop of his new expectations, the latter replied, "Why waste time, my dear son, in going to Mexico and the end of the earth—time you might be giving to God?"

John interpreted this remark as another call to the priesthood, and once again Mr. and Mrs. Selby-Hall pleaded with him to accept financial help. Because of his wife, Charles Selby-Hall could not without great difficulties have become a priest himself, but the two of them wanted to give a priest to God. "Finally they broke down my stubborn pride and independence," wrote their friend. "May God bless and reward them."

John went to talk with the Bishop of Southwark, who arranged for him to go to Rome and enter the Beda College without further delay. He arrived there toward the end of January 1912, and on Candlemas Day he accompanied the rector, Monsignor George, to the Vatican, and had an audience with Pope Pius X. On being informed that this student was a convert clergyman, the Pope laid his hand on his head, saying, "Bravo! bravo!" He gave John his special blessing and prayed that God would grant him all manner of consolations.

To a man of John Hawes's varied experiences it must have been far from easy to settle down to the life of a Roman student at the age of thirty-six after the independent existence to which he had grown accustomed. But that he fit easily into the life at the Beda is amply shown by the testimony of one of his fellow students, Father Henry E. G. Rope, who spoke of him as modest, yet strong, self-possessed, companionable and charitable. Of his many-faceted personality and gifts Father Rope wrote,

"I used to say that he had every talent save that of languages, in which his concords, genders and accents were apt to stumble. . . . Even here, however, his skill in sign language helped him out. He told me he had once been benighted in some north Italian countryside, and sought shelter in a cottage. Having little Italian, he leaned against the doorpost and pretended to snore. A small child at once divined and interpreted to her parents his petition; their generous hospitality was his. . . . "

Father Rope went on to detail some of John's pen-and-ink jokes. "Poking fun at my too uncritical zeal for medievalism, he drew me saying Office by the light of a glowworm, with a large box in the corner inscribed, 'Best Glowworms—Keep Dry,' from—shall we say—'Messrs. Urns and Boats.' Another time, noting my fondness for the Byzantine Mass at the Greek College, he pictured the 'Beda Chapel' transformed to the Greek rite. . . . Yet another sketch showed me sleeping calmly on a bed protected by a rim of prickly pinnacles, and 'No more holy water required. . . . ' I need hardly add that his brave, cheerful and kindly presence greatly enhanced the happiness of our college life in that old Rome in which death speed and din were not yet deemed the *summum bonum.* . . .

"Truly Franciscan was his ever-fresh joy in God's creation, his love of wild creatures, his keen sense of beauty in nature and true art. Like Chesterton, he kept through life the open heart of childhood. . . . " [1]

During his first year at the Beda John took a step which, considering his attachment to Franciscanism, it is surprising that he waited twenty months to put into action. He sought admission to the Third Order of St. Francis and on the feast

[1] Henry E. G. Rope, "John C. Hawes: 'Father Jerome,' O.S.F.," *The Beda Review,* September, 1956, p. 11.

of the saint, October 4, 1912, he was clothed as a tertiary in the basilica of San Francesco at Assisi. The following year, on December 8, "Brother John Francis Xavier Hawes" made his tertiary profession in the Capuchin church of St. Lawrence of Brindisi, Rome. In spite of Anglican failures and Roman rejection, John Hawes had at last realized his strongest desire: to be formally united to the Franciscan Order.

Several months after his clothing, in March 1913, word reached John of the corporate reception into the Catholic Church of Abbot Aelred Carlyle and twenty-two out of the thirty-three men who made up the Caldey Benedictine community. Two months later John went to meet his old friend and one-time religious superior when he arrived in Rome. "We went straight to St. Peter's," John wrote to Selby-Hall. "The Abbot of Maredsous said Mass at St. Peter's tomb; Aelred and I served him vested in cottas. Then we all had breakfast in the sacristy." What a joy it must have been for these two men who had traveled such a long road to Rome to meet in the heart of the Church of which they had so long considered themselves a part. Nevertheless, John with his customary incisiveness wrote later, "Abbot Aelred Carlyle and the Caldey Benedictines might have put off their submission to the Catholic Church if Abbess Scholastica Ewart had not helped to give them a good shove."

This meeting between the two friends was brief, however, for in May 1913 John was off to Malta for a "wonderful experience" at the Eucharistic Congress. In an attempt to live up to his Franciscan ideals, he spent the night aboard the steamer propped up against a pile of baggage on deck. He mentioned that "the first-class saloon was full of American priests and bishops. The Reverend Clergy walked about on deck in all sorts of queer cloth caps—some (American, of course) in English clericals, with opera glasses hung over their shoulders. One priest wore a gray suit."

Several pages of one of his letters were devoted to vivid descriptions of Malta and the wonderful Catholic atmosphere of the island, the whole of which "seemed to be given up to God and his Grace." He marveled that half the inhabitants received Holy Communion daily, and that there was no drunkenness and apparently no sexual immorality.

It is easy to understand how the Maltese ceremonial appealed to John's eclectic and baroque taste. He mentioned the brass and string orchestras in the west galleries of the larger churches; the credence tables arranged with silver flagons and plates—just like the Communion table at Westminster Abbey on royal occasions; except that here there were miters in addition to twelve solid-silver statues.

Most of the altar frontals, tabernacles and candlesticks were of solid beaten silver. The high altars all had a beautiful hanging canopy or baldachin. Never had John seen such immense candles, very long and thick, soaring up, and all miraculously straight! He was fascinated by the surplices worn by the priests, tight around the neck, with long, full sleeves folded back over the wrists. Even more exciting was the sight of all the canons of the cathedral at Citta Vecchia, and also at the Co-Cathedral of St. John, Valetta, wearing white miters at Mass. He could hardly believe his eyes when the deacon and sub-deacon walked in with miters on their heads, but he supposed they happened to be bishops.

He told Mr. Selby-Hall that whenever the Viaticum was taken to the sick, whatever time of the day or night, the church bells rang and the Sacred Host was borne solemnly under a square canopy with a crowd of men and boys in front carrying candles and lanterns, with numbers of men and women following them. No matter where he went at any period of his life, John showed unusual powers of observation and a retentive memory for details. He reveled in every manifestation of beauty, and had no narrow prejudices.

From the moment John had decided to enter the Beda he began to dream of returning to the Bahamas as a Catholic priest. When he wrote to Cardinal Farley, Archbishop of New York, regarding this possibility, however, he was informed that since the missions in the Bahamas were served by Benedictines of St. John's Abbey, Minnesota, there would be no place for a secular priest in these islands. In June 1912 he wrote to Mr. Selby-Hall that a great weight had been taken off his mind, saying: "God's will is now quite clear as regards that course for me. *Deo gratias*. I am really very thankful. I had such weighty misgivings that it would have been a mistake to go back to the Bahamas. . . . Affection for the dear people of my late flock made me desire to return to them, but now I see that it is clearly not God's will. I know He will provide all that is best for them, and He will bring them or their children into His True Church in His own good time—there is no hurry with God."

John's next move was to write to the Bishop of Regina, since he knew from experience how great was the need of English-speaking priests in the west of Canada. He could easily form a mental picture of himself engaged in rough pioneer missionary work on the prairies of Saskatchewan, but the Bishop showed no eagerness to accept this convert Anglican clergyman for his diocese.

It was not until shortly before his ordination to the priesthood that John discovered where his future apostolate would be. One day Monsignor George, rector of the Beda College, happened to meet Bishop Kelly of Geraldton, who talked to him of the spiritual needs of his vast diocese in Western Australia. On the next occasion when the rector came to join the students at recreation in their common room he spoke to them of this bishop. Turning to John, he said, "That would be the Bishop for you, Hawes; it would be worth your while to see him."

John replied, "But what about Canada? The Bishop of Regina has not yet given me a definite answer."

Monsignor George answered: "I could straighten that out later."

So the following day John called on Bishop Kelly, and they went for a long walk together, and the student, now more familiar with Rome than was the Australian prelate, piloted him through the streets. He recorded that "to the multitude of beggars that accosted him for an alms, the Bishop never refused one, but stopped and dived into his pockets and courteously handed the coin to the beggar as to Christ. He reminded me of the good bishop in Victor Hugo's *Les Misérables,* but how he could ever carry so many *centesimi* in his pockets I don't know! And he even asked me to say a prayer for him!

"That was the first of many daily long walks we had together. How Bishop Kelly loved Australia—and it was not exactly the land of his birth because he had been born at sea. His diocese, so he explained to me, was the biggest, poorest and wildest on the southern continent. 'Well,' said the Bishop, 'if you want real apostolic missionary work I can offer you that, but not much more.' I replied that this sort of thing would suit me perfectly. Then he spoke of the cathedral he hoped to build in Geraldton. He wanted it *round,* with the seats converging on the high altar. Next day I brought along some sketches to show him. He was delighted, and remarked: 'Why, you understand at once exactly what I want, and when I consulted an architect at home, he drew me out a plan of an oblong building with five domes.' "

John had received the first of the major orders, the subdiaconate, when he had returned to England for the summer vacation, just before World War I broke out in August 1914. Had he not been definitely bound, he would have volunteered for service in any capacity, but he had to go back to Rome and continue his studies. The rector excused him from doing the full course of philosophy, remarking, "You won't need much philosophy in the back blocks of Western Australia!"

On Ember Saturday, February 27, 1915, John was ordained priest by the Cardinal Vicar in the Lateran Basilica. He wrote to Mr. and Mrs. Selby-Hall: "Well, my dear friends, I am a *real* priest at last. The service at St. John Lateran was most beautiful. There were a great many to be ordained, so the choir stalls were full. The Mass was sung unaccompanied, all the clerics joining in with a thundering volume of sound, when the organ played the grand old plain-chant tune for the *Veni Creator*. When my hands were being anointed and tied up, I felt I must weep, but I gulped down the sobs and managed not to show tears. We were fourteen from the Beda, including those for minor orders. We were in church from 7:15 A.M. to 12:45 P.M. I had a racking headache all the afternoon, but felt quite happy. . . . I shall be very sorry to leave dear holy old Rome, and to bid a last lingering good-by to St. Peter's."

Once again the urge to go tramping reasserted itself, so with another student the newly ordained priest set out from Rome to Montefiascone. From here the pair walked on to Bolsena and Orvieto, covering a distance of about fifty miles in each direction. Most of the time the weather was wet and stormy. As Father Hawes "waded nearly knee-deep through little streams crossing roads, getting lost among the hills, and following mule tracks," he must have recalled his first tramp through England. In a letter to Selby-Hall he told of how he and his companion sat around a huge open fireplace in a great beamed room at Bolsena, surrounded by peasants. A woman cooked a meal on the fire, and sheep dogs strolled about the room. John never failed to notice dogs of any breed. He was passionately devoted to them.

In this same letter he gave details of "a grand concert at

the Beda on the Saturday night after the ordinations, for which Percy Gateley (another convert from the Anglican ministry, and also a Benedictine novice at Caldey) concocted one of his inimitable songs for the occasion, taking us all off. His verse on me was:

> Builds cathedrals at his ease,
> Loves, although they harbor fleas:
> Cats and aborigines:
> Can you tell me who is he?

Shortly before John left Rome for England, the Reverend Vincent Eyre turned up on a holiday pilgrimage to shrines in Italy. "We visited Frascati, among other places," Father Hawes related. "On the feast of St. Aloysius Mr. Eyre accompanied me early in the morning to that saint's church, where I said Mass at a side altar and my dear old vicar knelt with great devotion hearing my Mass. There was nothing clerical about his costume, only a dark suit with a turn-down collar. A day or two previously he was kneeling at his devotions in one of the smaller Roman churches, when the sacristan (struck by the priestly-looking face), and in spite of the lay clothes, approached him, saying that an altar was all ready for him if he would like to celebrate Mass. Mr. Eyre smiled, shook his head, and waved him away. Until his death he always longed to find himself in communion with the Holy See, but he was never granted the gift of faith."

Before he said farewell to Rome, Father Hawes obtained the necessary faculties from the Minister General of the Friars Minor Capuchin to establish congregations of the Franciscan Third Order in any parish of which he might find himself in charge. Then he set out for England, where he spent about three months with his parents.

On the feast of the Guardian Angels, October 2, 1915, he embarked at Tilbury Docks on the long voyage to Australia.

5.

Gold-Fields Missionary [1915–1920]

IN 1915, when Father John Hawes first arrived in Australia, the diocese of Geraldton of which he was to be a priest consisted of a vast territory of about 314,500 square miles set squarely in the center of Western Australia. It had been created in 1898, and by the time Father Hawes began his work there it still boasted no more than twenty-eight churches served by ten secular and four regular priests. The Irish Presentation nuns had twenty-eight members divided among six houses, while the Dominican Sisters from New Zealand, who numbered twenty-four, conducted four convent schools within the diocesan boundaries.

Bishop Kelly welcomed the new priest and turned over to him the so-called "parish" of Mount Magnet, which included the Yalgoo gold fields to the east of Geraldton. Father Hawes's district was 160 miles long and almost as wide. Within the parish lay four little towns, four churches (but only two presbyteries), and two convents on the gold fields. The country around Mount Magnet was given over to stock raising, with "stations" or ranches at which Mass was celebrated four times a year. Within Mount Magnet itself was a church and presbytery, but Father Hawes gave up the latter to be used as a convent for three Presentation nuns who came up from Geraldton to open a badly needed Catholic school.

At Yalgoo, seventy miles southwest of Mount Magnet, he had another presbytery, which he described as "a very comfortable little bungalow with a veranda all around, a sitting room, bedroom, kitchen and bathroom." Yalgoo church, so he stated, was certainly the prettiest little building of corrugated iron he had ever seen, "white walls and red roof, with a stately altar and spacious sanctuary, as long as the nave, even an apse with leaded stained-glass windows." There were about 250 inhabitants, nearly all of them Catholics. Camels and emus strolled along the street, and the camels emitted weird groans. From Yalgoo a team of nine camels would drag an enormous wagon, carrying about eight tons—balks of timber, and other equipment for the gold mines—to places more than fifty miles away.

In one of his first letters to Selby-Hall, Father Hawes explained that it was far too hot to do anything but "flop about struggling to exist, with a temperature of 110° in the shade all the time." He had tried to write once but his hand stuck to the paper and it was too much exertion! Mosquitoes kept him awake most nights, but sometimes he managed to get sleep by saturating his pillow with oil of citronella. "I have hauled my bed out and slept under the stars," he wrote. "I have said Mass daily at six, but after breakfast it gets too hot to do anything but alternately drink out of the water bag and lie down in the bath. I feel too exhausted even to start saying my Office until after sunset. Of course it is possible to sit in a draught between doors and windows, but the burning wind dries you up! Then you see a 'willy-willy' coming, and rush to close the windows. A 'willy-willy' is a whirlwind of red dust. You see a great pillar just like a waterspout sweeping down through the bush or up the road. If it passes through a house, everything is covered thick with a fine dust. These moving pillars of dust are a familiar sight—red against a clear blue sky.

"But a 'willy-willy' is nothing to a dust storm; in the latter the wind blows like a hurricane, and you can do nothing. The sky is darkened, verandas are torn off, and instead of the ordinary flocks of little green parrots, or gray and red cockatoos, the air is filled with hurtling sheets of corrugated iron, kerosene tins and empty rain-water tanks, and the little corrugated-iron closets that adorn every back yard and decorate vacant spaces in the gold-fields towns. If one of these architectural gems, or an empty 5,000-gallon tank, happens to descend on your head, you might have the misfortune to be consigned to the nearest hospital. If the local doctor is like the dentist—well! The one-and-only remedy the dentists have here is to pull out *all* the teeth you've got, so that you can't suffer from toothache any more, and they do it at one sitting. The Australian character is simple and straightforward and likes thoroughgoing remedies!"

Even if he found the physical discomfort hard to endure, it was clear enough that Father Hawes enjoyed writing about his new and strange environment. He went on to describe the two mining towns of Cue and Day Dawn, which lay about fifty miles northeast of Mount Magnet. To reach them the railroad had to cross a great "lake," sixty miles long. It usually was filled with sand, salt and yellow clay, but once or twice a year, after thunderstorms, it became a real lake, filled with water.

"Cue is the end of the earth, and Day Dawn even more at the back of beyond," he wrote. "My first day in Cue a man said to me, 'Well, Father, I wonder how you'll like it? I remember my first impressions of the place twenty-one years ago. I'd come straight out from Ireland, and when I got here I thought this place was the abomination of desolation spoken of by the prophet what's-his-name. I'd have gone straight back home to dear old Ireland if I could have, but I'd nothing to go with; but I like it all right now—it's the people that count."

At Cue, Father Hawes found a brick presbytery, a fairly good church "of the Gothic variety," a Dominican convent, and a large school. He describes the convent as "quite a picturesque place of tropical aspect, clothed entirely in Dominican white: white walls in shade under the low-sweeping veranda covered with creepers and flowers, little palms in front and whitewashed roofs sparkling in the sunshine."

Day Dawn was very different. Here his "heart sank" as the sun rose over the dreary, flat, treeless wilderness of baked red clay, red ironstone rocks and dried-up patches of brown grass, and over the "corrugated tabernacles" of the misnamed "town." It consisted of the usual rows of "hotels" and stores, with a town hall, fire station, and the Anglican and Methodist chapels roped together with the same telephone wire! Father Hawes noted that the Protestant churches generally snuggled up close together in the gold-fields towns, and were usually on the opposite side of the road from the Catholic chapel. There was one train a day, and this had "shot him out at Day Dawn at midnight." During the remaining hours of darkness millions of mosquitoes buzzed merrily around. They came from the town reservoir, which, as elsewhere in Western Australia, was called the dam.

The outstanding feature and pride of Day Dawn was the Great Fingall Dump, said to be 200 feet high. Father Hawes described it as "a mountain of powdered white quartz—refuse from the gold battery. But the Great Fingall has fallen on evil days. It now employs only fifty men, where formerly 500 worked." He went on to say: "One great consolation is that in the beastliest of places you will find some of the very nicest and dearest people. I like going to Day Dawn now because the Catholics there are so devout and so keen on their little brick church, dedicated to St. Joseph. Their hospitality to a priest is overwhelming."

It was both a surprise and a great consolation to the priest-architect to find that all his four churches were well supplied with good statues, fine Stations of the Cross, rich vestments and valuable altar vessels. Each possessed a splendid monstrance. The women kept the presbyteries or the sacristy lodgings clean and tidy. The only exception was at Cue, where nobody had even touched the presbytery since his predecessor departed. Father Hawes wrote, "When I arrived it was full of rubbish, dust, old papers, etc., so I turned to myself in the sweltering heat and spent two days clearing the place out. The movable furniture consisted mainly of empty beer bottles. I carted them out to the end of the garden, where small children came daily with little wheel carts to remove them, and thereby made their fortunes (getting something for the bottles at the hotels). The broken bottles left by the children have been consumed by stray goats!"

The missionary realized that he would get accustomed to almost anything. He began to grow quite fond of the wild, desolate bush scenery. He saw new beauties and fascination in everything. Then the first rain for nearly five months fell, filling up the water tanks, freshening the feed of the stock and cattle, and cooling the air. Father Hawes now felt that there were far worse places in the world than Western Australia in which to live. He was finding his feet.

Yet he confessed that he found it impossible to work up any interest in mining, minerals, reefs and gold nuggets, which were the usual subjects of conversation among his scattered flock. On the other hand, because of his love for animals, Father Hawes got on well talking to the stockmen and picking up bush lore from them. There were a fair number of blacks about in the bush, "the queerest-looking people I ever saw in my life," so he described them. Very few of the

aborigines in his parish were even nominal Christians, unlike those who had been converted by the Benedictine monks
of New Norcia. Most of the hotelkeepers were Catholics of

Australian Aborigine

Irish origin who would never accept a penny from a priest for
his board and lodging. Taken as a whole, Father Hawes found
the Catholic families very kind and hospitable, and soon
formed the highest opinion of them.

In several letters he wrote of their loyalty to the Church
and of their faithfulness in fulfilling their religious obliga-
tions. He mentioned a Scotsman and his wife at Cue who
thought nothing of driving seventy miles from their cattle
station for confession, Mass and Holy Communion. There
was another man, Paddy Morrisy, often called "The Saint" or
"Priest Morrisy," who never missed a Sunday when the priest
came. He usually drove in fifteen to twenty miles with his

wife and children, but sometimes, when he failed to catch his horse in the bush, he walked the fifteen or more miles by himself, rather than miss Mass.

This story is all the more remarkable, because Cue claimed to be about the hottest place on the gold fields. There was a saying that when its inhabitants reached hell they would send back to Cue for their blankets!

Father Hawes, as has been related, had ceased to wear his beloved brown Franciscan habit just before he left the Bahamas in 1911. Since his arrival in Western Australia he had adopted an equally picturesque costume—a thin long coat of pale brownish silk, white wide-brimmed hat, and pale brown holland trousers. He explained in one letter that the color had nothing to do with Franciscanism, but had been chosen because of the dust. White clothes were impractical, since it was not long before they were covered with dingy red dust stains.

Many of his early letters show that he saw everything and everybody with the eyes of an artist. Here is a typical paragraph: "Yesterday morning I went for a walk out a few miles in the bush, and really enjoyed it, because the sun was completely hidden under a sky of gray rolling clouds. It was like dear old England (the sky, I mean). And the bush was full of beautiful color, but there's no 'color' in the artistic sense when everything swelters all day long, scintillating under a fierce, pitiless, cloudless *glare*—low green scrub from six to eight feet high, and a vast rolling waste *without a tree*."

On Sundays the priest visited the different towns in rotation, so that each had Mass every third Sunday and several weekday Masses. The main part of the Sunday collections was used to pay railroad fares. Father Hawes got an average of thirty shillings every week, and also a very occasional Mass stipend. Altar wine, candles and other necessities were paid for by the altar societies in each town.

A good idea of the busy life of a mission priest in Western Australia about forty years ago is given in the "program" drawn up by Father Hawes after he had got to know his enormous parish. This is how it reads:

First Sunday

Cue—Confessions 6.30, Mass 7.30, motor to Day Dawn 8.15.

Day Dawn—Confessions 9 and Mass 9. Short sermon at both places. Catechism in the afternoon. Rosary, sermon and Benediction 6.30 P.M.

Monday—Confessions 6.30, Mass 7, Rosary 7.30 P.M.

Tuesday—Leave Day Dawn by 3 A.M. train, arrive *Mount Magnet* 6 A.M. Confessions on arrival, Mass 7. During the week visits to Catholic families in cattle and sheep stations. Mass at *Yowergalbie, Mumbinia, Edah,* etc. Loan of horse to ride to these stations.

Second Sunday

Ride on horseback to *Boogardie* (five miles) for Mass at 7.30 A.M. Back to *Mount Magnet* for Mass at 9.30, with sermon. Catechism 3 P.M. Rosary, sermon and Benediction 7.30 P.M.

Spend three days visiting Catholic families, then by 6 A.M. train (seventy miles) to *Yalgoo,* arriving there by middle of the week.

Third Sunday (an easy one!)

Confessions and Communion from 7 A.M. Mass and sermon at 9. Rosary, sermon and Benediction, 7.30 P.M.

Train back to *Mount Magnet* about the middle of the week, and then on to *Cue* (120 miles), arriving there about midnight. Then the round again as before, only with some different stations. Several of these are mines fifty or more miles from the railway. The men send a motorcar to fetch the priest.

One of the things that surprised Father Hawes was that he had to eat plenty of meat in the very hot weather. He wrote: "You get an awful sinking feeling in your middle if you don't take food regularly." He got another surprise when the Australian climate in the month of May moved from its extreme of heat to bitter winds morning and evening and brilliant sunshine alternating with rain. Having been nearly roasted alive, even in the shade, he never expected that he would welcome a fire to sit beside in the evening.

It was a surprise to him, too, that the people looked so healthy, and his Franciscan spirit reveled in the absence of any class distinctions. He said in one of his earlier letters: "The men are quiet but very sociable, and all is free and easy, yet there are real good manners and a rough sort of courtesy. When drunk, the men are usually quiet, and oddly enough the drunker they are, the more silent they become!"

There were so many little things that amused him. The local Methodist minister was clean-shaven, wore a Roman collar, a "Trilby hat," and dressed entirely in black—even in the hottest weather. The Church of England clergyman at Mount Magnet always wore a clean, stiff starched white suit and a white helmet. Father Hawes formed the rather harsh impression that most of the Anglican missionaries had little to do beyond collecting their Christmas and Easter dues from the Freemasons, but perhaps his observations were colored by the antipathy which he had developed since his conversion toward everything connected with Anglicanism. Somebody at Mount Magnet had told him that on a Sunday the parson often rang the bell and went into church where he read the service alone. This certainly has an apocryphal ring! In one of those earlier letters he judges that "where the Anglicans cannot have *attractive* services with an organ and a good choir (as in Geraldton), the C of E churches don't seem to 'draw out' in these back places, but Catholics need none of these things. I sometimes think how intensely dull our services are from the 'natural' point of view: no hymns, no music unless perhaps what is worse than none at all, a couple of devoted but earsplitting squalling 'prima donnas' painfully torturing the *Kyries* and the *Gloria* or the *Tantum Ergo,* to some soulless operatic twiddling. But *our* people come to *pray,* to offer sacrifice to God, and to be eased of their sins. The supernatural is really evident."

Father Hawes thought it odd that, considering the abundance of beautiful wild flowers in Western Australia, most of the little Catholic churches generally had their altars adorned in a homely style with "large brilliant and varied concoctions of paper and rag, springing out of assorted china vases between the long, topply judases." This exhibition of chiefly artificial flowers brought back to him the "delicious aroma of Italy and the Eternal City. . . . *Dear* old paper flowers, you waft me away in spirit, as I say Mass, from these torrid wastes to those altars amid the soft blue mountains of Umbria and Tuscany, to the time-worn sanctuaries of Assisi, Loreto, and San Gemignano."

There was definitely no Teutonic stiffness in the churches. Big, sturdy-looking lads of fifteen or sixteen were quite happy to go on wearing the same garments they had worn when they were eight, and first "on the altar," to use the favorite Irish expression. Scarlet cassocks, shrunk to the length of an episcopal mantelletta, showed brawny bare knees and stout calves. The children were charmingly unsophisticated. Father Hawes tells the story of a little boy of eight who had made his first confession most thoroughly and intelligently. He asked the boy:

"And there's nothing more, my child?"

"Please, Father, you'll come in to breakfast after Mass? I'm sure Mother would ask you to . . ."

"Never mind about that now, we can think about that after Mass. Say three Hail Marys for your penance, and make a . . ."

"And we still got those pictures you drewed us last time . . ."

"*Yes:* now make a good act of contrition, while I give you absolution."

It was remarkable how this convert Englishman got on with his mainly Irish flock. How much he loved them is evident from many of his letters. His first St. Patrick's Day at Yalgoo was described in great detail. It started off with a full church at seven-o'clock Mass, with the altar a blaze of candles, followed by a lively hymn to St. Patrick. In spite of not having a drop of Irish blood in his veins, so far as he knew, Father Hawes proudly displayed all day an elegant harp of green ribbon with a sprig of shamrock thereon, and a bit of shamrock sewed into his coat. After a strenuous afternoon in grilling heat, the kindly Presentation nuns brought him a festal meal—scones and cakes and grapes, black and white, and a watermelon with chunks of ice to keep it cool. The day ended with a grand concert and public dance. Nineteen couples came all the way from Mount Magnet, and danced all night, returning home by the 6 A.M. train.

The Presentation nuns are often mentioned in Father Hawes's letters, and described as "grand women." All were Irish "out from the old country." Their pastor added: "It's a wonderful thing, refined and educated women, leaving comfortable homes, and then giving up even the ordinary spiritual consolations of the cloister to live out in these dreary back-block places where they are often a fortnight without Mass, but with the consolation of having Our Lord in the tabernacle with them. They do a power of good, and the Protestants recognize it, in that so many of them withdraw their children from the state schools and send them to the nearest convent school, knowing that not only is the standard of secular education higher, with music, painting, dancing, etc. taught, but that the children learn better manners at the Catholic schools, including obedience and courtesy."

After a year or two Father Hawes made friends with all sorts of curious characters, among whom was a former mayor who had returned to the bush, where he cut sandalwood, sank wells, and drank a lot—but not water from his wells! The first time they met the former mayor resembled a dirty laborer; the following night he was a great swell in evening dress, acting as master of ceremonies at a charity dance. Another good friend to the missionary priest and the nuns was Jim Burgoine, the publican at Boogardie—a huge, burly fellow ever so hearty and good-natured. He and the priest shared a common love of horses. The two of them would sit around for hours, drinking cold beer and talking of horses, but it was not so easy to get Jim to Mass. If he did turn up, it was generally after the priest had taken the ablutions or when he was about to give the final blessing.

It was the publican of Boogardie who lent Father Hawes a fine, big, powerful stock horse for his first long ride around some of the outlying mines and sheep stations. On this trip he covered more than 240 miles through the bush, and had some hair-raising adventures. We can picture him with his altar stone and vestments, a thin pajama suit, sponge bag, razor, a breviary and missal, all done up in a roll of brown canvas strapped in front of the saddle. A blanket was under the saddle, a flask of water and a billycan on one side, and a small bag with sundry things in it on the other. He would take off his coat and Roman collar and tie them on top of the canvas roll so they would be handy if needed, and ride in his shirt sleeves and khaki trousers, with a white pith helmet perched on his head.

Father Hawes rode through the lonely bush all the first day, and it was not until nearly 9 P.M. that he found his way to a house, where a kindly Irish family gave him a bed for the night and a grand meal of hot tea, creamy milk, eggs, scones and rich cake. The following day he had the misfortune to lose the one absolutely essential item in his gear, the canvas water bag, and consequently suffered from thirst. Once again it was an Irishman and his wife who put him up for the night. On Candlemas Day Father Hawes celebrated Mass at one of his remote stations, where he blessed both holy water and candles for a dozen faithful Catholics. He was rewarded by an offering of five pounds, a welcome surprise.

After a Sunday at Yalgoo, Father Hawes set out again, taking with him some flour, sugar and tea in his saddlebag, and making a start by sunrise. He rode all day, except for a halt between noon and four to escape the terrific heat. Sunset found him at a lonely wild spot with a well, called the Shadow of Death, forty-one miles from Yalgoo. There had been a cattle station there once, but now he saw nothing but the ruins of roofless buildings, composed of sun-dried bricks. The ruins lay in a valley filled with eucalyptus trees whose boughs were dry and withered. A tall erection within some broken fencing looked like a gallows but had probably been a hoist for branding cattle, for the Shadow of Death had once been quite a big station.

Father Hawes writes: "I had to work hard hauling up a windlass to bring the water bucket up from the well—a heavy iron bucket. The well was about sixty feet deep, with horrid brackish water. My horse had a drink and I filled my water bag, after which I mad up to a little hill behind the ruined houses. Here I unsaddled the horse and turned him loose with hobbles on his forelegs and a large brass bell round his neck. Then I gathered some sticks, any amount of dry withered branches lying around, and in a few minutes I had a blazing fire. I mixed up some flour and water on a bit of newspaper, and made a 'Johnny Cake' or 'Damper,' as they call it here—a flat cake of bread which I laid on the embers and raked more ashes over it, and boiled my 'billy' for tea. It tasted very salty from the water of the Shadow well.

"It was quite dark by then, and a clear starlight sky over my head. I said the fifteen mysteries of the Rosary instead of the Breviary, and then curled up in a blanket and lay down near the fire. . . . In the morning at dawn I made tea and finished last night's 'Damper.' Then I went to look for the horse, heard his bell tinkling not very far off, down by the well. So I made my way there with my sponge bag, wound up a bucket of water, and had a refreshing bath—didn't trouble about a towel, but got wet into my shirt and trousers, which soon dried."

Among the many people Father Hawes met on this long, adventurous ride was at least one Protestant family, who mistook him for a policeman because of his big horse, khaki clothes and white helmet. Once they were told that he was a priest they could not do enough for him, saying that they had never been visited by their own Church of England clergyman. When he left them he rode on across great, flat plains and across the beds of dried-up lakes, where big kangaroos bounded about among scrubby bushes. He passed mining works with their skeleton towers, and many abandoned buildings, their iron roofs stripped off and hanging, flapping in the wind, like torn brown paper. On and on, mile after mile, until he reached a lonely whitewashed iron house, which turned out to be a hotel, run by two Irish Catholic brothers, each with his own family, and an old grandmother, only a year out from Ireland. Needless to say they welcomed the priest with open arms. As Mrs. Harvey, the grandmother, prepared supper she said, "Oh, Father, this is a wild, lone place, a wild, bad place, and they don't think of God at all, at all, but all their thoughts is down under the ground after the gold. God bless and save your Reverence."

"Poor old thing," commented Father Hawes, "after going daily to Mass all her life, no wonder she found Western Australia a 'godless country.' " She said to him: "I pray the Lord He'll just spare me to get back to the old country, so that I may not die in this terrible place and be buried over the hill yonder. Oh, Father, I couldn't rest there!"

Still, it was an intense joy for the poor old lady to be able to assist at Mass the following morning, when quite a large congregation assembled, most of whom made their confessions and went to Communion.

After another long ride in intense heat, passing Lake Monger glistening silver-white in the sun from the salt caked on the surface of its dry bottom, the missionary landed at a mining camp. Here the men were most friendly, and Father Hawes admits that it was not easy for him to refuse the rounds of drinks pressed on him that first evening. There were more mining settlements to be visited, so he changed over from his horse to a shaky old motorcar with a trailer, which he found much more uncomfortable, and which nearly bumped him to bits.

Here was a different hilly sort of landscape, a welcome change from the deadly monotony of the flat plains. The far distances took on a wonderful blue, so that Father Hawes could fancy to himself that the rolling country was the sea, and almost began to look out for white sails. The journey was worth while because he discovered fifteen Catholics, some of them Italians, who told him that this was the first visit paid by any minister of religion since they had arrived there eighteen months before.

Another drive in the ramshackle automobile took him to a hotel at Payne's Field, where the following morning enough Catholics had been "roped in" to make it worth while to celebrate Mass in the hotel eating room. Father Hawes recorded that "the tables were cleared out, except one that stood against the east wall, under a large colored almanac print of a rosy-faced girl fondling a Newfoundland dog. I could not help feeling that it lacked the devotional tone of a Raphael or a Fra Angelico, so I moved the table to the middle of the side wall where there was nothing but whitewash (and flies) above the crucifix. My congregation was entirely of the sterner sex, but at the Offertory I became aware of a flowered hat stealing in, which knelt down quietly in a far corner—it was the Irish kitchenmaid with red hair whom I had overheard remark the evening before that she 'had done with all that sort of thing' since she came to this hotel! There were no Communions at Payne's Field. For most of the men it was grace enough to get them to Mass—it would have been too much to expect this tough crowd to go to confession and Communion. At the ablutions I gave a five-minute sermon, as simple as I could make it, just on holding on to the Faith in these back blocks, and the duty of remembering that they were Catholics and the only witnesses of God out here. I said that man was something more than a brute beast, and begged the men to remember what they'd learned long ago at their mothers' knees, and how in the past they had often sung 'Faith of Our Fathers'; they must try to keep this Faith alive here, if nothing else. An offering of a couple of pound notes was presented with many apologies that it was not more. 'You've come at a bad time, Father, if you'd come a fortnight later, when the government crushings is on, we might have given you far more.'

"The red-haired girl got me tea and toast, and all the rest of the morning till dinner I heard her humming, singing and whistling 'Faith of Our Fathers' over her pots and pans. Perhaps my sermon had done some good? Beer and greyhounds seemed to be the only Sunday occupation for the rest of the inhabitants that Sunday."

After riding four more days, camping out in the bush on

two nights, and suffering from hunger and especially from thirst because his water bag had sprung a leak and none of the water in the few wells was drinkable, Father Hawes finally got back to Mount Magnet. He realized that the only way to keep in touch with his widely-scattered families was to buy a horse, so that he could make more of the apostolic journeys whenever he could spare the time. He had saved twelve pounds given him by the bishop the previous Christmas, and returned from this first long ride with thirteen pounds in his pocket. Jim Burgoine promised to look out for a good horse, and not long after this Father Hawes took his savings and bought the animal Jim selected.

He was amused to hear that his first tour of the distant stations had provoked much heart-burning and criticism in the Anglican fold. Some of the Church of England "squatters" were reported to have said, "Here's the Roman Catholic priest not been here two months yet, and he's got out to these back-block places, and our clergyman has been here two years and never visited us yet." The result of such grumblings was that the local parson paid a visit to one of the fairly distant stations, a fortnight after his Catholic opposite number had been there. This clergyman asked his congregation to present him with a motor bike, but they said times were too bad for such expense, and told him to make do with his horse and trap.

One of the results of Father Hawes's bush tour was a recurring worry about the many lonely Catholics of whose existence he heard from time to time. He often wished that he had several curates to help him, but this was a hopeless dream. On the whole, Father Hawes seemed happy enough, but very often he complained of the lack of peace and solitude. Was it that he had begun to feel already that his true vocation was that of a hermit?

In one of his letters he mentions that he longed for peace to say his Office and prepare his sermon, but little girls from the adjacent convent school came into the sacristy to practice on the piano, while a nun played the *Tantum Ergo* on the harmonium in the church! He would shut his door and window, only to be suffocated by the heat. Then he would take his chair out onto the shady veranda, but he was still distracted by the mixture of music. He would open his Breviary only to have the flies crawl over his face and hands. If he moved his chair to a place where he was in the path of a breeze blowing round the church, flap, flap, flap went the leaves of the Office book. The flies, borne on the wind, came back to torment him, adding their buzzing to the droning harmony of piano and harmonium. Then, driven to desperation back into the stifling room, but the music and the heat proved too much with the door shut, so out into the open air again. Where was he now—Terce or None? He just couldn't remember where he had got to with the Word of God.

"The tum-tum-tum-diddle-diddle ending of that waltz was repeated for the twentieth time," the priest wrote. "I cursed little Phyllis O'Brien—God bless the child! If my guardian angel finds two of my Little Hours are missing, he must blame Phyllis. Here goes for Vespers. Oh, drat those flies! No sermon begun. Return from supper at the hotel, and hurriedly hash up my Yalgoo sermon on charity and forgiveness of enemies—especially Phyllis O'Brien, as she is a dear child."

Throughout his life John Hawes had always loved taking long walks. One of his greatest deprivations in Western Australia was that there was nowhere to go for a walk, and nowhere to sit and admire a distant view. He mentioned this in several letters, but remarked in one of them: "Don't think I'm really complaining. I think the relation of our petty annoyance and inconveniences is a source of *amusement,* and the very relation of them makes one see how trivial they really are, and how absurd one is to fume and fret all the time over such trifles. Laugh at them and they are nothing."

If only he had kept a diary during those first five years in Western Australia! All we know from the scanty material available is that Father Hawes lived his busy life from day to day, brushing aside trivial irritations and discomforts, enduring hardship and privations which would have been too much for many priests. His people were generous and he never suffered from poverty no matter what he had to put up with in other ways. He loved his apostolic work, nor was there a dearth of artistic endeavor in this desolate country.

Bishop Kelly, having discovered that his English missionary was a brilliant architect as well as a devoted apostle, put him to work designing one church after another. These churches, which are his lasting memorial in Australia, will be described later, but needless to say Father Hawes, who loved "making things," put his loving care not only into the designs but into the practical building operations as well.

These first years in most respects were a fruitful period. They were also, from a physical standpoint, heavily taxing, and in 1920 Bishop Kelly told Father Hawes that he had earned a holiday. It was decided that the missionary should pay a visit to England, so with a light heart he began to make plans for the long journey.

6.

Bush Architect [1920–1937]

At the thought of the journey ahead and at the fact that money was so readily available for it, Father Hawes began to have misgivings about his lack of Franciscan fervor which seemed almost to have dried up in the torrid heat of the Yalgoo gold fields. "What had become of my Franciscan ideals?" he wrote in his memoirs. "A medal of Our Lady of Mount Carmel carried in the pocket had long been substituted for her scapular, but the Franciscan tertiary cord and scapular were too much bother to wear when you lived most of the day in your shirt sleeves!" Nevertheless, the Little Poor Man had not forgotten his disciple and eventually was to recall him to his primitive ideals.

As a matter of fact, he began to put them into practice as soon as he set off across the Pacific. The only passage he was able to get was on a troopship which, after a call at a New Zealand port, sailed for Panama where Father Hawes was transferred to a trading schooner on which he slept on deck, his pillow a coil of rope. The schooner landed him at Port Limón in Costa Rica and there he spent three days absorbed in plans for a new sanctuary, transepts and a side altar for the local Catholic church. Then he boarded a "banana boat" bound for Havana from where, after feasting on the beauties of the many baroque and rococo churches in Cuba, he went to Matanzas and thence to Nassau, once more aboard a schooner.

The Bahamas, as Father Hawes knew, from his previous work there, had been Protestant in religion since their settlement by England in the seventeenth century. There is no evidence of their being visited by a Catholic priest before 1845, and it was not until 1885 that the cornerstone of the first Catholic church in the Bahamas was laid and the first resident priest appointed. At that time the islands formed a remote part of the archdiocese of New York and, in 1891 at the request of Archbishop Corrigan, the Benedictines of St. John's Abbey, Collegeville, Minnesota, sent two monk-missionaries, one of them Father Chrysostom Schreiner, to Nassau. When these Benedictines took over the mission they found only about fifty practicing Catholics, children included. Father Chrysostom, having been almost miraculously saved from death when he and another priest were caught aboard their schooner between Cat Island and Conception Island during a terrible hurricane, made a vow that he would remain in the Bahamas as a missionary for the rest of his days.

From this time the advance of the Church in the islands was rapid.[1] As more and more churches were built and many natives were converted, the need for more priests became acute. When Father Hawes arrived, Father Chrysostom and the few monks who were working with him begged the missionary to stay and take up his labors in the Bahamas. Father Chrysostom begged him to take over San Salvador, that is, Watling Island, where Columbus had first landed in the New World, and there design and help build a church as a memorial to Columbus which the Knights of Columbus in

[1] Cf. Colman J. Barry, O.S.B., *Worship and Work* (Collegeville, Minnesota, 1956), pp. 205–12.

the United States had promised to finance. Although his earlier attachment to the Bahamas still persisted, Father Hawes regretfully explained that his Australian commitment would prevent him from contemplating any such thing, but he was careful to add that he hoped that things would work out so that he might return later.

Leaving them with this vague reassurance, he went on to New York to be the guest of the Collegeville Benedictines at St. Anselm's Monastery in the Bronx, where Father Bernard Kevenhoerster was the prior. Father Hawes took advantage of his stay to travel up to Peekskill to renew his friendship with Mother Rosina, now called Sister Mary Magdalene, and with Sister Mary Claudia, another of his former disciples. At last he began the final lap of his journey and landed in England, where he spent six months with his parents in Surrey.

One evening he was invited to supper at the convent of the Daughters of the Cross at nearby Carshalton, to meet with Bishop Amigo of Southwark and Abbot Bergh, O.S.B., of Ramsgate. The former recalled how, as a young priest, he was in charge of a parish in Texas, so big that it took the mail-train express three hours to cross it. "Well, my Lord," replied Father Hawes, "I can board the mail train at six o'clock in the morning at the northeast end of my parish, travel in it the whole day, and alight at the last little township in the southwest corner at 9 P.M. My parish covers 42,000 square miles, but of course most of it is inhabited only by kangaroos and emus. The Diocese of Geraldton covers roughly 300,000 square miles, but in the more remote parts some of the aborigines are still so wild as to be ready to spear a stranger and cook him for dinner!"

Father Hawes had hoped to meet Abbot Aelred Carlyle before returning to Australia, but was told that he had gone off to South America in a last desperate attempt to raise

money to pay the debts of his community. But before his
holiday was over and he had to return to Geraldton, Father
Hawes did manage to visit Father Rope, who was then in
charge of a remote parish on the border of Wales.

Toward the end of 1920 Father Hawes returned to Western
Australia, and shortly afterward Bishop Kelly died, a sad
loss to the missionary who had been devoted to the Bishop.
Then Archbishop Clune approached the priest-architect to
prepare plans for a new cathedral at Perth. Father Hawes
put much work into the designs, but eventually the scheme
fell through, so he was left free to devote himself uninter-
ruptedly to the building of a church at Mullewa, a small
town on the railroad, about fifty miles inland from Geraldton.

He records: "Day after day, toiling with sore and cracked
hands, tormented with flies and the scorching summer sun,
and clothed in lime-covered rags, all my interests are now
concentrated on this my latest church. Some of the piers and
walls are now ten feet above ground. God only knows how
I've toiled and sweated over it, all through the sweltering
days of summer. Often I have worked alone; mixing the
mortar, fetching my stones, often aching with lumbago and
hardly able to lift a stone without groaning. Often I've had
to knock off and go indoors to lie down on my bed for a
quarter of an hour and then drag myself out to work again
—to face the sun and the flies. But once I get going the enthusiasm and intoxication of the work carry me on. I become too tired out to eat anything except with a great effort.
People remark that I am growing thin.

"Thanks be to God, I never realized when I began (although even then I knew I was a fool to start on it) what I
was undertaking, or the magnitude and complications of the
task, otherwise I would never have had the courage to face
it. Not to speak of the financial anxiety and business worries,

or the stirring up of people to work on the quarry and carting stones and sand. There has also been the selfish apathy and indifference of so many Catholics. However, it's a reward to contemplate some portion of a wall a little higher every day.

"It's a great and noble labor, this piling of one stone upon another, semi-sacramental, one of the four primal occupations of man—that of the mason, the carpenter, the plowman, the fisherman. As a laborer I think of all those who have been at it long before: the Egyptians, the Greeks, the Romans, the Saxons, the Normans, and those giants of the thirteenth century. It's strange to think that when the Saxons were building their little 'Roman' churches, England was all 'bush' then, like Australia."

Father Hawes felt he was getting back again to his Franciscan ideals. Labor gave him a real friendship with the workingman. He was earning his daily bread; not only by his spiritual labor in his parish, but by the labor of his own hands. Moreover, each day was consecrated for him by beginning it, standing at the altar to offer the Holy Sacrifice of the Mass.

After the church at Mullewa was completed, visitors often annoyed the priest-architect. They gaped at him, saying: "And did you really build all that yourself, Father? Well, you will have a memorial behind you. You must feel a very proud man—doesn't it distract you when you're saying Mass to look around and think you raised all that?"

But Father Hawes felt very differently and, to quote his own words, "I thought to myself, God knows there's enough pride in my poor fallen sin-stained soul—pride and self-seeking in all I do. Yet as to pride of that sort over the finished building, I don't think I ever had it. Our Lady's church at Mullewa has always seemed to have an impersonal relationship to myself. Not as though I had designed it, because I prayed to St. Joseph every morning and commended the work to him. I was just *his* laborer. I always said that beautiful prayer of Pius X to St. Joseph. You can see his statue in the church now, with a ten-foot rule in his hand.

"I was continually altering the design and changing things as I went along. The building of it was a great adventure and a sort of pilgrimage: it was not something made but a thing that had *grown*. All I did was to *discover* it. And so, when at long last I stood before the high altar under the dome, it never occurred to me that I myself had built it—those rough, uneven gray walls—but that I seemed to be standing in some old church built by other hands in former times." [2]

From 1923 to 1926 Father Hawes's very infrequent letters to Mr. Selby-Hall were mainly concerned with the trials he had to endure—very good for his soul, no doubt—from the presence of a new bishop, whose views on art and architecture were very different from those of his predecessor. To be honest, it is not in the least surprising that Bishop Ryan, who came from a wealthy suburban parish of Melbourne, felt that this Englishman was a dangerous eccentric, if not quite mad. The astonishing little church at Mullewa, the like of which Bishop Ryan had never seen in his life, was enough to confirm his worst suspicions. No sane man could have designed such a fantastic building, only a lunatic!

It was an even worse blow to Father Hawes that Bishop Ryan maintained that everything was wrong with the new cathedral at Geraldton, which was still unfinished, and in which he took great pride, because he had managed to carry out in stone the dreams of the late Bishop Kelly. The new ordinary denounced the cathedral's peculiarities, as well as those of the new churches at Mullewa and Yalgoo.

"Art!" he exclaimed one day. "It's just wasted on these people. What do they understand of it?" Father Hawes wrote

---

2 For a detailed description of this church, which sums up all its architect's eclectic ideals and proves his unique knowledge of historic styles, see p. 222 ff.

in one letter about this date: "I fear my good Bishop thinks I'm a cracked idiot wasting my time, and that I would be far better employed in book study or preparing sermons. But he is very generous and gives away his money everywhere to this or that object of charity."

However, there were some consolations. The Sisters at Yalgoo reported that two old bushmen came to have a look at the convent chapel, and that they were quite enraptured over it, saying they'd never seen anything like it, or so pretty, since they left "the old country," and that it reminded them of the chapels at home. This cheering news delighted the priest-architect. He felt that, after all, his new Bishop might not be infallible in matters of art!

Alas! It was not only Father Hawes's architecture that annoyed Bishop Ryan, but also his liturgical peculiarities. For instance, what did he mean by having the *Asperges* before the Missa Cantata on Sunday mornings? No other priest in the diocese did so. The Bishop went so far as to maintain that the *Asperges* was a complete novelty in Australia. He said that he had never heard of it, except in cathedrals, and he lost no time in abolishing it at Geraldton. Father Hawes pleaded that the rite was quite common in most village churches on the continent of Europe, even in Catholic churches in England, but this did not convince Bishop Ryan. He then fell back on the argument that "the *Asperges* only lengthens the service." He could say nothing when the parish priest of Mullewa pointed out that it took only two minutes, and that even with the reading of long notices and a sermon his Mass was over in less than fifty minutes. But after a moment the Bishop remarked: "That's much too quick; you ought to preach a longer sermon."

In Geraldton Cathedral, where before Bishop Ryan's advent plain chant had been the rule, the music was changed to something not exactly liturgical. Father Hawes wrote:

"The ladies can now warble to their hearts' content Con-coni and other such operatic Mass murderers. They never get further with the *Credo* than down to the *Incarnatus.* The so-called 'High Mass' is now a Low Mass—*missa bassa con musica."* In his own churches the choirs sang the *Missa de Angelis,* but it had been a hard struggle to get them to learn it.

What with one thing and another he was getting plenty of hard knocks, but he could write, "However, it is all so good for one's soul. God is breaking me up to teach me greater detachment. I remember reading Tauler and his similitude of the dog shaking the bone or rag, making a play-thing of it.

"As to my cathedral at Geraldton, I feel more or less re-signed now to the idea of having nothing more to do with it. I never go down there now, nor do I feel I want to see it any more; yet it used to mean so much to me. It still does, I sup-pose, but this is probably not detachment or resignation, merely chagrin and wounded artistic pride. Perth may have to go, too, because the majority of the clergy don't want and certainly don't understand my design. Twice I have asked the Archbishop to relieve me of it and obtain the services of an architect more acceptable to the *vox populi,* but he is very kind and says, 'No, I want *you* to do it.' "

Once again it was the simple people—those supposed to have no artistic taste—who never ceased to praise the churches designed and largely built by this priest-architect. He tells the story of how one of the men who had helped to build the church at Mullewa brought a pal to have a look at it. "I sez to 'im, come an' 'ave a look at Father's church. It don't look much from the road, but just come an' see 'ow thick the walls are—ain't that *bonza* now? From out there you'd think it was jus' an ordinary buildin' . . . but this 'ere's different from any other church." It was these unsophisticated folk who agreed with Eric Gill that "Art is skill," that "beauty is a quality of things," and that "the artist is simply the responsible workman." [3]

Bishop Ryan remained at Geraldton only from 1923 to 1926. In March of the latter year he was transferred to the diocese of Sale in Victoria, not sorry to get away from Western Australia where he never felt at home. Despite their frequent differences of opinion on art and architecture, Father Hawes was the first to admit that Dr. Ryan was "a good bishop," and, above all, "a splendid missioner." The following three years the Archbishop of Perth acted as Administrator Apostolic of the Geraldton diocese. Then, in 1930, the Reverend James Patrick O'Collins was appointed to the see. He soon became a loyal and devoted father and friend to Father Hawes. The relationship between the two men was most happy.

One day in April 1929 Father Hawes received from Sister Mary Magdalene an American newspaper containing an account of the erection of the Bahamas as a prefecture apostolic, and that Father Bernard Kevenhoerster, O.S.B., had been recommended by Cardinal Hayes as first Prefect Apostolic, although it was not until November 1933 that Monsignor Bernard was consecrated bishop in St. Patrick's Cathedral, New York City. This reminder of the scene of his labors as an Anglo-Catholic Franciscan missionary inspired Father Hawes to write to Monsignor Bernard, asking if he would accept him for work in the islands subject to his obtaining a release from his own bishop. Monsignor Bernard replied that he would be delighted to welcome this Australian missionary to his poverty-stricken prefecture where more priests were badly needed. He explained that there were promising openings for fresh work, and that the people were most responsive. The fact that Father Hawes knew the Bahamas already, and

---

[3] Cf. *Sacred and Secular* (1940), p. 82.

was remembered by so many people, as well as the fact that he was a convert from Anglo-Catholicism, would have a great influence.

Shortly after this Bishop O'Collins came to Mullewa, where Father Hawes laid the whole matter before him. He told his ordinary that he had begun to feel that his apostolate in Western Australia was finished, now that the church and presbytery at Mullewa were completed. "I had built the house for my successors," he wrote in his memoirs. "It was far too comfortable and un-Franciscan for me. I had grown very unsettled." The upshot of this interview was that Father Hawes agreed to remain until there were a few more priests. The Bishop said that he could not be spared at the moment, and he wrote to Monsignor Bernard pointing out the difficulties in the diocese of Geraldton, above all the scarcity of priests.

There were a number of reasons for Father Hawes's state of unsettlement. Most of his people were of Irish extraction, and rejoiced to find that their priest shared their own love of horses. For some years Father had owned a splendid mare. From a race horse he had bred a fine filly, and from her a good colt. He also bred fox terriers, and got the name of being an authority on all dogs and their ailments. As for the horses, Father Hawes was not content with using them for apostolic work. He trained some of them for the track, rode them himself in races, and once won the Geraldton Cup! The men of his flock used to say that a grand jockey had been lost in him.

His ecclesiastical superiors do not seem to have objected to the priest becoming an amateur jockey. Both Bishop Kelly and Bishop O'Collins attended the races and applauded his successes. As to the people—they just went mad when the priest's horse came in first. At Yalgoo, on Sundays, a "bookie" took up the collection at Mass in the prize silver cup that

Father Hawes had won at a race! But to quote his own words: "Almighty God was waiting for something more from me. I had become far too wrapped up in horses and riding and races—I a priest and a Franciscan tertiary."

So his conscience pricked him again and again, but he was kept much too busy with architectural work to have time to wonder about the near or distant future. During the brief period that Bishop Ryan had ruled over the Geraldton diocese, the priest-architect thought he had done with his T square and drawing board forever, but Bishop O'Collins took a different view; insisting that Father Hawes design more and more churches, convents, and other buildings. The supervision of buildings in process of erection entailed not only extra journeys, but also the worry of endless correspondence. It is hardly surprising that Father Hawes's letters to friends at home grew more and more infrequent. He was happy enough designing and working out plans, and seemed to thrive on this work, although he often sat up at his drawing board half the night. With his parochial duties, riding, the breeding of dogs, and architectural work, he was burning the candle at both ends. One day his doctor remarked: "I don't like the look of you; if you don't stop all this and get right away you'll have a bad nervous breakdown."

The architectural work began to interfere with his priestly duties. Father Hawes wrote. "Niceties of design and problems of building construction obtruded themselves into all my prayers and attempted meditations. I had quite forgotten that the Art which was now again my first thought and absorbing preoccupation was the idol from which Our Lord had called me as a young man to go forth and serve Him in some other way. For instance, I would suddenly wake up to the fact that I had run on continuously through the psalms of three nocturnes of Matins and on to the end of Lauds without having read the lessons and canticles, while I was men-

tally revolving the arching over of some space, or the construction of a roof truss."

In 1933 his doctor and his bishop persuaded him to make
a trip to England for a much-needed rest. Once he arrived
in Europe he felt he must do a three weeks' tour of Spain to
study the architecture of that country, and he continued to
mull over the same sort of architectural details that had occupied him in Australia. In a long letter written from the
Hôtel de Inglaterra, Seville, on June 6, 1933, illustrated with
many sketches, plans and sections of churches, he wrote that
"Milan is still the Queen of Cathedrals and Seville is grand
and immense." Yet he had been convinced that "the Spanish
architects have executed in most marvelous masonry what
the Italians (would have liked to do but) only did in scenic
painting."

What thrilled him above all else was the sight of the choir
boys at Seville, dressed as pages, dancing in the sanctuary
before the Blessed Sacrament exposed. He described how the
Cardinal Archbishop came in after Lauds, vested in magnificent state, and sat on his throne at the west end of the coro
where he blessed the incense. Never in his wildest dreams
had Father Hawes imagined such splendid ceremonial. There
was a "full orchestra and sublime music," also "a tremendous
lot of going up and down all the time between the coro and
sanctuary. When a canon goes to preach he is escorted to the
pulpit by a mace bearer, half-a-dozen choir boys, and three
minor canons. The latter wear black capes and soutanes with
red-edged buttons—the canons are all in purple. The thurifer
and acolytes wear apparelled albs and amices and dalmatics.
The ladies go in for very pretty high combs in the back of
their hair, and black lace mantillas over them. At dinner in
the hotel there were some ladies in full dress with sort of
crinolines. One was bright green, another pink with three
white flounces."

He mentioned that he had been in Burgos, Toledo, Segovia, Cordova, Granada, and Barcelona as well as Seville. Wherever he went his observant eyes noticed and his memory retained details of architecture or religious ceremonial. Never had he seen "such glorious sanctuaries, with huge Gothic retables soaring right up into the vault." He could hardly find words in which to do full justice to the sanctuary at Toledo, with "its apse, carved retable, and two glorious rood screens with the two thieves." But Seville had "the noblest altar and steps, and the most *gorgeous* gilded bronze screen you ever saw!" This tour of Spain had a lasting effect on Father Hawes's architectural designs. After 1933 his affection for baroque became far more pronounced, and it came out especially in the altar furnishings he planned for his churches.

Then followed a tour of Ireland, where Father Hawes made a careful study of primitive Celtic architecture. What interested him most was the stone barrel-vaulted roof of Cormac's Chapel at Cashel. He even felt it worth his while to investigate some of the ancient monastic cells on the coast of Kerry. Their beehive shape and domed stone roofs in horizontal courses fascinated him. In years to come he would make good use of his knowledge of early Christian buildings in Ireland.

Father Hawes admits that by the time he had concluded his English visit and returned to Australia he had lost all further desire to go back to the Bahamas. To quote his own words: "I was getting old, and I felt I would not be much use now as a missionary. I dreaded the thought of the almost-continuous heat, the mosquitoes and the coarse, repugnant food, such as hominy. I tried hard to excuse myself, but all the same I knew quite well in my inner consciousness that God *had* called me. Never before had Western Australia seemed such a fair and lovely land to me. There was no nicer place under the sun than the Geraldton diocese. I had no more desire to travel or to see new sights; no dear relatives or kind friends. I felt I had no further ties with the old country."

Other things helped to encourage him to remain on the southern continent. Bishop O'Collins was so kind and considerate; always ready to discuss, understand and appreciate questions of art, archaeology and liturgy. Moreover, the Bishop and Father Hawes had other interests in common— above all, a love for dogs and horses. Finally, the diocese of Geraldton had been "put on the map." Hitherto it had been the despised Cinderella—the most forlorn diocese in the whole of Australia. Visitors now came from Europe and North America. There was always something to show them —including all the churches and institutions designed by the famous priest-architect. They departed interested and impressed with the signs of progress. Father Hawes enjoyed all the bouquets and the limelight; realizing that he had helped in no small way to bring about this change. By 1934 he could regard himself as a "star!" He had achieved a name for himself. No longer was he despised as an eccentric convert clergyman. In fact, he had become one of the most important ecclesiastics on the continent, of whom everybody had heard, and who was constantly praised. He was definitely of "news value," not only as a priest-architect, but as a priest-jockey!

Plenty of money rolled in, and he had quite forgotten what it meant to be poor. So he built a cottage in a lovely spot outside Geraldton, with the idea of retiring there to end his days as chaplain to the nearby Hospital of St. John of God. At the same time as he designed the Church of Santo Spirito he chose the place for his own grave at the foot of the rood screen, and even went so far as to have a memorial brass made, with his effigy clothed in vestments, and set into a marble slab. Meanwhile, the brass was hidden by a carpet. Yet he admits that he could not cheat his conscience even over this grave. He knew that he could never reside for long in this luxurious so-called "Hermitage," nor would his body ever lie under the pavement in the Church of Santo Spirito.

Eventually the "Hermitage" became the residence of Father Hawes's closest friend in Australia, Father James Prendergast, after the latter was appointed chaplain to the hospital. Father Hawes retained a room for his own use, and whenever business or pleasure called him to Geraldton, he occupied it. He described himself and his friend, sitting on either side of the big fireplace, contentedly smoking their pipes, with two dogs at their feet, stretched out in the firelight. There was nothing to suggest Franciscan poverty in this comfortable setting.

Bishop O'Collins, having decided to relieve Father Hawes of the burden of the vast parish of Mullewa, appointed him to Greenough, fifteen miles east of Geraldton. This town lies in the center of a long-established farming district, with solid stone houses and farm buildings, almost reminiscent of a bit of English countryside. Here the new parish priest could enjoy the sight of clumps of gnarled and twisted trees, with dense, shady foliage. The course of the river was marked by a serpentine procession of dark gum trees. On either side of the plain on which Greenough lies is a long range of hills. Just beyond them is the sea.

Father Hawes reveled in these surroundings, and here he designed St. Peter's Church, which, unlike most of his Australian churches, is in the Gothic style. He served two other churches about six miles distant from the town. Only his uncomfortable two-roomed presbytery reminded him of his Franciscan ideals. Here he set up his drawing board, and was soon immersed in more plans: first for the proposed convent and chapel to be built for St. John of God's Hospital, and then for the new Nazareth House at Bluff Point. Father Hawes had reached a pinnacle of fulfillment and contentment in his work. Only the thorn of the idea of Franciscan poverty remained to prick him.

7.

The Bahamas Beckon [1937–1939]

FOR some time Bishop O'Collins had felt that Father Hawes deserved some official recognition for the many services he had rendered to the diocese of Geraldton. Through the Apostolic Delegate he put the matter before the authorities in Rome, with the result that on December 28, 1937, Pius XI nominated this Australian priest as one of his domestic prelates. In the document, signed by Cardinal Pacelli, then Secretary of State, it was stated that this honor was imparted especially because of the great work done in designing the new cathedral at Geraldton, not forgetting many other churches and diocesan institutions.

Shortly after news of this distinction reached Father Hawes he wrote to Mr. Selby-Hall, "The blow, alas, has fallen, and my life is made a burden by a hail of congratulatory telegrams. It's astonishing the amount of money people in this country waste on telegrams, and the dear local folk awkwardly address me as 'Mon-sig-nor'—*sig* rhyming with *fig*. It's an overwhelming honor, when one is personally so absolutely unworthy of it, to be made a 'domestic prelate,' when you consider that many really eminent men like Hugh Benson were not given more than the distinction of a 'domestic chamberlain,' and here am I, the worst dressed and shabbiest

102

of all the priests in this diocese, supposed to be dressed in 'purple and fine linen' just the same as a bishop only without the pectoral cross—mantelletta and all! Well, you and I have always had a special devotion to the papacy from the time we met at Lincoln as Anglicans. It was our love and daily prayer for the Pope that helped to bring us into the true Church, and now the Pope has repaid me, a poor convert, a hundredfold for that devotion by bestowing on me the Roman purple of his own household—that purple that I kiss humbly on my knees as the colors (the school tie?) of the church of the catacombs, and the blood of the martyrs, and the doors of St. Peter's tomb.

"Yet, please God, if I live, I hope yet to shed my fine purple feathers and, as a Benedictine oblate, to end my days in the Bahamas in a patched old habit as plain 'Brother John' *(and the beard)* !"

It is easy to understand how this beloved English priest was nearly buried alive under congratulatory letters and telegrams. He longed to escape and hide himself, if only for a brief spell.

One day, he recalls, he accompanied Bishop O'Collins to Perth, where they lunched with the Archbishop. The latter had just lost (none too willingly) one of his priests, his private secretary, to the novitiate of the Friars Minor in Sydney. In the hope of gaining a better understanding of the Franciscan spirit, the Archbishop had been reading Ernest Raymond's recently published book entitled *In the Steps of St. Francis,* and said that the Monsignor might be interested in it. The latter admitted that at the moment he had too many other things to bother about to read another life of the Little Poor Man of Assisi, but that he went off with the book.

"That same evening," he wrote, "my Bishop and I went to the cinema. It was a typical and silly Hollywood film—how

different from the beautiful *Snow White* we had seen together some months before! As we hurried out after the
show, I saw before the entrance a poor young fellow with
a sad face playing the violin. . . . Alas! I had nothing in my
pocket. When I got back upstairs to my bedroom in the Archbishop's palace I was disgusted with the whole day. I thought
how worldly and grand I was becoming—lunching in state
with two bishops, and being sped luxuriously around the
city of Perth and its suburbs in a magnificent automobile.
The face of that poor young fellow with the violin outside
the cinema haunted me. I sat down sadly to recite Vespers
and Compline. Then I picked up *In the Steps of St. Francis,*
bound in Franciscan brown, and opened it at random. The
passage on which my eyes fell ran more or less as follows—
I have not the book with me so I cannot give the exact words:

"And I little brother Francis, useless servant, beg and pray humbly all who in the Holy Catholic and Apostolic Church wish to
serve the Lord God, that they will persevere in the true faith and
conversion, for otherwise they cannot be saved. I beg and beseech
you that with all our heart, with all our strength and power,
with all our desire and will, we love the Lord our God Who has
created and redeemed us. Let us therefore seek nothing else, wish
for nothing else. May nothing restrain us therefore, nothing
separate us, nothing drive us from Him.

"We may read passages such as this—exhortations and
pleadings—dozens of times without their making any real impression on our minds or any appeal to us, just as we read
such momentous words in the Holy Gospels, the words of
Jesus Christ Himself. But there comes a day sometimes when
those same familiar sentences seem to bring, standing over
us, the very writer himself—or the living speaker, his eyes—
fire; his tongue—a sword!

"Now the Little Poor Man had come for his lost sheep.

All my past devotion to him surged up within me—to him who walked so closely in the steps of The Master. I prayed that night in a way I had not done for many years. About half-past three in the morning I lay down for a couple of hours' sleep. It had been arranged for me to celebrate Mass at the Convent of Mercy Chapel, after my Bishop. It was the Octave of the Feast of the Epiphany, 1939. As soon as I began the Introit, my soul was flooded with light and consolation. I could hardly get through the Mass; I wanted to burst into tears. I blew my nose continually. I choked and coughed to hide my emotion. Our Lord in His pity gave me a momentary joy on Mount Tabor that the memory of that Mass might strengthen me afterward in all that I knew I must go through. The great chapel was full of nuns, and the bishop was kneeling at a *prie-dieu* in the doorway of the sacristy. It was terrible, but at last I got through. The Sister-sacristan said: 'You've got a bad cold, Father.' At breakfast in the parlor the Bishop remarked with a smile that I'd been very slow saying my Mass."

Bishop O'Collins had for some time been suggesting that Monsignor Hawes take another trip to Europe and even urged him to go. The priest kept putting it off, explaining that he could not get away until this or that church was built. Bishop O'Collins had come to the conclusion that the Monsignor had given up all idea of the Bahamas missions, just because he never mentioned the matter. And why should he do so, now that he was a domestic prelate to His Holiness the Pope? He had earned the right to settle down comfortably and spend the rest of his life, enjoying himself designing churches, and living in ecclesiastical luxury. It seems that Monsignor Hawes could not bring himself to reveal to his Bishop what had happened to him on the night when he had realized so clearly that he must follow the star wherever it guided him.

Anyhow, it was impossible for him to get away until the vicar-general of the diocese returned from a holiday in Europe. He considered later on that he had been subconsciously hoping that circumstances would conspire to prevent his responding to the call from the Bahamas. One day he summoned up his courage to ask the Bishop for permission for a holiday, because the latter was due to make his *ad limina* visit to Rome in 1940. The request was granted without any hesitation, so Monsignor Hawes was free to leave whenever it suited him.

At the next diocesan retreat for the clergy, the Monsignor made up his mind to give up smoking, in view of the sort of life which lay ahead of him. One night, when the other priests had retired to their rooms, he went into the chapel, and laid his pipe on the altar step. He never smoked again.

Next came the sad task of fixing the date for sailing to Europe. He allowed himself four months to put his house in order and to complete his work. The days sped past, and with a sinking heart he marked them off on the calendar. In after years he wrote: "I ought, of course, to have laid bare my soul to my dear Bishop and told him that what I hoped to do was to become a Franciscan tertiary and cast off the purple and lace which I wore on ceremonial occasions in virtue of being a right reverend monsignor, but my nerves were so strung up that I felt I simply could not face any arguing out of the matter. Nor could I face the additional pain of saying good-by to my many dear friends, knowing quite well that it did not mean just a 'God be with you till we meet again,' but a real 'farewell' forever. Nor could I put up with the questioning and the fussy farewelling of the crowd, however kindly and sincerely intended."

Just what Monsignor Hawes was visualizing at that moment was described in a letter written to Sister Mary Magdalene. He said, "I no longer think of a striving or combative life on Long Island, but picture an entirely new field—some smaller out-of-the-way and unfrequented island where the people are not visited by other missionaries, Anglican or any Protestant sect, but to retain their own primitive unsophisticated type of Baptist or 'Holy-Roller' meeting under ignorant local preachers. I have in my mind's eye the Island of Mayaguana, quite isolated out in the ocean, and marked on the chart with an apparently high hill—'Abram's Hill' [Guana Hill]—and two lesser summits. I can picture an isolated palm-thatched cell beside a tiny stone church on Abram's Hill whence the hermit would descend on weekends into the settlements or village to minister to Catholic converts in their former Baptist (or whatever it might be) meetinghouse, transformed into a humble Catholic place of worship, and from which village the hermit-priest would in true Franciscan style beg his food, such as maize, potatoes and bananas. Sunday Mass and Benediction for the converts in their village; the Blessed Sacrament in the tabernacle and the hermit's only daily Mass in the little church on the top of Abram's Hill."

As time wore on, the Monsignor felt he could not personally disclose the true facts to his Bishop and decided to write to him once he was on the high seas. He relied on the promise made seven years before that when the time arrived the Bishop would place no obstacle in the way of his taking up work in the Bahamas. As to the ultimate decision— whether he could leave the diocese of Geraldton for good, or must return to Australia eventually—that must rest with Bishop O'Collins or his successor.

This is how the Monsignor summed up his convictions at that moment: *"When God calls us* (speaking by His Holy Spirit in our conscience) *to do certain things,* we *must* do them or deteriorate in our spiritual life. I admire the life around me (in which I have been taking a part), but there is an inward movement planted by God in my soul, so I believe—*an inescapable impulse which for so long and for whatever I may do against it* has been forcing me in another direction. I know not (nor does it matter) whether God is calling me now for any more work to do, or any sphere of usefulness—it may be only in order to *uproot* me, for the good of my soul. Even though I may now be useless as a missionary in the Bahamas, I can, amid the poverty and simplicity of the people on the out islands, live a real Franciscan life in the strict and literal observance of holy poverty according to the Gospels, which would be impossible to do in Western Australia in anything of the same literal way."

Perhaps the hardest thing that faced him was to say goodby to his beloved "Dominie," to whom he was utterly de-

Monsignor Hawes and Dominie

voted. He writes: "Dogs have the gift of second sight, they can read our thoughts. When the beginning of the last week came I was feeling utterly miserable. I was at work, finishing some plans in the library of the Bishop's palace. My fox terrier would not leave me for a moment; if I went out of the room for only a minute to fetch something, she was after me. She would not, as usual, settle down to sleep in one of the armchairs near me, but must come and lie against my feet all the time. Now and again, when I spoke to her, looking up she gave me a glance so full of love and sorrow that it filled my own eyes with tears. Did she not understand what I knew and was grieving over the hour for the parting drawing nearer and nearer? It was an agony of mind for me to leave this faithful friend who for nine years had been my constant companion everywhere I went. However, I knew I was leaving her in good hands, with friends who would take care of her. It was on a farm near Greenough in such surroundings as she loved, with the company of little children and horses, and plenty of rabbits to chase.

"When my indoor work was finished at last, Dominie and I forgot our troubles and for our last three days together, joined by her son Rory from the Hermitage, we had some delightful rambles over the sand dunes, swimming in the sea, and digging for crabs in the sand. Was there ever a fox terrier who could climb trees like Rory, or such a fearless little swimmer through the breakers after a stick?"

At last the day came and after a cheerful little dinner party at the Bishop's palace, Monsignor Hawes piled his baggage in the back seat of his little green Ford and drove down to the railroad station, Dominie beside him. Bishop O'Collins was awaiting him and the Monsignor knelt down for a final blessing. The next day, when he reached New Norcia, he called at the Benedictine abbey to say farewell to the Abbot and monks. It was the end of twenty-four years as a missionary in Western Australia.

John Cyril Hawes had reached his sixty-second year when he left Geraldton on May 9, 1939. Three days later he sailed from Freemantle, and as he crossed the Indian Ocean he began his *apologia pro vita sua* with these words: "These notes are the confessions of one who was called and who put his hand to the plow—and looked back. He is not fit for the

Kingdom of God. But God has been very patient. . . . 'Forty years long was I grieved with this generation. . . . ' In my age Our Lord sent His bold servant St. Francis to call me back into the way, to give me another chance to become again as a little child. I mistrust so much all that I do now that I am doubtful whether I ought to write this. Am I being egotistical? May Our Lord deliver me from self-deception and pride, from being too self-centered."

The little black-bound notebook, which was entrusted to the author of this biography by Bishop O'Collins for whose private use it was intended, covers the whole of the life of John Cyril Hawes from his childhood until his farewell to Australia, stressing in particular the more important spiritual graces he had received, and laying perhaps too much emphasis on the countless occasions when he felt he had resisted God's grace and failed to answer His call. Again and again St. Francis appears, or, rather, the urge to follow the Franciscan way of life—a persistent call to embrace holy poverty. One is conscious on almost every page of a dual personality in the writer: the artist, and the lover of God and souls. The one is ever striving to master the other. At least this is how Monsignor painted his own portrait on that six weeks' voyage back to Europe.

The book ends thus: "I am well on the way now. As I write these words, the ship is nearing Suez. On my left rise up the red clifflike barriers of Egypt. On my right are the blue, misty peaks of Sinai against the morning sun. The waters of the Red Sea are nearly past. There can be no turning back now.

"I hope soon to kneel in the Holy Sepulcher and to visit the other holy places in the Master's steps. Then to Rome to get the Holy Father's blessing. Then, Assisi. And thence, on to what Our Lord may have in store for me. *Domine quo vadis?*"

All went according to plan. Monsignor Hawes arrived at

Jerusalem early in June, dressed himself in a Franciscan habit, and thus disguised made his pilgrimage to the holy places of Palestine. When he finished he set out for Italy, and arrived at Rome on June 28. There followed an audience with Pius XI and a general confession to Father Benedict Williamson, whom he had looked to as his spiritual director for many years.

These two priests understood each other. Father Williamson, like Monsignor Hawes, had practiced as an architect before he was received into the Catholic Church in 1896. After his ordination in 1909 he had designed many churches in England, most of them as original as those of Monsignor Hawes. He had tried and failed to revive the male branch of the Bridgettine Order. Some time before 1939 he had settled in Rome as chaplain to the Little Company of Mary at their hospital in the via San Stefano Rotondo.

He now advised Monsignor Hawes to "put yourself entirely and absolutely, without any conditions, in the hands of God. His Will will be made known to you through the external authority of His Church, speaking to you through your Bishop. Submit the whole matter to your Bishop (when you write), and remind him of the promise he made you seven years ago. Pray to God (not that He will make your Bishop do this or that, according as you want it to be), but that the Bishop may, by his decision, make known to you God's will for you. If the Bishop abides by his former promise of years back, and sets you free to leave his diocese, then you will know that this vocation, as it seems to you, is from God and you can confidently follow the new life that beckons you."

With this encouragement from Father Williamson, Monsignor Hawes left Rome for Assisi to spend a week revisiting all the places associated with the Little Poor Man. It was the hermitage of the *Carceri,* on the slopes of Monte Subasio, that drew him most strongly, for this was the model of a retreat which he hoped to build for himself.

On his way to England he stopped for a few days in Paris, where he arranged to meet his old friend and fellow student at the Beda, Father Henry E. G. Rope. The latter recalls that "to my wonder he had grown a beard. I knew whither he was destined, but he said nothing about any hermitage, and I wondered why a missionary in the Bahamas should be unshaven. However, I doubted not he had his own good reasons, and did not ask him. . . . It fell to me to pilot him by omnibus and underground and afoot to the Luxembourg Gardens and several of the churches. We had a simple meal at an outdoor restaurant, and heard Vespers and Benediction at St. Etienne du Mont. I had also to tell Hawes the values of French money. Indeed I was in grave danger of imagining myself for once, in a small measure, quite businesslike!" [1]

Father Rope parted reluctantly from Monsignor Hawes who, after a short pilgrimage to Lisieux, arrived in London on July 14. The following day he wrote a long letter to the Bishop of Geraldton, describing his visits to the Holy Land, Rome, Assisi and Lisieux, and said, "I have made it a real pilgrimage and have had plenty of time for thought and prayer, and have screwed myself up now to write this, to remind you of a promise you made me seven years ago: that 'when the time came you would put no obstacles in the way of my going to take up missionary work in the Bahamas Islands.'

"I have waited to see the vacant places of the diocese filled up by the younger priests who have since come out, and I may say that during the waiting I have grown still more attached to, and interested in, the Geraldton diocese, and especially since you . . . have always been so particularly kind and considerate to me . . . a very dear friend.

[1] Rope, *op. cit.*, p. 14.

"It is no feeling of unsettlement or desire of change that moves me in this matter, but purely a matter of *vocation* (as I feel). When I first became a Catholic I copied down some words of Father Isaac Hecker (Founder of the Paulist Fathers): 'The Holy Spirit is the *immediate guide* of the soul in the way of salvation and sanctification; and the criterion or test that the soul is guided by the Holy Spirit is its ready obedience to the authority of the Church. The Holy Spirit acting through the external authority of the Church is the infallible interpreter of divine inspiration in the soul.' When there is a question of vocation, it is no longer a matter depending on likes or dislikes. If the inner call is disregarded, the soul will deteriorate in the spiritual life."

The Monsignor went on to tell his Bishop about the advice given him in Rome by Father Benedict Williamson, and how he had written down the chief events in his spiritual journey in a notebook which he was about to send by air mail to the Bishop. He said that it might help the latter to read these confessions, adding, "Defer your decision until you have read them and treat them as confidential; do not discuss this matter with anyone else—as indeed I know you would not."

Having explained that Bishop Bernard, O.S.B., Vicar Apostolic of the Bahamas, had not influenced him in any way since they began to correspond in 1932, he ended this letter: "I am upset at the thought of causing you any pain or disappointment but, as I said, I am compelled by the strong conviction of vocation. I leave this matter in your hands as the one having the authority and ultimate right to decide. Let me know your decision, by air mail, when you write. Don't bother to return the notebook (you might put it in the safe along with my will)."

It was not until the early part of September 1939 that Monsignor received the first of two answers from Bishop

O'Collins. In the first letter the Bishop assured Monsignor Hawes that, having read the notebook mailed to him on July 15, he was prepared to grant the priest unlimited leave of absence from the diocese so that he could make a full trial of the life he visualized in the Bahamas. Nevertheless, the Bishop remarked that he doubted if the sixty-one-year-old priest would be able to adapt himself to this austere and literal interpretation of the primitive Franciscan way of living. "You anticipated to a certain extent what I desired," he wrote, "but your notebook is only part. Hence, as your Bishop, I request you to write a full autobiography in humility and in detail."

Bishop O'Collins followed this generous acceptance of Monsignor Hawes's plan with a second letter limiting the leave of absence to June 1941, with the proviso that it could be extended if the Monsignor felt he had found his true vocation. "You may find out," he cautioned him, "after a short time that you are not wanted in the Bahamas. You have tried before, and you may yet live to learn that a return to the poverty of the life in this diocese may be better for the progress of your spiritual life. I myself should be delighted to see you return. . . . My prayer for you shall always be that you may be happy in the Lord. Pray for me."

It was indeed hard for the Bishop to give up his missionary with whom he had worked so closely for so long. In 1948, in a letter addressed to the author, Bishop O'Collins remarked, "I always found Monsignor Hawes a most colorful character. He is an extraordinary person. It went very hard with me to allow him to stay in the Bahamas. I grew to like him much and I, as the Bishop, could never have accomplished the many works in the way of building in the diocese of Geraldton. He was an architect, painter, sculptor, stonemason, decorator, poet, horseman and horse breeder. . . . On one occasion we two left Mullewa, his parish, between

3 and 4 A.M. to travel to Geraldton on a goods train. We sat on the floor of the brake van with our legs dangling over the line and our backs resting against the side where the doors were slid back. The atmosphere was just right, and he proved wonderfully interesting as he talked about the far-off days as an Anglican novice on Caldey Island. . . .

"His life has always been a very austere one; the harder and more difficult the more he liked it. I always had the impression that he never let up. The result of his austerities was that he was often nervy and required careful handling. I have wished often since I came (to Ballarat) that he was with me. . . ."

Of this latter tribute, however, Monsignor Hawes was to remain blissfully unaware, and the two letters which he himself received were all that he needed: God had spoken to him through the external authority of His Church. Now with a clear conscience he could follow the new life that beckoned him. But first there were many old friends in England whom he wanted to see before he sailed across the Atlantic, probably never to return. He must also make a retreat, which he chose to do at Buckfast Abbey, since for several years he had been corresponding with Brother Peter, the German lay Brother, who had trained other Brothers in masonry, and who, with them, had built most of the great abbey church. Monsignor Hawes also planned to visit Prinknash Abbey, but time was limited and instead he made the long journey to Tintagel, the high, rocky promontory on the north coast of Cornwall where were the ruins of a castle famous in the Arthurian romances. Here his imagination was fired by the traces of hermits' cells dating from Celtic times which reminded him of similar cells he had seen in the west of Ireland. He pictured erecting something of the same kind when he had chosen a site on one of the more remote islands in the Bahamas, visualizing himself as another St.

Brendan the Navigator, living in a stone beehive-shaped hut, like the monastic cells on Skelligs Mhicil off the coast of Kerry.

On October 16, 1939—six weeks after the outbreak of World War II—Monsignor Hawes boarded a liner bound for New York to begin a new phase of his colorful and varied career.

8.

Cat Island [1939–1940]

WITH his major decision now behind him, the next problem
that confronted Monsignor Hawes was the choice of a site for
his hermitage. Once in New York at St. Anselm's Priory he
was able to talk over the matter with Bishop Bernard Kevenhoerster who was in the United States on a brief visit. The
Bishop suggested to him that he make a leisurely tour of the
Bahamas and report on conditions and prospective openings
for missionaries. As for his hermitage, he could please himself as to its situation, although the Bishop thought that the
northern half of Long Island or perhaps Cat Island, with its
few lonely Catholics, might be suitable. With his mind filled
with these possibilities, the Monsignor went off to spend a
week with the Franciscan Missionary Sisters at Peekskill, then
returned to New York and boarded the S.S. *Munargo* bound
for Nassau.

On the evening of November 12 Monsignor Hawes, arrayed
in his purple sash and rochet, assisted at first Vespers and
preached the sermon for the feast of All Saints of the Benedictine Order in the little cathedral at Nassau. The congregation
was made up chiefly of poor colored people with a scattering
of whites, and he was delighted by the lusty singing of the
English hymns before and after Benediction. "The whole

service was very homely and hearty," he wrote, but even this could not hold back a wave of homesickness for Australia. The entry in his diary for that day ends, "Feeling very lonely and miserable. Experience no pleasure in the beauty and pleasantness of the place. This is a help to detachment— Jesus, my *truly* joy be Thou."

At that time the Nassau Benedictine community consisted of Bishop Kevenhoerster, nine resident priests and one lay Brother, with five more priests situated on other islands. Monsignor Hawes's interest was piqued by the fact that the younger monks went about on bicycles; he was impressed by the missionary zeal displayed by the whole community. It pleased him, too, to find that "Brother" Christopher, "a huge big Negro in minor orders . . . was at the Propaganda College in Rome, and knows all the younger of the Geraldton and Perth priests, having been their fellow student. He is also a sergeant major, and drills all the volunteers and recruits for the Bahamian Army. Giving evening classes in Spanish, Italian and French is another of his jobs." [1]

He wrote down his newly refreshed impressions of Nassau, describing it as "the loveliest and pleasantest little town I've ever seen—so bright and cheerful and picturesque. . . . Pretty houses, the stone and plastered walls distempered in pinks and yellows or dazzling whitewash; gray, pine-shingled roofs, hips and gables and quaint dormers; overhanging balconies with every type of shutters, jalousies and trelliswork . . . all the colors of southern Spain with the neatness, trimness and cleanliness of old-country England." And the landscape, ". . . palm trees, casuarinas and every species of gorgeous tropical flowers . . . and such quaint little narrow, winding streets, uphill and downhill, with cuttings through the natural rock, and steps hewn into it."

[1] Christopher Foster, "Brother" Christopher, actually was not a member of the community, but was only a candidate for the Oblates of St. Benedict.

Then the harbor in "masts and rigging between every block of shops or market buildings: trim white schooners and sloops at anchor on the transparent blue and opalescent green waters of the harbor, which, with its wharves, is a busy place. Ships are always arriving or leaving. Yesterday there were half a dozen or so island mail boats, and I saw a big Canadian steamer painted wartime gray with a gun mounted on her poop. Airplanes arrive three times a week from Miami, and come down onto the water in the harbor."

In spite of the charms of the scenery, Monsignor Hawes did not remain long at Nassau. Within three days of his arrival he had boarded the mail steamer, *Monarch of Nassau,* to visit some of his old friends on Long Island. After a very stormy passage, the steamer anchored off Arthur's Town, Cat Island, on the morning of November 17.

That same day, about 2 P.M., when approaching the Bight, the seasick passenger had his first glimpse of his future home. He recorded in his diary: "As I viewed the shore from the *Monarch's* deck, two things struck my eye at once: the *high hill* at the back, and a *large square ruin* in the center of the settlement. The latter suggested a fine place for the Catholic church, and the hilltop for a retired hermitage. . . . I asked the captain how high the hill was and he said the government survey chart marked it at 420 feet, the highest land in the Bahamas. Most of the islands are low, with little hills of 100 or sometimes 200 feet, but they look higher than they are because of their steep and rocky outline, like miniature toy mountains, especially as the houses are small and lend scale to the scene. Trees are small, too."

When the steamer docked, Monsignor Hawes found a rough track that led eastward out from the settlement and curled about through the "bush" until it ended at the foot of the last bit of steep summit. Leaving the track, he fought his way for three quarters of an hour through the thick bush,

climbing over irregular, jagged faces of rock, until he was
about a mile and a half from the sea front. It was a wild and
lonely spot with a magnificent view, including the ocean on
the east side of the island. The priest surveyed the terrain
carefully, then made his way back to the sea to inspect the
ruin. Here bushes grew inside and a tall wild fig tree had
climbed one inner corner. "The ruin reminded me of some
of those on the site of old Panama city," he wrote. "Good
thick walls built of squared stones. House of some planter in
the early slavery days."

The *Monarch* sailed about sunset, and after a rough passage made San Salvador the following morning. Here Monsignor Hawes was welcomed by Father Herbert Buerschinger,
O.S.B., and he celebrated Mass in the new stone-vaulted
church, which he greatly admired. Late in the evening of
November 18, as the mail steamer entered Clarence Town
harbor on Long Island, on a distant hilltop he caught sight of
St. Paul's Anglican church which he had designed nearly
thirty years before. The next morning—Sunday—he beheld
its twin baroque towers, gleaming white in the brilliant sunshine. "The Pearl of the Bahamas," the out-island people
and sailors called this church, so he jotted down in his diary.
But now he could not worship in this lovely church, and had
to say Mass in the ground-floor room of a former store that
served as a temporary Catholic chapel.

Many of the older people on Long Island remembered
their one-time Episcopalian pastor. Some of them fell on their
knees and hugged him. One old blind woman threw her arms
around his neck, crying out: "Father Jerome! Father Jerome!
To think I live to this day that you come to see me again! O
my good Jesus, I thank You!" The Monsignor was told that
the Catholics at Clarence Town were all colored people. At
Deadman's Cay they were mostly poor white folk. Here a new

church, dedicated to Our Lady of Mount Carmel, had been built in 1938.

Long Island proved to be in a desperate state. Droughts, followed by heavy rains, had destroyed all the seeds planted. A plague of worms had eaten all the roots and fruit. There were no crops, and no price for sisal. A disease had killed all the sponges. The sponge fleet was idle, and the boats laid up. The people were literally starving. There were no peas, no beans, no sweet potatoes or bananas. The poor could earn no money to buy any sugar or coffee. All they lived on was the yield of their little plantations, supplemented by gifts of corn and flour from Father Arnold Mondloch, O.S.B., who had the charge of Long Island. Nearly all the out islands were in a similar state of destitution, but Long Island had been hit the hardest. Andros was very bad, too.

Monsignor Hawes described the plight of Jonathan Knowles, a white man, who had been struck with blindness and was now eighty years old. "I found his former good stone house had been destroyed by a hurricane in 1926. He was now living in a miserable wooden shack, about nine feet square, with a palm-thatched roof—a 'picturesque' enough scene, with its setting of palm trees and rich foliage on a rocky eminence looking down over the sparkling waters of the great lagoon. But wide cracks gaped between every ant-eaten board and daylight through the thatch. The old man lay on his bed, just a skinful of bones. His good wife said, 'He's got such pain inside from emptiness, he's just turned his face to the wall to die—there's nothing else for us!' She told me that they shivered at night with the cold winds, and were often soaked with rain. I looked at the few cooking utensils; not one grain of corn enough for a mouse to nibble. 'Don't the neighbors help you?' I asked. She replied, 'They don't come to see us now, because they can't; they've nothing themselves.' "

The effect of being confronted by poverty which was more austere than that of any Franciscan community had an immediate effect on the Monsignor. It drove home to him what was demanded of him as a tertiary and a follower of the Little Poor Man. The first thing he did was to make a resolution to sleep on the floor instead of on a bed. He tried it for the first time on hard concrete, and admitted that the mosquitoes and sand flies did not leave him much peace.

He jotted down in his diary: "We must follow the example of the Holy Father who offers himself to do penance for the war, which in itself is a punishment for the nations' forgetfulness and rejection of God. . . . Here on Long Island the people are simple, unsophisticated and religious-minded. They live in great poverty, whites as well as colored people. They go barefooted and eat very little. . . . They remind me much of the Arab and other native people in Palestine. With such primitive conditions as are to be found in most of the out islands of the Bahamas one could not attain to a closer Franciscan observance of the Gospel poverty than simply to live among the people *as they live,* and to share their privations and hardships as cheerfully as they bear these themselves."

Even Father Arnold had not much to offer his distinguished guest in the way of food. The meals consisted of hominy or boiled rice, with white beans and onions, and black coffee. But the Monsignor felt he was "indulging in gluttony in the midst of such abject poverty and want all around."

In the midst of new preoccupation, Monsignor Hawes had not forgotten his dog Dominie in Australia. He wrote, "The loss of her companionship is the greatest cross of all. That I should feel the separation from an animal far more than that from any living human being . . . is, I suppose, a sign of my unspiritual mind. I thank God for His goodness in letting me have the enjoyment for nine years of such an affectionate and loyal friend. If only I could love God and be content and happy when in His Presence as the little bitch was in mine, then I should do well. I can't help grieving, and I feel *so* lonely, but I try not to fret, because Dominie is in good hands.

"Tin-pot theologians are never weary of emphasizing that animals have no souls and no rights and no future. Well, I know my theology enough to know that an animal has not got a *rational* soul, but it has an *'animal soul,'* and of such a sort that those most beautiful of God's gifts of *love* and *loyalty* (virtues not found in cabbages) shine out in a pre-eminent degree in the said animal soul. Love is not a perishable thing. Whatever some professors of theology may say, the Catholic Church does not, nor has need to, lay it down that there is no future existence for the animal creation. Well! To the end of my life I shall hold firm to this sentiment, because love, *per se,* is a gift for eternity."

Monsignor Hawes returned to Nassau for the feast of the Immaculate Conception to find that a friend had sent him a copy of the Christmas number of the *Western Mail* containing colored pictures of West Australian ranges, forests, farms and gum trees. Once again he felt "very, very homesick." But this feeling partially disappeared when on December 15 he sailed for Harbour Island, Eleuthera. At Dunmore Town, a lovely spot, with a perfect conjunction of beauties of land and sea, he found a fair-sized stone church, a convent with three Sisters of Charity, and good school buildings. Eleuthera was "a real garden Paradise." Conditions were very different from those on Long Island. There was plenty of food. Bananas sold at six for a penny. Coconuts were cheap and plentiful. The presbytery was comfortable and modern.

The garden contained some fine palm trees. Father Leander Roerig was the perfect host. Then there were enjoyable sails over blue waters to some of the out stations, for instance to the Lower Bogue where there was "such a gem of a little church, with the altar excavated out of the solid rock of the hillside by cutting away down to the steps and floor of the sanctuary."

Father Leander went off for Christmas and left the Monsignor in charge of Dunmore Town. After the midnight Mass, which was sung amid clouds of incense, the youth of the settlement ran wild, exploding firecrackers. The result was that the priest got no sleep before it was time to rise again for his second Mass at seven-thirty. He wrote in his diary that he was "reduced to a complete nervous wreck, with the heart pumping furiously."

In the solitude of the presbytery he opened his diary and made the following entry:

"December 25, 1939. God has now called me to the greatest cross of my life and the greatest separation from the world. I look back too much, and am longing again for that which I have surrendered to God. I must make these thoughts on the past an act of thanksgiving and gratitude. How *good* God has been to me. And now He wishes to be more so in another way, new to me, if only I will but trust Him.

"How happy I was last Christmas. I had moved into my little presbytery at Greenough. I arranged my books and my drawing things in the sitting room. I cooked 'spaghetti à l'Italienne' and had a bottle of claret the Bishop had given me. There was a nice plateful of meat for Dominie, with a real good bone. Then I sat down comfortably in the easy chair, lit my pipe, and my dear doggie jumped up on my lap and buried her nose between my knees. I read the *Universe* and the *Catholic Herald.* Then got into the little green car, Dom by my side, and set down over the river bridge to fetch a paralyzed girl and her mother and the 'old man' for midnight Mass. How beautiful was the service! There was no kerosene for the lamps, so the church was as dim and mysterious as the cave at Bethlehem, with only the flickering light of the six candles on the altar and two tapers each before the images of Our Lady and the Sacred Heart. There was another candle on the confessional and one on the closed organ case. No distractions as to marshaling into order a lot of altar boys. No directing of a procession to the crib, with all the worry and anxiety as to whether everything was going all right, as it used to be at Mullewa. There was no music and singing—just the dim, spacious church, well-filled benches of silent worshipers, and the glorious liturgy.

"Then, after running people home in the car, I returned to the presbytery. Next a refreshing sleep, with the soothing music of Dominie's gentle snoring in the basket beside the bed where I could reach out my hand to pat her. In the fresh morning the sound of the sea beyond the dunes and the lovely warm air, sunshine and scuttling rabbits as we went over the hill and down to Bootenal and Walkaway. And in the afternoon a delightful run up to the Hermitage to see dear old Jim, with an uproarious meeting between Dominie and her son Rory. Then on down to the palace, and a joyful Christmas reunion with the Bishop and some of the clergy. So happy and settled was I at Christmas. But then at the octave of the Epiphany all this peace was upset by the vision of the star, the *call* within my soul. Ah! the Hound of Heaven!

"Well, why am I writing all this down? My pen is running away with me. I suppose it is to follow my heart, which has flown home across the oceans. Last week I was delving into a life of St. Teresa which I found on Father Leander's bookshelves. The saint says: 'St. Peter lost nothing by throwing himself into the sea, though he was afterward afraid. God loves courageous souls, but they must be humble and have no confidence in themselves.' "

Monsignor Hawes went on to describe two ways of looking

at the missionary and apostolic life from the point of view of the priest or religious: (1) *The Way of Prudence* and (2) *The Way of Divine Folly*. He was absolutely sure that he had been called to give up the former, which he had adopted for many years because he had not been courageous enough to try the latter. It was just a matter of vocation. Now he knew that he had been called toward the contemplative and eremitical life. God had shown him the way; he dared not turn back to the way of prudence. He confessed on paper: "I am a *priest* of God but not a *man* of God. I have not been a man of *prayer*. I am 'a well without water, a fountain dried up,' self-centered, self-seeking, a lover of pleasures, recreation, ease and comfort; immersed in outward activities. The ears of my soul are stopped up with active works lest I should halt and listen. What pleases me or serves my ends I labor for, especially architecture, with an intensity and devotion that looks like fervor. I love work more than all else. I look at the life of a St. Francis of Assisi, or a Charles de Foucauld, and either such lives as theirs are an illusion, or else mine is!

"Be courageous. Those holy saints I admire; sinner, miserable sinner and backslider as I am, I will start to try to imitate them in their love of solitude, silence, abnegation and penance. When, and not until after, I have done this will I know whether there is any definite work for me to do among others. Come ye apart into a *desert* place and rest awhile; to rest (not the body) but the soul, to refresh it. Put ye on the Lord Jesus Christ, 'I live, yet not I, but Christ liveth in me.' "

So on December 28 he returned to Nassau on the mail boat. Here he found a letter saying that the storekeeper on Cat Island was prepared to sell five acres of land on the top of Coma Hill, as well as the block with a ruined house which would do as a church. Bishop Bernard raised no objections. The Monsignor went on praying that it would not be long before he had found a place apart in the wilderness to go to, and where he might come nearer to God.

On the last day of the year 1939 he noted in his diary that his hermitage must be called "La Verna, because it is the highest hill in all the Bahamas, and must be consecrated to God. It must be a beacon, a holy place in the keeping of His Church. *Ara Coeli—Monte Alvernia.*"

He recognized that conditions were very different from those in the days when penitents and solitaries went out into the mountains or woods and built their cells where they fancied. Now, if you wanted to camp in the middle of a lonely place you must find the owners and get the title deeds and have the ground surveyed. Blessed Bernard of Quintavalle, the first disciple of St. Francis, got rid of his house and all his earthly possessions on the very same day. But Monsignor Hawes, after nearly five months of negotiations with his lawyer, still had not managed to wind up his affairs, including the selling of his railroad shares and other investments. What worried him most was an annuity—he could not rid himself of that. He decided that all he could do was to arrange for the money to be paid to Bishop Bernard, and ask him to make use of it for charitable purposes, and at the same time to give the hermit such alms as would be needed to disburse among the poor, or for carrying on public worship. A visit to the leper settlement across the south side of the island of New Providence gave Monsignor Hawes further inspiration for imitating the life of St. Francis in the most literal manner possible.

On December 30 he drew up yet another series of good resolutions, confessing that he could not resist looking back almost daily, and wishing he could return to his easy, comfortable existence in Australia. There was still time to change his mind and inform Bishop O'Collins that he realized he had made a mistake in thinking he was called to be a hermit. But he knew he could not turn back, for Father Benedict Williamson, his spiritual director, had written from Rome: "Welcome to your new home and apostolate. I am sure in embracing your life of real Franciscan poverty you are following the call of God. It is a great vocation—one this poor world needs more than all else."

So Monsignor Hawes resolved, "The new life I am called to begin must be more hidden-solitary. To preach the Gospel in silence, living not only as a priest but as a hermit. *Beati pauperes*: that is the beatitude I want; and on a secluded hilltop, upraised as an altar, yet withdrawn from the habitations of the settlement. I have now found a corner where I believe my soul will be well. Solitude, Poverty, Abjection, Obscurity. That is my vocation now, that of a Franciscan hermit. Charles de Foucauld was called to be 'a hermit and not a missionary,' yet laid the foundations of missionary work in the Sahara. If I live the life God shows me, I may bear fruit. It will be made clear to me what sort of missionary work (if any) I am to do. But I must not throw myself into the work, but wait for it to come to me from the Lord. . . .

"Since I have not attained (and perhaps my temperament may not be suited) to that *interior* mortification that accepts with equal indifference all experiences whether pleasing or contrary to nature, therefore I return very gratefully into God's hands those gifts he has showered on me so plentifully in the past: the enjoyment and fellowship of my brother priests; human respect; the solace of horses and dogs; delight in my little car and driving it; and the absorbing interest of architectural work . . . also minor things, but things to which we are apt to become enslaved. . . . I fear that they may absorb me to such an extent as to deny me leisure or inspiration for that constant attendance upon the thought of God that the Christian who is striving after perfection, and still more the priest, ought to have. This is the prime motive of St. Francis in his love of poverty."

Then he recorded his New Year's resolutions for 1940:

"I offer to Thee my God my soul and body as a reasonable holy and living sacrifice in union with that of my Saviour on the Cross and in the Mass. I wish to unite my intentions with those of Our Holy Father the Pope, Pius XII, especially for peace. He has offered his life to God for the peace of the world. I would likewise offer mine, poor and worthless as it is, but I have no desire to live—no wish at all for a long life. I put myself absolutely in Thy Holy Hands, O Lord. I offer my life to live it in suffering or pain or disease, to accept anything Thou sendest me: rheumatism, cancer, blindness, stroke, drowning at sea, to become a leper. Give me absolute resignation to Thy will—to be ready to accept disappointment, frustration of all my plans; misunderstanding from others. *Fiat voluntas Tua.*"

The first week of the new year dragged past slowly. It was a relief when Bishop Bernard told Monsignor Hawes that he wanted him to go to Long Island to give help to Father Arnold. For the time being he was to take charge of the settlement at Deadman's Cay. But this was not to be until after Easter, so he could stay on Cat Island meantime. He calculated that coming and going from one island to the other would be expensive if he was dependent on the irregular and infrequent services of the mail boats. It would be more economical to run a boat of his own, which he could sail with a colored boy to help him. He recalled that between 1909 and 1911 he had sailed his own boat the *Hispaniola* up and down the coast of Long Island, and even once to Nassau. There was no reason why he should not adopt the same mode of transport, even if he was now in his sixty-fourth year, and not quite so agile as he was as a young Anglican Franciscan missionary.

What worried him was: could he, as a Franciscan hermit, vowed to holy poverty, become the owner of a boat? He wrote in his diary: "There is no way of getting from Cat Island to Long Island except by sea. One can do without a horse or a car and can walk. Our Lord and the apostles used to sail across the Sea of Galilee, even though they *could have walked* round by the coast as the crowd of people did. The boat would be for mission work, and as there are no Catholic stations yet on Cat Island, I can sleep in the boat—a hermitage on the waves. But I regard it only as a *temporary expedient* until such time as I can settle down permanently on one or other of the islands and be rid of the necessity of crossing. If I can settle on my miniature 'mountain' top at the Bight of Cat Island . . . all will be perfect."

The maritime-minded Monsignor found out that Abaco was the best island for picking up a good boat. Many boats were built there for the sponge fisheries, and it was then the off season. Boats could be bought cheaply. He began to study books on navigation in the Bahamas, and smiled when one author informed him that "anyone condemned to travel regularly on these waters goes in constant danger of his life." For practical reasons a boat was essential. It would enable him to carry all the tools and building materials needed for erecting the hermitage. They would not have to be dumped ashore at once. Again, if the boat should be caught becalmed and then struck by a gale on some open "tongue" of ocean, or stove in on the rocks of a lee shore, or run on a sunken reef, the seaman-priest would be safe in God's hands. "After all, one can be drowned but once, and it eliminates the funeral." At the end of these jottings came the prayer: "Our Lady Star of the Sea, I take refuge under thy mantle, there will I live and die. St. Nicholas, patron of sailors and St. Christopher, patron of travelers, pray for me."

No time was wasted. On January 10, 1940, Monsignor

*Fra Jerome,
e Hermit of
Cat Island*

Father Hawes and Dominie (1933)

Monsignor H

(

John C. Hawes (1919)

On a journey in Western Australia

Hawes boarded the mail boat *Priscilla* bound for Marsh
Harbor, Abaco. His companion was a twenty-five-year-old
colored man, Victor Fergusson, a good seaman who had been
loafing around Nassau when the priest met him. A ship's
compass was packed in the priest's bag because he hoped to
return in a sailing boat if he managed to find one that
seemed suitable. He had also taken a papal flag and a red
ensign, given him by Mr. Selby-Hall. The following day,
after examining several boats, he bought the *Olga* for forty-
five pounds cash down. This sum included a well-built
dinghy. In his diary were noted most carefully the measurement of the boat, which was twenty-two feet over all, with
an eight-foot beam. Having purchased a cracked Dutch oven,
a quart of corn grits and a loaf of bread, filled up the water
keg and put his suitcase aboard, the Monsignor told Victor
to up anchor, and the *Olga* sailed at midday.

Twelve pages of his diary are taken up with a detailed log
of this first voyage of the *Olga*. It took nearly five days to
make Nassau. Every change of wind is recorded, every shifting of sail. One can picture the boat racing along as the big
ocean waves loomed up behind and rolled under her, rising
ahead like the serrated ridge of a mountain range. One can
almost hear the wind whistling in the rigging and the flapping of the sails.

"We anchored the first night under the lee of Falcon
Crags. Up anchor at dawn and sailed after breakfast of coffee
and bread; anchoring again in a small sandy cove near the
ruins of Wilson City, once flourishing lumber camp. Victor
went ashore to get firewood, and filled three bags with sand
for extra ballast. Then wind ahead, and short, heavy seas
rolling in. Victor stood on the bowsprit to keep lookout for
reefs and rocks while I steered. He could tell the depth of
water to a nicety just by the different shades of color. At
4:30 P.M. we ran into Cherokee Sound and anchored for the

night. We slept on the bare boards with damp sand bags for pillows. Victor snored all night. I had a very stiff neck and rheumatic shoulder."

The sailors spent two days in Cherokee Sound, hoping for a change of wind. At dawn each morning Monsignor Hawes celebrated Mass. He hoisted the papal flag on the mainmast and the red ensign over the stern. The altar stone and cloths were placed on the cabin top, while the celebrant stood in the hatch, facing forward.

"It was so beautiful," he wrote, "so still, a pall of white mist over the land, with only the hilltops and the tops of the

Mass Aboard the Roma

forest trees visible above it. The sun rose as I came to the *Sanctus.* I said these Masses for peace, and for the conversion of the Bahamas to the Faith, and for a blessing upon the inhabitants of the settlement at Cherokee Sound."

Then it was discovered that the upper gudgeon of the rudder was worn to the thinness of a wedding ring. It would have been unsafe to risk putting to sea, so the Monsignor decided to wait until the next mail boat called, and get her to tow the *Olga* back to Nassau. To fill in the time, he painted out the lettering on the stern, substituting ROM for OLG until the *Olga* became the *Roma*. But he grew tired of this delay, and having tied up the rudder head to the deck rings as a precaution, hoisted sail, and ran down the coast to the coconut palm-fringed bay, near which was the settlement of Crossing Rocks.

A young man came out in a boat, and invited the visitors to come ashore with him. Such a welcome! In the ramshackle old Baptist chapel an informal concert was held that evening, with much clapping and loud applause. "Two young ladies, black as the stove, in great wide-brimmed feathered hats and smart frocks, sang a duet: 'De wall it am so high you cannot get ober it; de wall am so low you cannot get under it; de wall am so wide you cannot get wound it. Only de Lord can let you in.' Apparently they referred to the New Jerusalem."

The skipper and his mate once again boarded the *Roma*. Sixty-five miles of open ocean now lay between them and Nassau harbor, once they had passed "Hole-in-the-Wall" lighthouse, seven miles out of Cherokee. The wind dropped. Heavy black clouds hid the sun and obscured the land. A squall was not far off.

"I called up Victor, who was asleep below, and we reefed the mainsail. Drops of rain. Sound of approaching wind and waves. Drenching downpour about 5 P.M. Three quarters of an hour to sunset, but almost dark already. The gale coming from right aft, due north. Heavy sea. Just the wind for Nassau, but pretty tough. Danger of jibbing, so lower mainsail more and haul in boom. An extra big wave crashes the dinghy (towed behind) into *Roma's* stern, breaking its bow. The rebound of the rope with a terrific tug pulls the stem right out of the small boat. The wreck disappears in the inky darkness. A bad loss—five pounds 'gone west.' At any rate, we are safer now and make more speed.

"Then a big crash and flapping. Our jib tears away from the jib sheets. I go forrad and struggle with it. Get soused as waves break over the bow. Let go halyards and tie the jib down to the bowsprit. Far too busy and alert to feel seasick! Pitch-dark night. No moon. No stars. Hurricane lamp (an old one left on the boat) goes out. I try, but fail to get it alight again, so can't see compass. Victor proves to be a splendid seaman—absolutely fearless and never flurried, but he's now overcome by sleep, although he did have a nap in the afternoon. Young men need more sleep than we old fellows do! I've had none since the previous night, and precious little then, owing to stiff neck.

"We reef down some more of the mainsail, and I send Victor below at 11:30 P.M. There's a faint glow on the skyline right ahead. *Deo gratias.* Nassau light on the great concrete water tower, still about thirty miles away. How my eyes ache, fixing them on that glow. I see the light on the weather bow to starboard. Then, as a great white-crested roller heaves us up as it surges up and throws her stern round a bit, I see the light next right on the port bow beyond the edge of the mainsail, and have to wear away again to bring it back ahead—on the starboard bow. One hallucination that pressed in on me continually was the impression of a flat white plain lying beyond a solid black wall, with a pine-clad mountain rising on the right. The foam from the boat and the nearby curling sea horses showed up with a phosphorescent glow.

"*Deo gratias.* Now the actual light itself (of the lighthouse) appeared above the black, watery horizon. It was a fearful struggle to keep my eyes open; but how fascinating! I recalled those words of the Psalms and murmured to myself: 'I am come into the depth of the sea; and a tempest hath overwhelmed me. . . . Thy way is in the sea, and thy paths in many waters. . . . Thou, who troublest the depths of the sea, the noise of its waters.' I tried to pray to the God that rulest the power of the sea; and begged Him to appease the motion of the waves thereof.

"One seemed very near the borderland of the other world, and quite indifferent, and without fear, as to whether one crossed over. In danger and hardship (amidst nature) one has an intuitive faith in the existence of God and the immortality of the soul. 'They that go down to the sea in ships, doing business in great waters, *they* shall see the works of the Lord, and His wonders in the deep.' I was certainly beholding those wonders that night.

"I had seen one day into another, and now one o'clock, two o'clock, and soon the lights of the town are visible, so I shout down the hatchway and call Victor up to give me a spell. My eyes are so tired. How we seem to be rushing on, nearer and nearer, and so many confusing lights in front. Victor knows his way in—good pilot. When we get close to the lighthouse he stands forward and cons and I steer again. What a relief to get under the lee of the raging breakers on the bar! We have to jibe, and a big wave nearly sweeps us both off the deck. Now a peaceful run up to the anchorage among other boats under the lee of Hog Island. It's 3 A.M. After the loss of the dinghy, freed from its pull, the *Roma* must have made nearly eight knots (ten miles) an hour. '*O Roma felix!*' Victor replies, 'God be thanked!' He reckons the *Roma* is 'a bird!' In the words of the Psalmist I say: 'They rejoiced because the Lord brought them to the haven which they wished for.' "

This first of many adventurous voyages in the *Roma* reveals the character of the sixty-four-year-old priest and would-be hermit. The odyssey speaks for itself, and needs no comment or explanation. The boat was beached for repainting and repairs and Bishop Bernard came down to inspect her. Everybody thought she had beautiful lines. As for her skipper, he suffered from a stiff neck and bad rheumatic pains for several weeks.

About this time he wrote to a friend in England that from now on he must be addressed as "Reverend Father Jerome," explaining that "there are no *monsignori* known on Cat Island; neither is there any such person known there by the name of 'Hawes' or 'Reverend John' or 'J. C. Hawes.' " From this time he was known by the name that he stuck to for the rest of his life: "Fra Jerome."

On February 1 he and Victor sailed at 4 A.M. for Cat Island, with about forty-seven miles of open sea ahead of them. The following morning he celebrated Mass at daybreak on the boat, having anchored the previous night in a little cove at West Shroud on Cistern Cay. The voyage took nearly four days, for the wind shifted continually. Again and again a great black wall would roll up, towering so steep that it looked as if it would break right over the little ship, but the *Roma* just slid up the steep slope. The hours went by slowly. Hot meals were out of the question. Fra Jerome and Victor were reduced to munching hard ship's biscuit.

All day, as they sailed past Great Guana Cay, and went out east through Galliot Cut, the seas got rougher. They had to haul the new dinghy on board and lash it down on the weather side of the cabin trunk. The sun was hidden beneath an inky black sky. Both Fra Jerome and Victor were soaked through. Then the jib sheets tore away. It was not until after 9 P.M. on the night of February 3 that Victor caught sight of the lighthouse on Devil's Point, Cat Island. They ran into smoother water under the shelter of the land about midnight, but it was too dangerous to anchor. All they could do was cruise up and down until dawn. As soon as it was light enough Fra Jerome steered the *Roma* through the reef off Port Howe, where they anchored near the long, sandy shore. It was Sunday morning.

"We landed in the dinghy. I felt utterly weary and exhausted; no meal since breakfast the previous day, but a swim restored me a bit. We rigged up an altar on two short bits of board, out of the dinghy's flooring, in the bush fringing the shore. Here I celebrated Mass, facing east across the sparkling opal-green water of the harbor within the bar. Toward the end of Mass I saw another man standing beside Victor, gazing intently at me. I had avoided seeking the people, but the Mass had brought them to me. The stranger besought me to visit his settlement a few miles farther on. I went next morning, and he offered me a plot of land with an unfinished house on it, begun before his father died. So this was to be the first Catholic church on Cat Island."

Refreshed with a breakfast of hot black coffee, pancakes and bananas, the skipper and mate lay down for a well-earned sleep. Then in the afternoon, having hoisted the papal flag, they sailed on to Port Howe. "I stepped ashore in my tertiary habit," Fra Jerome wrote, "a plain, shapeless, sacklike gray tunic with the Franciscan cord, and a large crucifix hanging from it attached to the rosary beads. I was wearing sandals." He was welcomed with open arms, and the people crowded around, begging him to "hold church" that evening. A Mrs. Deveaux offered the use of her fine eighteenth-century house for services. There was only one Catholic woman with her baby in the congregation. "I gave out some hymns that they all knew—'Rock of Ages,' 'Nearer, My God, to Thee,' and 'Lead, Kindly Light.' They were sung very heartily. I preached on 'The Rock of Peter': the Church that Our Blessed Lord founded on St. Peter and the Apostles. A great many said they would like to become Catholics if I'm going to remain on the island and if a Catholic church is built. Some of the people have friends or relatives in Nassau who are Catholics. Also they are acquainted with the good work done by the Benedictines in visiting the sick in the hospital, and among the lepers. They seemed to know all about the good works of the Catholic Sisters of Charity in Nassau."

By the end of a week more than enough people had come forward to make quite a big congregation, and Fra Jerome immediately began to give them simple religious instructions and to teach them a few hymns. A room in the Deveaux house served as his temporary quarters. His hostess, Mrs. Deveaux, a mulatto who was the second wife of the last of the line of Deveauxs, was much distressed because he refused to sleep in a bed and preferred the bare boards. But on the second night he compromised with a mattress stuffed with native grass, which proved very soft and comfortable.

On Shrove Tuesday, February 6, Fra Jerome walked overland to the Bight, a distance of fourteen miles, carrying a small suitcase containing everything needed for Mass. That evening he met the three owners of the property that embraced Coma Hill and, after much bargaining, they agreed to sell eight acres for thirty-five pounds. Then, having borrowed a hurricane lamp and a blanket from Commissioner Wells, Fra Jerome found his way along the narrow, rocky path through the brush. There was starlight, but no moon. At last he reached the top of the hill, with much clambering over the rocks. He lay down on a narrow ledge of rock, partly sheltered by bushes, to sleep beneath the stars.

"*Ash Wednesday*. At dawn I chose the most sheltered place I could from the wind—a ledge of rock on the northwest side of the summit. Here I laid out the altar stone, clothes, etc. I began with the *Asperges,* and walked round the site of the future oratory and blessed it, according to the directions given in the *Roman Ritual.* Then I lit a little fire in a hole in the face of the rock beside my altar and burned some leaves and blessed the ashes. After this I celebrated Mass, standing barefooted, balanced on the upper edge of an overturned slab of rock. It was rather like saying Mass on the

topsail yardarm of a ship! What a glorious view I had right
below and behind me—land and sea, hills, woods and inland
lakes." This diary entry marked the practical beginnings of
Fra Jerome's eremitical existence. Now the hermit wasted
no time in working out the details of the labor involved.

February 13 he sailed the *Roma* up into the Bight, along-
side the jetty, and unloaded all her cargo, including eight
bags of cement, tools, shovels, picks and crowbars. The people
crowded around, eager to be given paid jobs. Work started
at once. Some men widened the track of approach from the
sea to Coma Hill; others using ponies "toted" up water, sand,
lime, etc. There was plenty of work involved in clearing the
brush from the summit and in constructing a water tank.
Fra Jerome, his gray robes tucked up, sped from one group
to another, giving directions, aid and encouragement.

"The work begins at seven o'clock," he wrote. "That
means actually about 8 A.M. in the normal run of things.
Then they knock off an hour for breakfast at nine, and again
from 1 to 2 P.M. Finally they knock off about 4 P.M. according
to the foreman's watch. According to mine it is often nearer
three-thirty. . . . But what does it matter? They are dear,
simple people and very willing. Our days are short: sunrise
at six-thirty and sunset soon after six. I give them little
presents of tobacco, and they present me with papaws, bananas, eggs, beans, peas, etc. I willingly give a day's work
to some old man who talks a lot and does very little!

"I am also providing and endowing a school for the Deadman's Cay people on Long Island, and paying for the materials to finish the little church at Baintown. I hope to have
enough money to convert the old warehouse at Port Howe
into a church, which will be a good-sized one. When my hermitage is built and *all the money gone,* then I can feel I am
a real Franciscan. I will plant a little field of red corn (maize)
below the hermitage, and grow some casavas, beans and peas,

and make my own 'tea' of lime leaf, and be self-supporting as well as self-laboring."

For the first few days the architect clerk-of-the-works returned each night to his floating hermitage, lying at anchor offshore, and slept on board. But after a strenuous day's work this was an exhausting process, and when one of the natives mentioned the existence of a large cave on the northern side of the summit with an entrance in a low cliff of rock, Fra Jerome went off at once to explore its possibilities. It was even better than he had hoped, and he took possession at once, dragging in tree branches to sleep upon and constructing a rough altar of loose rocks under a natural funnel-shaped skylight. Fra Jerome was delighted with this realization of such a Franciscanlike hermitage; enthralled with the view and the singing of the birds on his own hilltop, he felt transported to Mount Alvernia.

Then almost immediately below the walls of his rough chapel he discovered a smaller cave, about twenty-five feet long, which he decided would make a perfect burial crypt. "Anyone coming up and finding a dead hermit has only to put the body on a board and shove it right into the far end of the cave, and then wall up the same with stones lying ready to hand," he wrote. "No coffin, no undertaker or funeral cortege, no trouble or expense to anyone. Everything is wonderfully provided for." And, in the meantime, he could use the cave to store bags of cement.

In spite of the joy the hermit felt in his anchoritelike dwelling, physical discomfort kept him from any unrealistic contemplation of his existence. When the wind was from the north, the big cave was very cold, and even clad in his habit and covered with a rug, Fra Jerome found sleep impossible. His insomnia was increased by the pain in his fingers, which were raw from the lime and cement and throbbed constantly. Then, too, the sandals he wore chafed his feet, which developed sores during his long tramps to and from Port Howe. To make matters worse, he cut his head badly against a piece of jagged rock while he was readying his altar.

Nevertheless, he was at peace with his world when on February 27 he celebrated his jubilee Mass in his cave

Jubilee Mass in the Cave

chapel. Standing before the rough altar, with twenty-five years of the priesthood behind him, he had a mental picture of how this jubilee Mass might have been celebrated if his life had taken a different course—a picture that he translated to paper at the first opportunity.

The jubilee Mass was but a momentary interruption of Fra Jerome's labors, however. He threw himself into the completion of the hermitage and by the end of March a tiny four-foot-square kitchen had been started and a small wooden hut erected. The hermit made himself a table and bunk and, now that the land crabs were on the move again, took to sleeping in this "cabin." The walls of his cell rose rapidly, supporting, like the kitchen, a domed roof, and on April 2 he finished off the gateway in the boundary wall with two circular lettered medallions surmounted by a cross.

What with the dirt and heat Fra Jerome was having an uncomfortable time of it. He complained of his unkempt beard, remarking that "The only thing to be said for a beard out here is that the mosquitoes evidently have the same opinion of it as I have, and it prevents them from biting my face." He disparaged himself as "a disheveled, dirty, horrid-looking old man, just like a moldy Coptic monk in the streets of Jerusalem. My skin, face, arms, hands have turned a chocolate color with the dust and dirt off the building, and the sweat in the heat mixes it into an indelible grease. No matter how hard I scrub with soap and water, or bathe in the sea, I can't get it off." Water was scarce, too—and expensive if one lived on a hilltop as Fra Jerome did and had to pay to have it brought up by mule. He began to long for a good downpour to fill his cistern.

But he was not to be discouraged by such trivial disadvantages. By the Feast of Pentecost his oratory was finished and the first Mass was said in it three days later. Then heat and overwork took their toll. Fra Jerome found himself prostrate from exhaustion and was out of action for a week, unable to eat or sleep. "I am growing old and worn out," he confided to his diary. "After a few spasmodic flashes of energy, I won't be able to stand up to things. . . . I am so utterly tired and exhausted. All I want to do is to lie down and sleep."

He pulled himself together in spite of his fatigue and by January had completed the rock steps and the Way of the Cross which he had begun earlier and whose most imposing station was the twelfth: a twelve-foot crucifix of which the figure had been cut from a sheet of iron and painted. On Good Friday of 1941 a large crowd gathered to make the stations and the hermit passed out holy pictures to all his friends and assistants. Then he transformed the wooden hut into a guesthouse for his first visitor, Father Callahan from San Salvador, whom he described as "a tough old missionary who has fallen in love with Mount Alvernia."

The natives did not share Fra Jerome's unbounded delight in his spare quarters. One afternoon, he reports, as he was working on the construction of the kitchen, "a Negro woman full of curiosity went inside. I heard her laugh and say: 'What sort of a building dis?' A young man who was clearing away the debris on the floor replied: 'A prison cell, I guess!' So to the natives it appeared as *Carceri*, i.e., prisons."

He himself admitted that there were times when the solitude frightened him, especially during a gale when the wind moaned, howled and whistled around the hermitage, sounding like human voices outside the window. Again, lying on his palm-leaf mat within the arched recess on a breathless, steaming night of July or August, he sometimes suffered from hallucinations. The sight of a bush or an old tree stump in the darkness brought alarming visions of an old woman squatting down on the other side of the grass plot or a bent old man coming up the path.

But these were small things. The real discomforts arose from the construction of the hermitage itself. Fra Jerome had not foreseen that the rough, unplastered walls would harbor insects in their many cracks and crevices, and he was plagued by ants, centipedes, scorpions and hog lice, even occasionally by a large, black, furry, tarantula spider. Moreover, the rough walls absorbed the dampness of the atmosphere and many a morning when he awoke Fra Jerome's habit would be almost wet. "The place has quite the old smell of the Roman catacombs!" he noted. "But as I have built it, so it must stand and remain just as it is—for *me*, at any rate.

"What a luxury smooth white walls would be, and how I long for a floor that I could really sweep decently clean! One luxury I have, and am very thankful for, that is the wire mosquito-fly netting screens to the windows and doors. Without these life in midsummer would be almost unsupportable except for a completely mortified ascetic. The windows have fly screen inside and wooden shutters outside, but no glass. When a storm is raging and the wind keeps shifting all around, one has to shut up every window, so the little place is in almost complete darkness, to keep the rain out. The roof domes are quite waterproof, but the moisture seeps through the porous stonework of the side walls, thick as they are, and runs down in many places."

One consolation to Fra Jerome's aesthetic sense was that within a year or so the clifflike declivity in front of the hermitage became a little garden, sprawling with brilliant tropical shrubs and flowers of varying shades, predominantly scarlet and purple. Before long the flowering creepers climbed over the jagged rocks to the base of the weather-stained stone walls so that it was hard to say where God's rock ended and man's masonry began.

The steep, narrow, winding path prohibited any automobile or motorcycle from coming near the hermitage. Fra Jerome maintained that it was a relief to be free from all the exasperating gadgets of so-called modern progress. He had no telephone, no radio, no electric light, no water pipes, no gas-pressure lamps or stove—only the companionable flames of a flickering wood fire in the open stone fireplace in the little kitchen.

He could look around his hermitage with satisfaction, for it represented an isolation and an eclectic architectural inspiration that pleased the demands of his personality. Bits and corners of the churches he had loved best had found their way into his dwelling: the barrel vault of rough stones from the ancient priory church of Caldey as well as the hole in the wall with a little chimney on the gospel side of the altar where he placed the sanctuary lamp; the stone altar patterned after the one Fra Jerome himself had built at Caldey; the wooden stall where he recited his office from those found in Carthusian cells. And of course the influence of the primitive Franciscan hermitages in Umbria and Tuscany was evident in the whole layout of the hermitage—in the way it appeared to have grown out of the natural rock rather than having been built upon it. The sketches and rough plans in Fra Jerome's diary indicate the many modifications that eventually resulted in the picturesque and brilliant pastiche that his hermitage became. There is nothing quite like it in the world.

Mount Alvernia Hermitage

9.

Island Priest   [1940–1943]

WHILE the Cat Island building operations were going on, Fra
Jerome found plenty of opportunity for seagoing adventures
in the *Roma* as he sailed from island to island, making contact
with the unsophisticated islanders and recording his vivid impressions of treacherous seas and tropical scenery. He made
plans to spend his first Holy Week in the Bahamas on Long
Island, and on a perfect cloudless morning he and Victor set
out in the boat. Soon the sky turned dark and murky, huge
Atlantic rollers broke over the *Roma,* sousing the sailors, and
before long they had lost their bearings altogether. It was
the next morning before they sighted land about seventeen
miles away—the precipitous cays and forbidding rocks of
Conception Island.

Fra Jerome headed the boat toward the island so that he
could say his Palm Sunday Mass on shore, but the sea was
too rough to make a landing and they were forced to go on
until they reached a barren tip of Long Island. Here Fra
Jerome rigged up his altar among the mangrove bushes and
celebrated Mass; then he and Victor fell famished upon a
strange breakfast of coffee and bananas. They wasted no time
in launching the *Roma* again, but in spite of expert naviga-

On Mount Alvernia

he Hermitage, Cat Island

Laying of the Foundation Stone of St. Augustine's Abbey, Nassau (1946)

Lower left: St. Francis of Assisi, Old Bight (Interior)

Lower right: Church of the Holy Redeemer, Free

tion it was Wednesday evening before they sailed into the lagoon at Deadman's Cay.

Fra Jerome had always reveled in liturgical ceremonies, and here in the Bahamas he had ample opportunity to indulge his enthusiasm. The Benedictines in the islands, as part of their missionary technique, had encouraged the faithful to participate actively in public worship; consequently the people—even the children—answered the prayers of the Mass in Latin, directed by a trained leader. Most of them, despite the fact that they could not read, had memorized the prayers and could sing the entire Common of the Mass.

On Easter morning Fra Jerome was backed by his entire congregation singing the *Missa Cantata,* preceded by an incense-swathed procession around the church during which the people shook the rafters with the alleluias of the hymns. "My word! You should hear these people sing," he wrote. "The *whole* congregation, not frightened of hearing their own voices, and so very musical and harmonious. One could never get Catholics in Australia to sing; only a small 'select' choir."

The hermit had many confessions to hear at Deadman's Cay and he had also to take Holy Communion to the sick, "with full ceremony down the road—altar boys, candles and bell. There was one dear old lady who, although very sick, got up and dressed and knelt with her black forehead resting on the floor boards." It was easy to feel a deep affection for these people, and Fra Jerome said good-by to them regretfully when he and Victor stepped aboard the *Roma* on the Tuesday after Easter.

Almost immediately they encountered more stormy weather, and the boat got stuck on a sandbank in Blue Hole Channel, where she ran in for shelter. After three hours she was afloat again, but the grapnel would not come up, having got fastened under a ledge of rock. "It was only five feet depth of water," Fra Jerome explained. "I undressed and dived down, and struggled with the heavy iron under water until my breath gave out. I made three attempts, and then Victor stripped, too, and we both dived under and tugged until at last the grapnel came out with such a jerk that we both fell backward into the water, and had to make haste to clamber up on to the *Roma* again by the bowsprit stay. Not bad work for an old rheumatic clergyman of sixty-four!"

Strong winds drove the boat off her course, but eventually she made Port Howe, where Fra Jerome took a night's rest in an empty room of the old haunted house of the extinct Deveaux family. Instead of ghosts, some very noisy rats disturbed his slumbers. Then, after skirting the coast with a favorable wind for thirty-four miles, he returned safely to the Bight.

In April 1940 Victor Fergusson returned to Nassau and Felix Darville, son of the catechist at Deadman's Cay, took his place as general factotum. A second little wooden hut was built for him on Mount Alvernia. Fra Jerome soon discovered that Felix was not nearly so reliable as Victor, and his disillusionment was expressed in a general way in his diary.

"The colored people are unfathomable. . . . When I first came to the West Indies in January 1909, the deep sympathy I felt for the colored people, from freshly reading *Uncle Tom's Cabin*, had made the Negro an object of romantic interest to me. I thought more of them than of the poor white people out here. Returning to the Bahamas, I now find I am troubled with a feeling of aversion to the Negro. May God forgive me! Their aspects, manners, speech, intonation . . . repel me. Yet they are our own brethren, one in Christ—dear to the Sacred Heart of Jesus. Charity is no natural virtue, but a *gift* from God. How selfish and uncharitable I am, alas! O Lord, *give* me Charity—infuse into my poor cold heart that love for my fellow men that I don't feel for them. Am I unsocial and misanthropic? I want to be a Franciscan! St. Francis kissed the lepers' sores. *I* shudder to shake hands with some dirty and deformed black paw held out to me. I am bitten with the modern notions over carefulness and fastidiousness about hygiene, etc."

These sentiments, so unlike the hermit's later attitude toward his flock, stemmed partly from a certain homesickness for Australia that he had not yet conquered. "I feel absolutely no vocation to work on these islands, nor do I see any real need," he confessed. "Bishop Bernard wants me to work on Long Island or Eleuthera rather than on Cat Island . . . he points out in his letters that at the present time he cannot embark on opening new missions. He has neither priests nor money to spare. All I can do is to look after my few poor faithful catechumens. I shall be so glad when all building is completed on Mount Alvernia. Then I can send Felix home, lay up the boat, and be absolutely solitary on my lonely hilltop."

Fra Jerome had good reason for wanting to send Felix home. Not only was the unfortunate boy subject to epileptic seizures, but he was far too fond of rum and proved more than once that he was not a safe mate to have on the *Roma*. By June Fra Jerome had had enough. He resolved to send Felix back to his father and persuade Victor to return.

Victor, by this time, had become engaged to one of the Cat Island girls and both of them wished to become Catholics. He was pleased at the prospect of once again becoming the hermit's shipmate. Not only did he take charge of the boat, but he worked as a builder's laborer, cooked a midday meal for the priest, and looked after the old pack horse that carried loads of sand and cement to the summit of Mount Alvernia. Fra Jerome had indeed found himself an ideal helper.

In the meantime the catechumens at Port Howe had started to build a church and when it was ready Fra Jerome got permission from the Bishop to say the first Mass facing the people so that "in this way I can keep an eye on them and say: 'Stand,' 'Sit,' 'Kneel' and so on." He described the interior of the church as having a tabernacle on a little altar behind the celebrant with screen gates kept locked when Mass was not being celebrated and "curtains drawn across during Mass, as the priest has his back to the tabernacle and this saves genuflecting. I carpentered and painted a six-foot-long cross. . . . It is now hung up in the new church."

During the summer of 1941, while Fra Jerome was engaged on the construction of a church at Freetown at the Bight, his days followed a regular pattern that would have felled an ordinary man. "I say Mass about 4 A.M. (first streak of dawn in the sky). Prime, Terce, after which I gather sticks, light fire

" *Cold bath out on the lawn* "

and pump up water." He then describes his "one recreation and luxury," a daily cold tub between Mass and breakfast out on the smooth green lawn behind the chapel, the hermit vigorously scrubbing his back to the accompaniment of bird song. "Even if a solitary snake slithers across the carpet, for once you feel ready to hail him as your 'little brother.' "

Then a breakfast of cereal or grapefruit, "a bunch of bread and cheese" in hand for lunch, and the hermit was off down the hill to Freetown to begin work at 7:00 A.M. Invariably he carried with him little packets of corn, coffee beans or sugar for some poor old woman. He might arrive at the building site "to find that one of the two 'masons' has got his wall horribly askew and out of the perpendicular. So I have to settle jealousies between them. At last I get down to my particular job of building one of the round twenty-four-inch diameter columns. Hot sun tempts me to lay down my trowel and say I can't work any more."

After a swim in the sea just before noon and lunch at the beach, the old priest would return to his masonry until four o'clock; then the long walk home over the narrow, rocky path. "When I begin the ascent of the hill I am often so dead beat that I can hardly get along. Dripping with sweat, passing through the gateway, and arriving at the cross paths, I begin the stations (*very short* prayers) as I struggle up the steep path of loose white stones, then the zigzag flights of rock steps. Remove hat and genuflect at each station. At the twelfth I kiss the foot of the big cross. Having arrived at the top, I make a brief visit to the Blessed Sacrament, kneeling at the oratory door.

"Then, rounding the tower, where there is always a refreshing cool breeze, I sit on the steps of the doorway for a few moments in the shade, drinking in the beauty of the vast stretch of blue Atlantic Ocean. Sometimes (very rarely) a ship—a Canadian freighter going to Cuba. Very often I take another fresh-water bath (the third bath of the day) before drawing more water to quench the thirst of the young fruit trees, hibiscus and bougainvilleas. Then I light a fire, ring the six-o'clock Angelus, drink a lot of tea (sometimes three or four potfuls), eat some dry bread and a few bananas.

"After this I lie down on my bed about 7. P.M. I wake up fresh and alert around about midnight, walk out on the lawn to gaze on the beauty of the moon or the starlight tropical night. Then on entering the oratory I light the hurricane lamp and say Matins and Lauds. Having made a meditation, I return to the cell and sleep again until about four. I make no attempt to fight against sleep as many of the saints did, because I suppose their particular vocation was to do penance in that way.

"I can only say: 'Welcome, Sister Sleep! Holy Sleep, come to me a sinner. One day, one blessed night, you will come in festal array to me. You will come to me as Abiding Sleep— Rest Eternal. You will close the door on the repellent vision of the life of this world, with all its insincerity, stupidity and cruelty. You will open the door for your pale brother who will stand on the threshold waiting to be greeted with quiet joy. . . . O Death, true friend, it is consoling that I cannot escape you. You will take the Breviary, or the ax and trowel from my hand, and the working overalls from my body. But meanwhile I must try to carry on my work cheerfully—eating, sleeping, and journeying as a penance. I must not make a lugubrious burden of the communing of my soul with my Creator and Redeemer!'"

Fra Jerome was growing so weary of these almost daily walks down the hill to the Bight and up again that he resolved that once the Freetown church was completed he would "never, *never* touch a trowel, ax or modeling tool again." To walk even a mile through those narrow, winding jungle tracks over rough, uneven, jagged rocks underfoot was more of a strain than five miles on a good, straight, smooth road. After rain there were pools of water on the tracks, and one got soaked from the wet branches of bushes and trees.

But he was delighted at the great crowd that turned out for the laying of the foundation stone on Laetare Sunday, March 23, 1941. The people filled the air with little cries of admiration and pride at the sight of the walls of their church going up and were sure that it would not be nearly big enough for all who would want "to join and give in their names to become members."

The following month the hermit's labors were pleasantly interrupted by a visit from His Royal Highness, the Duke of Windsor, then Governor of the Bahamas. "I had a chat with him," wrote Fra Jerome, "walking along the sea-front road. We discussed Australia and his railway accident in Western Australia, and went on to speak of horses, dogs and architecture. He is very nice and very well informed on all subjects—so simple and unaffected. He was dressed in an old blue yachting suit and looked like the second mate of a yacht. He was much taken with the distant view of the hermitage and chapel."

The Duke and the hermit went on to discuss Fra Jerome's birthplace and his architectural studies, and the former spoke of Father Arnold's work on Long Island and of what an expert "doctor, dentist and builder he was." Fra Jerome was pleased at the Governor's admiration for St. Paul's Church in Clarence Town, especially his remark that "it looked so fine on the hill with its two west towers, just suiting the place. 'I'm glad you like it, sir,' I said, 'I built it thirty years ago when an Anglican clergyman, just before I left the Bahamas to become a Catholic.' The Duke then asked me what Order I belonged to and I told him I was a Franciscan tertiary. He showed me his three little dogs. A man was exercising them ashore." Fra Jerome was evidently delighted by this en-

counter with someone with whom he could again talk horses
and dogs.

The hermit had by no means abandoned his voyages in the
Roma during this period. He describes the "absolute confidence" he had in Victor, especially when sailing past Devil's
Point against a head wind. The young man would stand on
the bowsprit and call out "Luff a bit . . . hard a' port . . . keep
off hard a' starboard" until the danger was past. Once sailing in deep water the boat swung round and her skipper
shuddered as he saw a brown-green patch with a claw of
jagged rock sticking out above the water less than ten yards
away from them. On another occasion the *Roma* was escorted
by a school of porpoises whose playfulness was a novelty after
the usual dangers that confronted them.

One stormy voyage to Long Island was undertaken to pick
up Father Cornelius Osendorf who came to spend a week at
the hermitage. Fra Jerome realized that his guest was being
forced to live under conditions too primitive and made up
his mind that he must have a small cloister and guest cell. He
felt that better accommodations were in order for the Benedictines who might come to Cat Island after his death, and
when there was no visitor, "the hermit can use the room himself to get better nights' rest." This mitigation of his asceticism
gave him some uneasy moments, but he excused it on the
grounds that his bunk beneath the window sill was so hot
and airless in the summer, so damp in wet weather. Above
all, he was constantly pestered with hog lice. "I love and hold
in high esteem that most Franciscanlike of all the saints—
Benedict Joseph Labre," he wrote, "but his own particular
and peculiar vocation is not to be emulated in the toleration
of vermin. I turn to another of the saints—St. Bernard of
Clairvaux—who says: 'I have loved poverty, but I never loved
filth,' and likewise St. Teresa of Avila."

Suddenly, in October 1941, the full fury of a hurricane hit

Mount Alvernia, and for the first time Fra Jerome realized what damage could be done by the force of the winds. At dawn on October 5, when the hermit went down to Freetown to hear confession and celebrate Mass, the sky was overcast. The men working on the jetty warned him that a storm was approaching and begged him not to try to return home, but he refused to listen. As he struggled up the steep slope, the wind from the north had increased so much that he had to stoop down and cling to the steps with his hands. When at last he reached the hermitage, he was nearly blown off his feet, and it was all he could do to pull the door open and get inside. But—"the hurricane hadn't begun yet. These were only preliminary puffs." The hermit lit a fire, boiled some coffee and porridge, and read some of the newspapers received in his last mail. It was impossible, however, to ignore the elemental upheaval.

"The roar of the wind outside was now terrific. I crawled through the low hatchway in the back of the vestment press into the oratory, to pray for the poor people below. I knew their badly built houses couldn't stand this long. After two hours came a lull—this was the center of the hurricane passing over. . . . The first blow had come from the northeast, but as the cyclone passed over us in a northwesterly direction, we now got a battering from the opposite circumference of the moving circle—from the southwest.

"The second act was far worse than the first. When the terrible roar died away and the swirling mists of rain and sea water cleared away, I looked down on a scene of desolation. From a fresh, verdant green the face of the land was turned to a dull brown, as if it had been burned with fire. Big trees lay flat; bushes stripped bare of their leaves. Buildings roofless or nonexistent. My church roof had gone and only gaunt, ragged arches stood out, the gables on them torn off with the shaking. Mount Alvernia, exposed more than any other place to the full blast of the hurricane, carried its little buildings intact, but the low wooden (guesthouse) cabin was slewed right round on its foundations from northeast to east. Even more amazing that the big wooden crucifix on the Way of the Cross stood unharmed."

When at last Fra Jerome was able to descend the hill to Freetown, he found that a number of people had taken refuge in the sacristy of the church after their houses had been laid low. Several vessels had been caught in the gale and were never seen again, while others had had narrow escapes and were thrown up onto the land. As for the *Roma,* she capsized, sank and remained safely protected under water from the violence of the storm. All the natives declared excitedly that this was the worst hurricane within living memory that had ever struck Cat Island even though it lasted only four hours. The force of the wind had been more than two hundred miles an hour.

Of the other islands San Salvador was the only one that had been badly hit. There were very few people on that island who had not lost almost all their possessions, yet there was no moaning and groaning, but only, "Tank de good Lord he spared life; if it had come in the night, lots would have been killed." The church was a sad ruin with all the east wall torn down and broken masonry everywhere, but the damage done was nothing compared with the havoc wrought in the Anglican and Baptist chapels. Bishop Bernard lost no time coming to the relief of the people with a generous supply of corn, sugar, flour and clothing. The government sent over a shipload of lumber, shingles and cement for rebuilding the houses. So there was plenty of work and pay and food for some four months afterward. The local sloops and other sailboats could not be back and off fast enough with their piled-up cargoes.

"Well! That is my first hurricane," wrote Fra Jerome. "I

don't know but that we might get another this month; sometimes another follows on after only a short interval. Isn't
there some old saying: 'Troubles'—or is it 'bears walk in
pairs?' The cheerfulness, patience, fortitude and resignation
of the people are quite wonderful. No complaints, but gratitude to God that it was not worse and that He took care of
them through all the terror."

The impression made by the hurricane on the local religious attitude was amusingly brought home to Fra Jerome
by an old black woman, Henrietta, one of his stanchest
parishioners. She was an invalid and lived with her sister in
a little one-room house with a palm-thatched roof, but her
missionary efforts extended to her neighbors.

"I found Henrietta sitting on a tree trunk, holding forth
to a little crowd," Fra Jerome records. "So I greeted them
and sat down on a rock, while Henrietta went on with her
sermon. 'It's beautiful, de Karthlic Church. I wish I'd been
a Karthlic since I was five years old. It's all those years wasted,
wasted. Why did de Lord send the hurricane to knock all de
people's houses down? It's cos of their wicked goings-on, I
tell yer. De Lord, He punish them, but He spare my poor old
house, cos I all day serve de Lord in it and pray. Dese other
so-call churches let you do what you like, but de Karthlic
Church is strict, very strict, an' you got to keep de rules. Jesus
Christ was a Roman Karthlic.' I can report her little sermon
accurately, and without any embellishment, because I jotted
her words down as soon as I got home.

"At the midnight Mass—the first one in the new church—
during the *Adeste Fideles,* my eye happened to fall on Henrietta in a front bench, and her poor old black face was really
transfigured—something extraordinary and beautiful in it.
I am not sensible generally of seeing the people at all, but I
suppose it was just after the Priest's Communion, and I was
looking to see if those for Holy Communion were making a

move up to the altar rails, or I had to sign to the altar boy to tell them. The zealous server had rung his little bell so many extra times—in fact, almost every time I genuflected—so the people could hardly tell from the bell which was the *Domine, non sum dignus*."

That midnight Mass of Christmas 1941 seems to have given Fra Jerome great happiness. Of baptized Catholics there were still only twenty-two, but all received Holy Communion. On the morning of Christmas Eve he had baptized a dozen elderly catechumens, all of whom had attended Sunday Mass regularly for a year. He was never tired of writing about the wonderful singing, and the people made good use of the *Westminster Hymnals* sent out from England. Moreover, they had grown quite accustomed to afternoon Vespers in English, and reveled in chanting the Psalms, even more so the Litany of Loreto at Benediction, where they responded lustily *Ora pro nobis* to every invocation.

In February 1942 Father Leonard Hagarty, O.S.B., gave a fortnight's mission at Freetown. Fra Jerome wrote in his diary: "He was as good as any Redemptorist whole-time missioner I ever heard in Australia. The people turned up well, and just loved Father Leonard whose very solid and thorough instructions were so easy to understand; bright and homely, too." Father Leonard spent three days at the hermitage, and shortly thereafter Father Frederic Frey, O.S.B., came from Nassau for a week's rest and change.

Lent at Freetown, with the stations of the cross on Wednesday, Saturday and Sunday evenings, was a strenuous time for Fra Jerome. He wrote that the people loved these services when they were carried out after dark by the light of hurricane lamps only. "There are always loud groans and sighs. Between times I saw an old woman talking aloud to herself. She went up to the eleventh station, and hit the executioners in the picture, as the only way to show what she felt about them!"

Lenten fare for the hermit consisted of his own specialty: a bread that he baked from a mixture of whole-wheat flour combined with the locally grown Indian corn flour to which he added Quaker Oats or Kellogg's Corn Flakes and a dash of brown sugar and baking powder. Although he described himself as "a very accomplished baker," he also admitted that often, having placed his loaf in the Dutch oven, he would go off to write a letter and be recalled to the business at hand only by the smell of burning. In spite of what he ruefully described as a "quarter inch of charcoal biscuit on top and bottom," Fra Jerome insisted that it was "very nourishing bread and needs no butter or marmalade," its only drawbacks being that "sometimes one has to cut it with a hatchet."

Fra Jerome, like the other clergymen of the Bahamas, went to Nassau in July for the annual priests' retreat. There among his Benedictine friends he enjoyed the comparative luxuries of sitting down to prepared meals, drinking ice water, and "no washing up afterwards." He was introduced to turtle "meat" pies and wrote that he was having "quite a dissipated time . . . going out to dinner with the local naval boss, Commander Langton-Jones . . . who is in charge of all the lighthouses in the Bahamas." The two men found many common interests, particularly dogs and seascapes, and the hermit was delighted to discover that the commander was familiar with all the Australian ports. The naval officer told Fra Jerome of a book he was writing about the Bahama lighthouses and the many stories of pirates in Bahamian waters, and the old hermit sat fascinated long past his normal hour for retiring.

Fra Jerome's chief concern at this time was ridding himself finally and forever of all his worldly possessions. He had sold out the last of his investments and handed over the proceeds to the Vicar Apostolic of the Bahamas; the Hermitage had been made the absolute property of the Benedictines. All that remained was an annuity of one hundred and twenty pounds which he was unable to dispose of, as the capital belonged to certain trustees. He consoled himself by remembering that St. Francis had allowed tertiaries to retain a few necessary possessions. Nevertheless, he still had doubts. "What sort of a man of Gospel poverty is he who has a banking account— even if it only stands at one pound, seventeen shillings, and is offset by a bill of one pound, two shillings, threepence owing for groceries? I have two pairs of sandals, my girdle and three habits, whereas it should only be *one*. Also I have a few cotton shirts and pajamas, but this year I have got accustomed to wearing my habit only without any shirt, with only white cotton drawers. Within these last three years since leaving Australia I have lightened my ship of three thousand pounds. Now at last I am really a poor man."

Fra Jerome forgot that the *Roma* was another of his possessions from which he could not part, because she was essential to his mission work. Writing in October 1942, he says, "Victor has just brought back the *Roma* to her customary smartness—hull spotless snow-white, with bright red and blue lines, and red copper paint below the water line.

" 'I love her as I do my own wife,' says Victor! Fortunately his wife does not need painting—like the white ladies do! So a smart yellow cotton dress set off with scarlet bows is as good for her as a new mainsail is for the boat. It makes an artistic contrast with her chocolate-colored skin. A wide-brimmed palm-leaf hat is the topsail."

Victor, who could afford to buy new frocks and hats for his wife, was better off than most of the island folk in 1942. World War II had made its mark even in these remote parts. German submarines had sunk several vessels in Bahamian waters. The cost of living rose steadily, and there was little or no work for the people on the out islands. Many were on the verge of starvation. The supply of fish had run short; summer crops had failed; there were no bananas, plantains or other fruits, no work, and therefore no money to buy corn or flour. Families were forced to feed on roast land crabs supplemented by beans or cowpeas.

Fra Jerome wrote home that he had seen young girls dressed only in old corn sacks and that even these were rare, hard to get and valuable. "It is no fault of the people—they are *not* lazy and shiftless as some travelers say. 'Oh, they can live on very little; they are used to it!' What I feel is that it is high time that they got used to a higher standard of living; *why* should these poor creatures never have anything better?"

Haunted by the dire poverty and misery on Cat Island, the hermit resolved to add to his mortifications and penances. He limited himself to one full meal daily consisting usually of macaroni cooked with cheese, onion and tomato. But he wrote, "I still feel I fare much too well when I think of some of my poor people below the hill, and sumptuously as compared with the meager diet of that mortified hermit, Charles de Foucauld, who took his meals on the ground without even a plate and only dipping his spoon into the saucepan or pot. Neither did the first Capuchin hermits have tables; they took their food on the floor—no beds, no tables. In these degenerate days we shy at any sort of mortification. We are too pampered and fastidious."

As a result he also decided to cut down his supper to "tea and bread with perhaps some peanut butter or marmalade; *or* just a bowl of hot soup and some bread; *or* oatmeal porridge, *or* hominy with a little sugar and milk." But these ideas are blue-penciled out and over them in red is written: "Cut out supper."

The natives often climbed the steep slopes of Mount Alvernia, knowing that he or she would have only to ask and be given whatever the hermit could spare. One day a tired-looking old granny came laboring up the hill and sat down on a rock outside the chapel door, quite exhausted with the climb. "Good mornin', Farder, good mornin'," she said.

"Well, Uterpe, what has brought you up all this long way?" asked Fra Jerome.

"Farder, I did want to speak to you. Farder, I'se ashamed to ask you but you did tell us if things was bad and we had nothing, to come to you, and I got some sisal on the boat to send to Nassau to get me some flour, but got nothing now left in the house."

"What did you have for breakfast, Uterpe?"

"Farder, I didn't have nothin' to have—not a bite." So Fra Jerome mixed milk with the coffee in the pot, adding plenty of sugar, and gave old Uterpe a chunk of bread and two bananas to eat right away. Then he put some flour in a paper bag and some tobacco leaf, and wrote an order on the storekeeper for half a bushel of corn for the old lady, not forgetting to add lard and sugar. She departed happy, and full of gratitude.

Then, finding himself alone, the hermit went into the oratory to get on with his Office, but soon there was another "Mornin', Farder, is you dere?" and this visitor—a poor man —wanted medicine.

"What for? What's the matter with you?"

"Headache and fever—can't sleep."

Fra Jerome had to part with some of the few quinine pills and aspirin tablets left him. Now perhaps he would be able to proceed with his prayers. But no, looking down from the chapel door, he noticed a big straw hat bobbing about among the bushes—this time a girl. Having arrived at the top of the hill, she said she wanted to sell some eggs.

"How many have you got there, Esther May?"

"Five, Farder."

He gave her a sixpence, and sympathized with her on the

loss of a second baby, but warned her to "keep away from the men till you can get a good young man for a husband and get married. These eighteen months past you've been very faithful in coming to Mass, and I'd like to baptize you, but I can't do so until you've changed your life."

So young Esther May was dismissed, and departed down the hill with another sixpence. Once again the hermit made a fresh start on his interrupted Office, but he did not get much farther than a psalm or two. There was another call—round the other side by the kitchen door:

"Farder, Farder, are you in? . . ."

Many of Fra Jerome's friends in England and Australia pictured him living in complete solitude like an anchorite with all his days spent in prayer and contemplation, but more often than not he was preoccupied with such incidents as these. It was seldom that a day passed when he did not get at least one visitor. He wrote: "One after another they find their way up the hill to see the old hermit. It's little I do. I wish I could do more, dear Lord. How busy Charles de Foucauld used to be, and what multitudes he received every day and helped at his hermitage in the Sahara."

In August 1942 a little church dedicated to St. John the Baptist was opened at Baintown, Cat Island, and Fra Jerome took care of this church as well as those in nearby settlements. The *Roma* was in full service and it is easy to picture the skipper and his mate launching the dinghy and rowing out to the boat lying at anchor off The Bight. Then, after a few hours' sleep they up-anchor in the starlight, run out under the jib, and anchor again outside the bar.

"At dawn we are off again—full sail and a free wind and all clear ahead across the bay. . . . Suddenly there is a terrible grinding noise and we heel over, pounding up and down on a hidden outcrop of rock. We let down sails at once, and Victor jumps overboard in his clothes and, standing up to his neck

in the sea, tries to shove the *Roma's* bow round toward the
deeper water, and I shove with the long sweep. . . . *Deo
gratias!* A bigger wave heaves us off into the deep water.
Fortunately the *Roma* is well and strongly built and escaped
with no more than springing a leak. . . . As we got off the rock
and Victor climbed on board his legs were badly cut by the
sharp rock and bleeding profusely. Fortunately I had a tin of
carbolic salve ointment on board. . . . It was only St. Nicholas
and our Guardian Angels that brought us safe back to port."

These autumn voyages brought concrete results as far as
Fra Jerome's missionary endeavors were concerned. By the
end of October he had eighty-nine converts and more were
under instruction. But the hermit had his hands full with the
emotional Bahamians. He wrote that "here you have to get
back to the discipline of the primitive Church. You have to
keep drumming into them that religion is not a coat of whitewash but a new life." He was encouraged, however, by the
remark of the commissioner of the islands who told him that
he had noticed a remarkable difference in the Freetown people since Fra Jerome had opened the church there. Lawsuits
and court cases had diminished considerably—which may
have been because Fra Jerome himself acted as judge in quite
a few cases. He wrote down the story of one husband-wife
fracas that he settled amicably.

"A fortnight ago a young woman whom I had married in
June last year, Rosalie, arrived panting and sweating early
one morning at the hermitage. 'Farder, I don't know *what* to
do—me and Harold was just havin' a little fun togeder—just
play like we often does, and then I go into the house and take
up the knife to peel an onion, and the constable he come in
the door and say, "Give me dat knife," an' he wrench it out of
my hand, an' take it to put me in court before the chief' (the
local name for the commissioner).

" 'Well,' I replied, 'why did he do that?'

" 'I don't know, Farder, I was only peeling the onion.'

"I told her to go home and send her husband up to see me. In an hour's time Harold appeared and repeated exactly what his wife had said.

"So I went down to the village and questioned the people in all the nearby houses to find out the true facts. It proved to have been a nasty fight—husband and wife rolling on the ground, trying to strangle each other! 'I'll kill you,' says Harold. Getting up, Rosalie runs into the house and fetches the big sisal knife and makes a pass at Harold in the back. Then the constable arrives, having been summoned by Harold's mother. He just held out his hand quickly, and said: 'Give me the knife.'

"I knew it might go hard for the poor girl—perhaps six months' imprisonment—so I talked to the couple outside, and gave them a dressing down for telling me such lies, and that it was no good my trying to help them unless they told the truth and nothing but the truth, otherwise the magistrate would get cross with the contradictions and prevarications, and, having to cross-examine so many witnesses, it was sure to end with imprisonment.

"The next day was Sunday and I preached about the Bible —the Church's book, and with what *reverence* she treated the Word of God, and the very book itself, for example, the ceremonies (which some of them had seen in Nassau) at a High Mass—incense, lights, etc., at the reading of the Gospel. 'And when you were received into the Church you professed your belief, saying, "having before me the Holy Gospels which I touch with my hand," and some of you may have to go into court and lay your hands on the Bible, saying: "I swear by Almighty God to tell the Truth, the whole Truth, and nothing but the Truth." And you that are Catholics now, do you mean to tell me you will dare to do as you used to do before— to tell the magistrate a pack of lies?'

"Then I enlarged on *why* God did not strike a person dead at once, and on liars having their part in the lake of fire and brimstone, etc., etc.—a very necessary sort of sermon, because perjury just to back up friends, or clear yourself, is so prevalent and so little thought of.

"That same Sunday evening I walked along to the residency and had a friendly talk with the commissioner. The case was heard in the middle of the week. The delinquents owned up to all the constable charged them with. The 'great cloud of witnesses' waiting below in the basement, not one of them had to be called. The commissioner was well pleased with being able to settle the case so easily, and, after a good lecture, merely bound over Harold and Rosalie to keep the peace. On the following Saturday the pair came to confession, and knelt side by side at the altar rail next morning. So far, they have lived happily together again!"

This long story will set at rest any notion that Fra Jerome's life on Cat Island resembled that of St. John the Evangelist on the Isle of Patmos. If he ever fell into trances or had ecstasies he took good care never to mention them in his letters. He was no Angela of Foligno or Margaret of Cortona. Judging from his correspondence, Fra Jerome would have been horrified if anybody had called him a mystic. God, as visible in His creation, interested him far more than the abstract speculations of mystical theologians. All that mattered to him was that "the Word was made *flesh,* and came to dwell *among us.*" On Cat Island, in the beauties of the sky and the sea, and above all in the people, Fra Jerome almost always seems to have "had sight of God's glory, glory such as belongs to the Father's only-begotten Son, full of grace and truth." How often did he not refer to the "beautiful gifts of God," saying that God lets us have lovely things to cheer us on our way and to be a medium of education for us?

But he was convinced of the efficacy of the contemplative

orders, and as World War II went on he began to feel that, once peace was restored, there was little hope that people would be brought back to God in any other way than through the growth and expansion of the Benedictines, Cistercians, Carmelites and Poor Clares—and through the transformation of the Franciscan Third Order, "from a pious confraternity back to the original idea of a Catholic communist society of penance, voluntary poverty, and social welfare."

"I think," he wrote, "that many returned soldiers, sailors and airmen, after all the privations and horrors of this war and the futility of the world wrestling for economic domination and influence, may yet fly for peace and rest to such Benedictine communities of the primitive observance, which try to support themselves by agriculture or other forms of manual labor. But they must be housed in an austerely plain monastery, with the 'oratory' mentioned in the Rule of St. Benedict, not the great sumptuous and costly medieval abbey church. There must be no publicity or advertisement—no encirclement of the monastery with tea gardens or boarding-houses for sight-seers and trippers. In an abbey of the Cluniac type, the visitors would gaze open-mouthed at the gorgeous carvings and paintings of God and His saints—'look at the pictures'—and move on. In an abbey of the Cistercian kind they will notice more the *life* of the monks, and go away wondering *why!*"

The famous hermitage of the *Carceri,* visited by almost every pious pilgrim staying in Assisi, was always at the back of Fra Jerome's mind. And if anybody had asked this voluntary "prisoner" on Cat Island what was the hardest thing he had to endure, there can be little doubt that he would have replied that it was not having a dog as his companion.

In September 1942, three years and four months after his heart had nearly been broken on parting with his fox terrier, Dominie, he was still thinking of his "dearest cobber" and remembered clearly this "scruffy black and white fox terrier—tail up and head cocked on one side, with bright eyes" regarding her master. When Fra Jerome looked at a treasured photo of Dominie he admitted that the tears came into his eyes and a choking lump into his throat.

Mrs. Roberts, the wife of the farmer who had adopted Dominie, wrote him that the dog "had kept up a brave exterior," but after a whole year had passed and she could not hear again the voice she loved, the waiting was too long for her, and one morning Mrs. Roberts found Dominie curled up dead in her basket. She had passed peacefully in her sleep with no sign of any struggle, a fitting end for such a faithful heart.

Snakes, however, were put into a different category from dogs. Fra Jerome had no wish that these dumb creatures should be slithering around him as he passed the Golden Gate. In November 1942 he wrote that he had been engaged in "a proper 'snake week' around the hermitage, and had killed three out of four. One dropped from the porch roof, with a big frog in its mouth that was squarking loudly." The hermit seized his machete and chopped the snake's head off, and the frog jumped free. "Well! little fellow," I said, "you've had a narrow escape," whereupon the frog jumped flop, right onto my shoulder. Brother Frog and Brother Lizard are always good friends, but a snake is the very devil!"

A few days later Fra Jerome was doing some jobs around his little guest cabin, in preparation for the expected visit of Fra Nicholas Kremer, when, coming swiftly through the long grass, and heading straight for the cabin, he beheld the biggest snake he had ever met outside a zoological garden. He struck it with all his strength, but the cutlass, though sharp-edged, made no impression on its tough, leathery skin. He hit the reptile again and again. Then it slithered half under the floor of the cabin. Had it died there, the stench would have been unbearable for weeks. So Fra Jerome seized the snake by the tail, and pulled it out with all his might. Twice his hold slipped, but at last he hauled it out. Then the snake turned on its captor, who just managed to get a grip on its

& I loathe touching anything

The Snake Hunt

neck. It was almost seven feet long and as thick as a human forearm. Some of the natives who saw the dead snake the following day reckoned it to be the biggest ever found on Cat Island.

The incident provoked some other and sinister "snake yarns" outside the church after Mass on Sunday. One woman who had left her two little children under a tree while she was working in her plantation found that a snake had coiled round one of them and killed the infant.

The local attitude toward snakes was closely bound up with superstition. "Talking of snakes," Fra Jerome wrote, "the terror of 'Obeah' still remains with some of the people. Last Sunday an old, old woman came to me after Mass for some 'medicine' for her feet—very swollen and cracked. I gave her some epsom salts to bathe them in hot water with some healing ointment. 'I know why they come so,' she said, 'it's the Black Heart of the Seven Sisters. My brother read it in a book he found in a sailboat from Haiti, and he gets earth out of the graves in the cemetery and spreads it at night on my path between my house and kitchen. It's that what cracks my feet; so I'm a cripple now and can hardly walk.' So all I could do was to laugh, and tell the old lady that it was all silly nonsense and superstition. She and her brother Simon keep up a perpetual feud."

On January 14, 1943, Fra Jerome received a letter from Dr. Gummer, the new Bishop of Geraldton, informing him that he was still regarded as a priest of that diocese. It pleased him that the Bishop had retained his name as one of the "consultors," without interfering with his extended leave of absence from Australia. Dr. Gummer wrote: "Your leave will not be terminated by me. Should you wish to return at any time, you will be most welcome. You gave of your best to the diocese, and you have left behind an honored name here, and an example for the young priests to follow."

But the old hermit, far from having any desire to return to Australia, felt that he ought to do far more penance, and confessed that, after a visit from Father Brendan, he "fell to more relaxation again," that is, he moved into the little guest dormitory on his new cloister. Here he had been sleeping in pajamas between sheets with two pillows. But he admits that he tossed about most nights and got very little sleep. Even worse, the sand flies got in under the sheets and bit him! " 'The sergeants of the Lord' come in to punish me thus," he wrote. Determined to renew his efforts, he gave his rock bunk in the cell a thorough washing with a strong solution of permanganate of potash, and brushed the walls and soaked the corners. This rid him of the hog lice, and once more the hermit slept on the straw mat in his habit and cord.

But even this hard bed was not penance enough for him. Ever since he had cleaned out the small cave for a "burial crypt" Fra Jerome had intended to sleep there, but the longer he deferred doing so, the less he was inclined to relish the idea. Now, however, he resolved to go through with this mortification. On February 12 he peered into the narrow, irregular chamber at the far end of the cave—and it looked repulsive. A snake slithered into a side pocket of the rock; land crabs scuttled over the ground. With sudden resolution Fra Jerome lit a fire inside the cave that blazed up so high that to him, watching through the barred door, it looked like "the gates of Purgatory." When the leaping flames had died down to embers, the hermit tossed a few chips of paraffin onto the bed of glowing coals and immediately the cave was filled with a thick smoke that killed the mosquitoes and sand flies.

By midnight the air in the cave was clear of smoke and Fra Jerome began his preparations for sleeping within. He carried an armful of hay to the far end of the cave and crawling on his hands and knees arranged it as a bed. With his hatchet he chipped off some protruding knobs of rock from the floor, and filled up a hollow with loose, flat rocks before spreading a palm mat over the dried grass. He dispensed with a pillow, as the floor sloped downward and his head was higher than his feet.

"I knelt down," he wrote, "and said my short Litany of the Hermits and then lay down, first on my back with arms out straight as I hope I may be laid when dead in *forma crucis.* Then I turned the hurricane lamp to a faint glimmer. I kept my hood drawn over my head to keep 'varmints' out of my hair. I recited the Compline prayer. . . . When the time comes and my soul is in Purgatory (if my body is walled in here), worms and maggots will be ceaselessly at work on it until the bare white bones lie in the form of the cross. Perhaps a snake will wriggle through the empty eye sockets of the skull, and crabs, no longer dreaded, walk under the ribs."

This somewhat morbid picture is mitigated by Fra Jerome's further meditation on the happiness he drew from sleeping directly under the altar in the cave above, and by the description of his dream of awakening in the Bishop's house in Geraldton to the sound of the cook going about preparing breakfast.

"Then I really wake up and see the rough vault of rock some eighteen inches above my head. I draw up my knees and they hit the ceiling. But how warm and comfortable it is here. I feel grand, and the sore throat is really much better. I am lying on my left side and a faint glow comes from the lamp on the other side. I lie and doze a little longer and then turn up the lamp. I crawl down the cave on hands and knees. The door has swung to with the wind and outside it is raining. Climbing up to the oratory, I see the first faint glow of dawn in the sky. Well! One's grave is a very snug and comfortable place to sleep in!"

Perhaps the severities that Fra Jerome inflicted upon himself contributed to a certain "nerviness" that is apparent in some of his diary entries. He remarks that the devil had been piling up artfully a mountain of petty annoyances, trifling, but enough to upset his equanimity. The prior at Nassau had not responded to his plea for more candles; there had been no acknowledgment of a check he had sent to another Benedictine to defray the expenses of a blind girl; another monk had wired that he would arrive that evening—"like a thunderbolt when I am short of groceries and other supplies—no clean sheets ready or anything."

He grumbles on that just when he has arranged a trip to Long Island "comes a vague communication from the Bishop that he hopes to visit the Bight 'shortly.' He doesn't say *how* —plane, private boat, or mail steamer; if the latter, will it be for a few hours' stay over or a week until the mail boat returns?" He was disturbed that some of his flock were leaving to get work in Florida; that feuds were cropping up among his people. But that these were just passing irritations is clearly indicated when he writes, "First hand goes to the devil, but the second to me. For I have a most wholesome lesson in learning how far I am from religious detachment and humility."

One of the things that helped the hermit forget about minor annoyances was a new-found interest in gardening. He had planted orderly rows of cabbages, carrots and turnips as well as many local varieties of vegetables and fruits, and carefully watered and tended them. His cabbages gave him particular delight—their extraordinary sweetness, he was sure, came from the tropical sunshine. He toyed, too, with the idea of keeping goats but decided it would be too much bother and contented himself with urging his people to drink goats' milk. They obviously regarded this as an eccentric notion. As one woman put it, "I want *real* milk—not that dirty stuff from a dirty cow or goat, but proper milk in a tin."

Fra Jerome accepted this rebuff with secret amusement and turned his attention to more important matters such as the baptism of Victor's first-born, a handsome boy whom they named Paschal. Holy Week was upon him again. Fra Jerome had decided to perform the Maundy because "it's all there in the missal so I reckon it is meant to be carried out," and there was wholehearted congregational enthusiasm when the hermit washed twelve pairs of black feet on Holy Thursday.

A less liturgical project was a plan for a communal corn bin "plastered inside and out with a strong waterproofed mixture of cement. Padlocked manhole on top of concrete roof, thus sealed against weevils." The hermit urged the adoption of this upon the government authorities along with "public toilets," which he claimed were urgently needed in

Freetown. There was no danger of Fra Jerome becoming a "poseur and dilettante" with such practical problems constantly engrossing him.

He was engrossed, too, by the books and magazines that arrived on the mail boat, and commented critically on his reading. Of *The Song of Bernadette,* which he devoured in three days, he remarked that it "has made Lourdes live for me, and has given me a deep devotion and love for Bernadette Soubirous." *The Family That Overtook Christ* he dismissed as "melodrama—exaggerated and strained in style." But what appealed most strongly to him was a life of the Carthusian Dom Edmund Gurdon which in 1943 was appearing in the Prinknash Abbey magazine *Pax.*

Dom Edmund had written in his later years, "My days here are flowing by very peacefully. I am most of the day in my cell in utter solitude, all alone with God and my thoughts and my rich store of memories of the past. I pray a great deal more than I have ever done before. I do also a certain amount of manual work. Time never lags with me, nor has it ever done so. I have never in all my life known what *ennui* is. I find my days always too short. My life is indeed monotonous, but its monotony is only exterior."

Fra Jerome carefully copied these words into his diary and added, "I could make Dom Edmund's words my own."

10.

Soliloquies of a Solitary [1943]

LONG before Fra Jerome set foot on Cat Island he had been trying to clarify his ideas on the eremitical life: first, through his reading; later, through jotting down in his diary thoughts that had occurred to him. He was, of course, strongly influenced by the Franciscan eremitical ideal, but in accord with the eclecticism that had shown itself so strongly in his architectural exploits, his view of the hermit's life was drawn from many sources.

Just what the composite was is clearly revealed in a series of articles called *Soliloquies of a Solitary,* which first appeared in *Pax* in 1943, and which in 1952 was published in book form, with additional material, and a dozen illustrations by the author, by the Dublin Capuchins. Fra Jerome, with a cloudy idea of keeping his identity a secret, had signed the original articles "Troglodyte," but his references to an "island hermitage" gave a strong clue to the authorship of the *Soliloquies.*

Fra Jerome introduced his little work with a bow to Cardinal Newman, who had written, "Solitude is to be sought not because of the relief from those who are not there, but for His sake Who is." This, Fra Jerome felt, summed up perfectly the *raison d'être* for the eremitical life; its idealistic appeal, he thought, had been expressed in Richard Rolle's words, "The hermit's life is great if it be greatly led."

Then in his vigorous style Fra Jerome went on to discuss the meaning of the solitary life as he saw it. " 'A modern hermit! What a lovely romantic life!' some will say; or, 'How I envy him being free from all worries and responsibilities'; 'Such a calm and untroubled way'; 'A shirking of real life, I call it, a lazy, vegetating existence,' another will exclaim. They all miss the mark, understanding very little about it. The life of a solitary is, of course, that of a contemplative, and I write of it here as colored by the Franciscan outlook. I did not choose or plan or will to be a contemplative, but being a priest it was because I was not the man of prayer I ought to have been that, to save my soul, God in His mercy called me to leave the world. With real diffidence and, I hope, a true humility I make a record of my experiences as a hermit-tertiary of St. Francis . . . that they may perhaps be of some encouragement or consolation to a like-minded pilgrim; but let him not look to read any high matters herein, for my hermit feet have as yet tramped but on the Purgative Way."

Then for the "like-minded pilgrim" Fra Jerome traced the steps that led him to become a hermit, telling of his first glimpse of Cat Island and of his "Holy Mountain," and gave a detailed and highly romantic description of his hilltop. "The great clouds sailing overhead, painting the landscape with beautiful shadows athwart its sunshine" he used as a symbol of the heavy black storm clouds that blotted out the sunlight from the soul of even a secluded hermit.

He also confessed to the pull of a warmer, more temperamentally attractive existence such as he had experienced in Australia.

"I pictured the spacious, comfortable presbytery that I left, with its easy chairs and well-stocked bookshelves; the kind nuns and the laughing school children; the shouting boys at football; my car spinning along those long, smooth country roads of Western Australia. Sunday with the bells swinging in the church tower and the mellow pipe organ throbbing to *Missa de Angelis,* while at the altar the smoke of the incense curls above my head, spreading a bluish haze in the cupola of the dome. We never realize the full extent of our happiness in some particular place until after we have left it."

But, Fra Jerome pointed out, it is not by indulging in memories of this kind that a vocation is fulfilled, but by following the way of life to which God calls us. And with regard to his own particular vocation he pictured his past life as nothing—"just a little noisy bubbling over of the kettle with a show of spouting steam; so much of self mixed up with it all—self-esteem, self-satisfaction, self-delusion." Then the agonized self-question: "*Why* has our Lord touched me? *Why* couldn't He leave me alone?" Thus he revealed his struggle, his own dark night of the soul in which he was overwhelmed with the thought that he was suffering from a vain delusion that he had made the biggest mistake of his life when he left Australia. He went on to tell, however, of the resolution of this conflict when at last his vocation was confirmed by his spiritual director's counsel and encouragement.

Fra Jerome's discussion of the eremitical life owes much to *The Quest of Solitude* which, before he gave up his missioner's role in Australia, gave him a general idea of how Christian hermits lived from the earliest periods of Church history up to modern times. This idea he incorporated into his *Soliloquies* with the understanding that antiquity and modernity must be reconciled and combined, and he explained that he had tried to build a "hermitage of today which fits in with the original standard because it has no modern ameliorations or characteristics."

The hermit went on to lay bare his reasons for believing

so strongly in the solitary life. He pointed out that birds and wild creatures have their homes, monks their monasteries and individual cells, and itinerant friars their rude mountain hermitages to retire within. He stressed that Jesus, after He left Nazareth, had no home of His own; that many of the saints followed their Master in utter homelessness. Poverty as laid down in the Gospel must be the rule in order to counteract the spirit of acquisitiveness of which money is the symbol. For acquisitiveness is the soul of evil, not only in the individual but in corporate bodies and nations.

"Poverty, Solitude, Penance—that is the vocation of a Franciscan hermit. I feel that if I respond faithfully to such a call, and live the life God shows me, I may bear fruit; but if I am to undertake any sort of missionary work, God will make it clear to me: I am not to seek it, but to wait for it to come to me. In my old age I would like rest and quietness to prepare for death, but *Domine, si adhuc tuo sum necessarius non recuso laborem; fiat voluntas tua.* The fruit of the apostolate springs not from any action, not from any work, not from preaching, but wholly from union with Christ Jesus, Who says 'Without Me you can do nothing.'

"Meanwhile, I have this place apart in the wilderness to pray in. I go up into the mountain with Our Lord to pray, that I may come nearer to God. The new life I am called to lead, living as a hermit, is to preach the Gospel in silence."

The Hermit of Cat Island felt that his friends ought to understand just what was this new life he believed he had been called to lead, and went into it in some detail.

Fasting and abstinence from flesh meat were the basis of his life, and he wrote, "For a hundred years after the death of St. Francis supper was an unheard-of thing among the friars of the motherhouse of Santa Maria degli Angeli. Similarly, with the first hermit-friars of the Capuchin reform.

"In *Piers Plowman,* Langland says he will not give alms

to any hermit except those who eat only once a day after the hour of None. . . . We moderns have got so habituated to three solid meals a day that to omit or delay the regular hour makes us *imagine* we are hungry. Let the hermit, then, conform to the practice of those monasteries where the strict observance is kept up. After Mass he will take standing the monastic 'pittance'—a bowl of hot coffee and some dry bread. When he has had his one full meal after None, he will not feel the need of anything further before nightfall and bedtime. . . . Wartime affords additional opportunities for simplifying the menu. Here, at present, cheese is unobtainable; it is the off season for hens to lay eggs; and the sea has been too rough for any fishing. To my dish of boiled rice or Indian corn I add a sauce made with red peppers, tomatoes, shallots or onions out of my garden, chopped up small, and fried in cottonseed oil. Whether Habacuc would have passed my 'mess of pottage' as okay to carry to the reapers I couldn't say, but it is probably better than any mess that Charles de Foucauld ate in the Sahara!"

Fra Jerome goes on to describe the place where he prepared his meals, and gives further little domestic details. "In the tiny kitchen of his hermitage the recluse will be up against

The Solitary

the many inconveniences of real poverty: there is no room to put anything down anywhere, only one small table twenty inches square, a few narrow shelves in the corner, and a couple of iron bars across the fireplace with its smoke-blackened arch stones. It is raining, and he forgot to bring in any dry sticks from the now-wet heap of firewood outside. After the meal comes the washing up; the fried cotton oil congeals on the plate, and burned rice sticks in the saucepan like a sacrament that confers character! Thank God there's no rule enjoining two meals a day."

The hermit of Mount Alvernia attached equal importance to his clothing—or rather the lack of it. "Wherever I go I wear the gray habit and cord, donning an old torn and ragged tunic for nightwear, for the hermit must always be 'on duty' with his loins girded and his light burning. . . . St. Francis said his brethren were not to wear sandals unless compelled by necessity. Merely to substitute sandals for boots and shoes makes, in reality, for greater comfort. A few years ago I could not step barefoot even on the rounded shingle of the seashore without flinching; now I can walk (and have done fifteen miles at one stretch in a day) absolutely barefooted over the roughest jagged rock or loose stone rubble, and un-concernedly through pools of rain water. . . . The Franciscan hermit has his footgear perpetually being resoled and re-heeled by nature and needs no new ones.

"About twice a year, when my hair is growing too long down at the back of my neck, I cut it off myself in chunks with a pair of scissors, and without needing a mirror. My beard, after the Capuchin style, I regard not so much as an escape from daily shaving, but as a penance. How anyone could grow a beard for preference I cannot imagine! I sup-pose the hermits of former times must have looked a bit wild, so I was amused when one of the rare visitors who had climbed the hill couldn't refrain from blurting out: 'Well, really, you look just like one of the old prophets out of the Bible!' "

Fra Jerome continued to soliloquize about his longing for a good library, telling how much he missed the companionship of books. On the other hand, he remarked that he could manage quite well without "boatloads of spiritual books." After all, the Bible, Breviary, and the Missal are the three books containing "the one word of God." Another deprivation, a spiritual one, was that he managed to get to confession only about four or five times a year when a priest happened to be on the mail steamer going to or coming from one or the other out-island mission station.

It was a compensation that he had the privilege of saying Mass without a server, because he could take as long as he liked over it, "for how my server would fidget if he had sometime to kneel for an hour praying for *Ite missa est!* Nor is there a devoted cook fuming because the bacon is getting cold. And why should the hermit worry if the amice does stay around his neck more than half an hour? Standing before this table of squared stones on the hilltop, do I not reach back thousands of years to the *sacrificum Patriarchae nostri Abrahae; et quod tibi obtulit summus sacerdos tuus Melchisedech,* and forward to all eternity? So why need we hurry?"

Fra Jerome went so far as to maintain that "the keystone of the regular observance of a contemplative life is the night office." Although he included in the *Soliloquies* a description of his nocturnal devotions, his diary gives a more complete and informal picture of them.

"I always ring the Angelus bell at midnight. The old sick people down in Freetown tell me how they like to hear it in the long, still night. . . . The midnight hour I begin thus: 'God be merciful to me a sinner.' Taking holy water, I kneel on the rock floor against the west door of the oratory. I slowly make the sign of the cross. Then I look at Our Lady's image and repeat the holy words of Lourdes: 'Penance, pray for sinners, for a sick world.' I kiss the rock, and then move forward on my bare knees saying the Hail Mary. Halfway I stop, and holding out my arms in the form of a cross (fingers just touching the wall on each side) I say the Our Father, Hail Mary, and Glory Be to the Father for the intentions of our Holy Father the Pope. Then I go forward a little and kiss the altar step five times in honor of the Five Wounds (or seven times in honor of the Seven Sorrows of Our Lady), and twice more—one for our Holy Father St. Francis and one for St. Patrick. Then I shuffle on to the step and kiss the edge of the altar slab. Then again move backward, still on my knees, and below the step kiss the rock again, raising my arms high with hands joined, and begin the *Veni Creator Spiritus*. . . . I rise and kneel in the stall and say the Litany of the Hermits. . . . Then I rise and sit and begin my meditation.

"After an hour I light the big hurricane lamp and recite Matins, but leave Lauds for the morning, and it makes a good thanksgiving after Mass. If my eyes are tired, or if there is a shortage of kerosene . . . I only say the invitatory and one nocturn of Matins at night. It's not the correct thing, and may be a bit irregular to break up the Office thus, but why strain and tire one's eyes and use precious midnight oil when there will be all the day coming with the sun that God has provided for a natural light—better than a smoky old hurricane lamp!"

The diary also sets forth the hermit's method of intercessory prayer during the midnight hour alone before the Blessed Sacrament.

"I travel around the world. Prayer is the golden chain that stretches across the oceans and binds us around the feet of God. Australia: my two bishops—James Patrick and Alfred

Joseph; Geraldton, Dongarra, Mullewa, Tardun, Perth and the tertiaries; Ballarat, with the good Sisters and their sick ones. Jerusalem: the Convent of Our Lady of Sion and the orphanage. Rome: the Holy Father and Father Benedict Williamson. Assisi: with all its friars of the order to which I belong. England: my relatives and friends. Peekskill and the Franciscan Sisters. Vancouver. Wartime Europe. These islands: the Bishop, Fathers and Sisters; the Apostolate of the Sea, all sailors and fishermen; my own flock here on Cat Island and Long Island."

His commemorations finished, Fra Jerome would return to his cell "sometimes to sleep, sometimes to toss restlessly about until the first streaks of daylight." On one occasion he really felt so sick that there seemed sufficient reason for taking a dispensation from his Rule.

"I clamped the brake down on the alarum of the clock, and I had an extra sound sleep. I woke with a sudden start —how much of the night had passed? Is it near morning? I strike a match. The minute hand of the clock is exactly one minute to twelve. Well, if that's not my Guardian Angel I haven't got one! What are you here for? Your health and rest? Let us have no more relaxations and mitigations that have ever been the curse of monastic observance."

But of course these nocturnal observances were only part of the Rule he had set himself. He recited the rest of the Office during the day, read portions of the Bible or *The Imitation of Christ* after his frugal breakfast, and interspersed his prayers with vigorous manual labor. At the close of the day the hermit walked down the hill, then climbed up by the steep path to make the Way of the Cross, rang the evening Angelus, and finished his devotions.

The uncritical reader of *Soliloquies of a Solitary* would be almost certain to form the idea that the rule of life observed by the Hermit of Cat Island was more or less a literal imitation of that of the First Rule of the Friars Minor, or that Fra Jerome was trying to conform to the Third Order Rule. Actually the "Rule of Mount Alvernia" was a patchwork made up of bits and pieces taken from various rules. Fra Jerome interpolated anything that he felt would be helpful to his spiritual life without bothering whether it was Franciscan in origin. Nevertheless, even though there is no reference in the *Soliloquies* to the short Rule drawn up by St. Francis for all Franciscan hermits, Fra Jerome insisted that he was a hermit-tertiary of St. Francis.

His deviations from the Franciscan rule tended toward an emphasis on mortification. For example, Franciscans do not stand for their frugal breakfast; the "standing pittance" was a custom that Fra Jerome picked up from the Anglican Benedictines at Caldey. As far as the austerities of the hermit's fasting were concerned, he exceeded the Rules of both the First and Third Orders which advocated neither perpetual abstinence from flesh meat nor a "breakfast pittance and one meal a day."

Fra Jerome's sacklike gray habit and cord, patterned after that of the Capuchins, was quite unlike the costume of medieval Franciscan tertiaries who were bidden to "dress in humble, undyed cloth . . . their outer garments and furred coats without open throat, sewed shut or uncut but certainly laced up, not open as secular people wear them . . . their sleeves closed. They are permitted to have leather purses and belts sewed in simple fashion without silken thread, and no other kind." His beard likewise was a Capuchin inspiration.

Although Fra Jerome's belief that recitation of the night Office is "the keystone to the contemplative life" was consistent with strict Franciscan practice, he seemed to have forgotten that there are many contemplative orders which do not require their members to rise in the night to recite the Office. Moreover, the hour of mental prayer at midnight seems to have been adapted by the hermit from Cistercian observance, rather than Franciscan. And as is usual with Fra Jerome, he exceeded the Cistercian practice by half an hour!

But there was one observance that Fra Jerome dearly loved that was peculiarly Franciscan. That was the making of the Way of the Cross. Fra Jerome's carefully carved, open-air stations have their prototype in countless friaries all over Europe and particularly in Italy.

And in his isolation from his fellow tertiaries Fra Jerome was also following a tradition established in the Middle Ages when some of the Franciscan tertiaries were so loosely connected with the Order that after their deaths their bodies were claimed by Augustinians, Benedictines or Carmelites. The hermit, once he had retired to the Bahamas, failed to establish contact with any official branch of the Franciscan Third Order and seemed to prefer to regard himself as a solitary unit of a mystical world-wide "Order of St. Francis." He even, in 1950, requested that O.S.F. and not T.O.S.F. be added after his name, explaining that the former initials comprised all Third Order congregations and hermits.

In the *Soliloquies,* however, he writes not only of St. Francis, but of the medieval hermit Richard Rolle, of Dom Edmund Gurdon and of Charles de Foucauld, all of whom he considered guides to the eremitical life. And he goes on to say that if he loves his little hermitage and wishes to be buried in his cave, his want of detachment must be forgiven, "since a great and holy solitary, St. Cuthbert, expressed the wish for his remains to be laid to rest on his beloved Farne Island beside the oratory his own hands had fashioned."

Fra Jerome ended his unique little book on a note of humility. "The solitary has left the world in order to try to live closer to God. St. Francis was able to say to God, 'I would wish to love Thee more if it were possible, but I cannot give

Thee more than myself; I have given myself whole and entire.' How happy and blessed we poor earth-bound creatures would be if only we could truthfully say the same. Let the hermit kneel humbly behind little Bernadette Soubirous as she shuffles forward on her knees over the loose stones in the cave of Masobielle in order to hear more clearly the words of the gracious Lady: 'Penance! Pray for sinners—for a sick world.' *Sancta Maria, Regina Eremitarum, ora pro nobis.*"

Nobody could say that profundity is a characteristic of *Soliloquies of a Solitary*. Rather is it a collection of vividly drawn and highly colored sketches, like those which illustrated and enlivened most of the author's letters to his friends. The prose style is as quaint and original as the pen-and-ink drawings. Just because of his artistic temperament it was almost impossible for John Cyril Hawes to lead a "hidden life" in the strict meaning of the phrase. Neither could St. Francis, for that matter. Like the Little Poor Man, Fra Jerome could not resist making grand gestures and drawing attention to himself. Both these men were basically dramatist-poet-knights proclaiming that they were trying to be faithful to their Lady Poverty. Fra Jerome always saw *himself* in much the same way as he saw his buildings, carvings and paintings. He was so naïve and simple that it is improbable he realized that this little book might be regarded by unsympathetic critics as an amusing piece of exhibitionism! After the publication of the *Soliloquies* in 1952 it became extremely difficult for the hermit to lead a hidden life, yet even then he could not understand why people would not leave him alone on his Bahamian island.

11.

"In Journeyings Often . . . "   [1944–1948]

FROM 1944 Fra Jerome found his solitude interrupted more and more often. Both missionary work and architectural assignments drew him away from Cat Island until Mount Alvernia no longer seemed like his permanent home, but like a retreat to which he withdrew for a brief period of isolation before he had to be off again.

One of the problems that he encountered in his missionary work, and one that gave him a good many headaches, was that of administering conditional Baptism to converts from Anglicanism. He himself clung to the view that rites administered by High Church clergymen must be valid. "You can't go splitting hairs about their right intention—they mean to do what 'the Church' does. When Protestant ministers can imitate Catholic rites and ceremonial, and cense the altar with the 'correct' number of swings, etc., and probably more rubrically than the average priest does it, can you doubt their want of exactitude over what they know is so much more an important thing as Baptism? . . . It's very difficult to drum into the heads of simple folk the difference of a 'conditional' sacrament and what it means; and this 'rebaptism'—as they see it—makes for bitterness. . . .

"I venture to think that to accept their Anglican Baptism,

after proper inquiries, would bring more over; and supposing in one case out of a hundred that Baptism *was* invalid, would that be a more serious loss than one hundred people kept away *in toto* from the Church because of its enforced 'conditional' rebaptism? In the one aforesaid supposed invalid administration the Baptism of Desire would ensure the salvation of that soul. You can talk and instruct until blue in the face about the 'conditional' administration as precautionary measure against some possible flaw in so important a matter, but nine out of the ten will cheerfully think they are being baptized a second time—*two* baptisms for the remission of sins!"

But when Lent of 1944 came round Fra Jerome abandoned theological speculation to wonder despairingly if the conditional and unconditional baptisms he had administered had done much to cast out the devil. His flock had indulged in so much lying, thieving, adultery, gambling, drinking and fornication, that all he could do Sunday after Sunday was to denounce their wicked lives until he got weary of hearing the sound of his own voice. His self-imposed penances and his sufferings from colds, fever, sore throat and rheumatism did nothing to raise his spirits. He wrote that he felt like a John the Baptist in the wilderness. From the pulpit he preached to exceptionally large congregations, all agog to hear what he would have to say. The more pious purred in their seats until their priest let loose on *them,* because they gloated self-righteously over their neighbors' sins.

A succession of fiery discourses, with plenty of references to lions, tigers, jackals, and wolves and comparisons of some of the listeners to slimy serpents slithering in the long grass; then passing on to the beauty of brotherly love, Christian charity, and the love and compassion of the Sacred Heart for the lost sheep and the prodigal son proved effective.

"Well! *Deo gratias,* my sermons bore some good fruit. The

liquor-shop proprietors closed down their dance hall for the rest of Lent, and the ole-man 'hymn and hell-raiser' came along by himself to Mount Alvernia, sweating and panting up the Via Crucis under a broiling sun. He was very humble and repentant and made his confession the following Saturday evening. . . . And in revenge the devil's latest attack on the hermit came last Sunday, when I was away in Freetown. Thieves forcibly broke into the hermitage and stole four pounds I had left there in small silver and notes. My alms box for the sick and needy, containing a money order from some tertiaries in Australia, had been cashed a few days before."

By way of contrast to those hell-fire sermons with their denunciations of vice in its crudest forms, Fra Jerome was told by Bishop Bernard shortly after Easter that he must give the annual retreats in July to the two convents in Nassau— the Sisters of Charity of St. Vincent de Paul, and the native colored Sisters of Blessed Martin de Porres. No other priest was available. Fra Jerome wrote to Mr. Selby-Hall, "If you get this letter in time, please ask the prayers of the Carmelites for me and for the poor Sisters who have got to listen to me. I dread these retreats. I feel so helpless. I'd much sooner work ten hours a day in midsummer with my trowel, building a new convent for them, than this job of plastering the spiritual walls of souls! I'm only used to preaching to Australian bushmen and miners or to poor ignorant sinners on such subjects as Mass-missing, swearing, drinking, fighting, thieving and fornication. These are hardly helpful themes for holy Religious!"

But then the idea began to appeal to him. "Things have suddenly taken a turn. Ideas, pictures and thoughts are flowing in. These retreats will prove a good exercise and discipline for myself, even if of very little or no help to the good Sisters. I get more and more mixed up as to what mysticism and contemplation really are, the more I read about them. It's all very 'high flown!' The only sort for me that I can understand is that of the holy Curé d'Ars' farm laborer sitting in the church before the tabernacle, '*I look at Him, and He looks at me,*' or St. Francis praying all night, '*My God and my All.*' The present status of Adam's earthly Paradise, the Third Heaven, and the Seven Rungs of the Ladder of Perfection are quite beyond me!"

Fra Jerome now decided that he must sell the *Roma*. During the previous year he had not made much use of the boat and she had been too much of an expense, what with paint, ropes and pulleys. On her last two trips to Port Howe and back she had nearly been wrecked, and had lost her best big anchor. He wrote, "Much as I loved the boat, I am glad to be free of the last thing that might be imputed to me as a personal possession. I wish to have absolutely nothing to leave in my will, so I have sold her to Charles Rolle, the Baintown catechist. She is now a useful cargo boat. Good-by, little vessel. Many happy sails and adventures have I had in you these four years." It was not long, however, before Fra Jerome felt that he could not do without a boat. The *Roma* was superseded by a dinghy, the *Rocbird*, which he could sail himself.

Fra Jerome was overjoyed to receive a visit in June 1944 from Bishop Stephen J. Donahue of New York. "A great day!" he wrote. "We go down to the beach to meet the plane from Nassau, and conduct the Bishop in procession to the church." All of the native Cat Islanders turned out for the occasion, and Fra Jerome had fifty candidates for Confirmation ready for the Bishop. After the ceremonies were finished, the Bishop, the hermit and two Benedictines had lunch together. Then a visit to the commissioner who offered to put them up for the night. "No! They say they prefer to spend the night up on Mount Alvernia, and don't mind if they have to rough it at the hermitage."

So back they climbed to the hilltop, where sitting on the green lawn they had tea. Fra Jerome scrambled around making shift for the night for his guests. The Bishop, of course, occupied the guest cell; Father Ambrose bedded down in the shingled cabin where the hermit had laid out a sheet-covered grass matting and pillow for him; and Father Marcion crawled into the hermit's bunk under the window sill. Fra Jerome rolled up a towel for a pillow and fitted himself into the curves of the rock outside the south wall of the chapel where a soft breeze wakened him for his midnight devotions.

In the morning, after the four priests had celebrated their Masses, the nine altar boys who had climbed the hill to serve the Bishop fell to upon the sandwiches, cakes and Coca-Cola brought by the Bishop's party, while their elders contented themselves with a more conventional breakfast. When the episcopal group was ready to return to Nassau, they took Fra Jerome along with them so that he might give his scheduled retreats.

Fra Jerome was given a comfortable room and bath in the bungalow just below the Benedictine priory where, once the retreats were finished, he had plenty of space for a drawing board and to spread out his tools. Here he settled down to working out the plans for St. Peter's Church at Clarence Town, and, once these were finished, for the Ballarat Cathedral in Australia. It was grueling work and often he stayed at it till well past midnight, but by the middle of August the drawings were finished and the hermit found himself waiting impatiently for the mail boat to Cat Island.

Before he left Nassau, however, Fra Jerome went to see his old fellow missionary of Anglican days, Canon Devall. The two friends were overjoyed to see each other again and when Fra Jerome's visit drew to a close, very humbly the Canon begged his blessing. The hermit was deeply affected by this and wrote, "I, although a true priest, felt quite unworthy to give it."

His visit to the Canon turned Fra Jerome's thoughts to a comparison of Anglican services with those of the Roman Catholic Church. Although he was far from an enthusiastic "vernacularist," he was very much in favor of conducting funerals, baptisms and marriages in English. It pleased him that in the Bahamas congregational Vespers or Compline sung in English was encouraged. But when it came to the Mass, it was a different story, and the hermit was violently against the use of the vernacular.

"Latin is, of course, the common and universal tongue, essentially 'Catholic.' Some correspondents in the Catholic weeklies are talking nonsense about vernacular in Germany and Austria: there is *no such thing;* only rhymed paraphrases or translations sung by the congregation during the ordinary High or Low Latin Mass. Why all this talk? If people want more English, let them sing a few English hymns during Mass, and let an educated layman read the Epistle and Gospel in English while the priest is saying them at the altar."

This was the sort of thing Fra Jerome had started in his Church of the Holy Redeemer, Freetown. Every Sunday the catechist, vested in cassock and surplice on the greater festivals, read the Epistle and Gospel in English. On Palm Sunday and Good Friday he read the Passion. This meant that the priest did not have to shout his part and was saved a sore throat. "Nothing Lutheran or revolutionary here," Fra Jerome commented. "But for the ordinary weekday Mass, it is distracting if the priest reads the Missal in an extra-loud voice. I detest those so-called 'dialogue Masses,' and far worse, of course, are those yell gabbles of the Holy Rosary during Mass. No! Dim your abominable glaring electric lights and give me the old medieval 'blessed mutter of the Mass,' so conducive to prayer and meditation. Let the priest be quick or slow, I don't care, but don't let him shout. He stands before the altar, not to '*say*' Mass, or to '*read*' Mass, but to do it!"

These strong opinions on the manner of celebrating Mass are matched by his attitude toward money. "Was I wise to sell out all I had?" he asked himself, and replied without hesitation, "No, of course not—I was ever a fool, and intended to be one! But as I've never run short of the wherewithal to build and to help my poor souls, I order lumber and cement and haven't a cent left to pay my bills in Nassau. I never refuse anyone that asketh of me. I buy groceries every weekend for my old grannies and invalids, sometimes paying out to get a leaky part of a palm-thatched roof patched up; or it may be a pair of dungarees for a penniless old man, or cloth for a woman's dress, or a blanket or milk for the baby. Always so many asking, and I've got no money left, and I don't know where it is to come from, but with the aid of my Guardian Angel and St. Francis I manage to help everybody. The last mail brought a set of Mass intentions from the Franciscan Sisters at Peekskill, and a money order for five pounds from a friend in Australia." It was in fact amazing, almost miraculous, how gifts both in money and in kind dropped onto Cat Island—like St. Thérèse's shower of roses.

Throughout the autumn of 1944 Fra Jerome, despite the fact that he was now sixty-eight years old, kept himself busier than ever. One of his ventures was the production of a small book of prayers and meditations, lavishly illustrated with eighteen drawings. This he sent to his friend Father Rope. Then he set to work to carve a seven-foot crucifix for the Clarence Town church, using a pocketknife, since carving tools, or even a chisel, were not available in Nassau, owing to the war. He painted and gilded the crucifix, and while he waited for it to dry he busied himself with drawings for the proposed new priory at Nassau. He explained to Father Frederic that he felt that the monks' choir should be the first portion to be built, and that the twin towers would serve as sea beacons like those at Reculver on the north coast of Kent in England.

His solitary sails in the *Rocbird*, in spite of the dangers that they exposed him to, had such a beneficial effect on the hermit's health that by the beginning of Advent he felt that he could once again revert to a vegetable diet. The only mitigation that he allowed himself was a mug of hot cocoa before retiring on cold winters' nights.

And from his description of Mount Alvernia at this season, the cocoa was indeed a necessity. "Short, dark days now, and these north winds of Atlantic Ocean gales sweep with biting force over the hill. This time of year it is indeed Mount Alvernia—the Mount of Cold, of freezing! Of course to a well-nourished, meat-fed Englishman this would not seem really cold at all. But when you are of old age, and your blood is thin after a sweltering hot tropical summer, it is, in proportion, in contrast, different. Every time I have to open the kitchen door to fetch in water or firewood, I shiver in the blast of the biting north wind coming down from the icy waters of New York and the Hudson River." But there was one great relief—the hog lice had completely disappeared from the hermitage.

On December 13 he wrote that he had received no mail for more than a month, owing to the erratic movements of the steamer from Nassau. "Dear friends at home—what would you think of being three weeks and five days without a letter or a newspaper? The local storekeeper down below at the Bight picks up occasional news on his radio, but more often than not he is without batteries, or his set is not working properly. True, a hermit *ought* not to pine after any worldly news, but if you don't get any, how can you pray for the world and for sinners?" Having little to do, Fra Jerome amused himself by drawing a Christmas card, which he felt appropriate to the present author.

At the beginning of 1945 Fra Jerome found himself knee deep in building plans and operations. He left his hermitage to camp at the Old Bight where St. Francis Church was under way, and here, from January through March, he threw himself into the supervision and construction of the building. The tumbledown shack in which he slept was infested with ants and other vermin, the "jiggers" bit the old man unmercifully, and his bare feet became sore and scabrous from treading in lime.

It must have been a relief to him to finish the job and go off to Long Island to visit Father Cornelius Osendorf with whom he could restrict his activities to discussing plans for the new Clarence Town church. This new Catholic church would stand on the highest hill in the very center of Clarence Town, its twin towers higher than those of St. Paul's "the Pearl of the Bahamas," which Fra Jerome had designed thirty-seven years earlier.

But he was still more urgently needed at Nassau to draw up the working plans for the Benedictine monastery. Abbot Alcuin Deutsch, who was staying in Nassau, and Father

MONASTERY   COLLEGE

St. Augustine's Abbey, Fox Hill, Nassau, Bahamas. North View.

Frederic Frey, the prior, had many conferences with Fra Jerome which helped to crystallize their conception of the new monastery and make a start on the building. His stay in Nassau also afforded the hermit a much-needed rest, as he had developed septic ulcers on his insteps and had to get around with the aid of a stick.

Although his room at the monastery was comfortable, and life in Nassau was easier for Fra Jerome, he looked upon this exile from solitude more as a penance than a respite. *"Voluntas Dei,"* he wrote. "When called upon, I must use such gifts as God has given me for the general good in the service of His Church. So I must sacrifice my solitude and exterior detachment." This was hard for the old man, for the noise of Nassau bothered him and he complained of the earsplitting, deafening roar of planes overhead, of the hoots and grindings of motor trucks and lorries, and of the "ten thousand dogs" that barked loudly all night long.

"I sleep (or don't!) on a huge spring bed in a large, comfortable room and sit down to three square meals and eat meat, too. Everybody is very kind to me here. It is a most exemplary and edifying community, but the *Paupertas* of a Benedictine monastery is a 'second cousin once removed' from the Lady Poverty of St. Francis. I shall be quite glad to get back to the peace and quiet of my hermitage."

It was not until August that Fra Jerome was able to return to Cat Island, but all was not so peaceful as he had anticipated. Almost immediately he was called upon to settle a bitter dispute between two groups who were about to go to law. One man whom the decision went against was very disappointed. "He said to the others of his party: 'What you listen to that ole man for? What sort of priest is he? You dunno what crime he wasn't sent out here for, to have to live all alone up on that hill!' . . . Good for the hermit! Perhaps the best explanation as yet forthcoming of my settling here!"

Litigation of this kind, which the hermit found so unpleasant, was offset by his interest in enlarging the Freetown church. For the rest of the year Fra Jerome was occupied with the extension of the nave of the church and the construction of the south porch. And when he really wanted to get away from everything he took the *Rocbird* out for a sail.

In spite of his seventy years Fra Jerome often was forced to anchor his boat if the wind was onshore and, sharks or no sharks, dive into deep water and swim ashore. "The last time I did this it was very cold," he wrote, "but I soon got warm walking in the sun and slipped on my habit again. I admit I had neuritis extra bad that night. . . ." The truth was that Fra Jerome was too old for this sort of escapade, but he refused to take care of himself. It is not surprising that by Lent of 1946 he was "anchored to the anchorage" by a leg and foot "swollen as big as an elephant's, starred here and there by decorative boils." He was incapacitated to the point where he could not even gather kindling to light a fire, but he says that his Guardian Angel sent a man up the hill with a bundle of firewood and that this "heaven-sent messenger" returned every day until he recovered.

One morning, just after he had bathed his leg and bandaged it and was sitting writing, with his foot on an old box, who should arrive but His Excellency the Governor—Sir Charles Murphy—accompanied by his wife, daughter, and military aide-de-camp. Fra Jerome wrote: "There they were standing without the hermit's door. I felt worse than Eliseus did when he saw Naaman with his horses and chariots! I'd been too sick to sweep or tidy up the place for days, and I was in a very dirty old ragged habit (more than Franciscan). The party came in and sat on the only chair and on boxes and the cold rock seat in the corner. But I found them most charming people, and their sons had been at my old school —Kings School, Canterbury. Lady Murphy especially was quite intrigued with the 'quaintness' of the hermitage, and looked up its chimney and missed *nothing*, but was too polite to remark on the dirt and dust! They most kindly wanted to take me away with them to Nassau on their plane, but I couldn't have walked down the hill, because of my elephant's leg."

Eventually he did have to go to Nassau for treatment, leaving his catechist to carry on the Sunday church services, because no priest could be sent to take his place. By April 6 he wrote that he had made a marvelous recovery, "eating plenty of boiled cabbage, grapefruit, limes, lemons, and a concoction of salt and bitter wild sage." He wrote at great length about what he was doing, supervising the layout of the new monastery and boys' college. Much as he longed for solitude, he realized that the most acceptable thing to God and himself at that moment was to place his architectural knowledge of design and building at the service of the Benedictines. It was a big job and entailed plenty of hard work and headaches. Fra Jerome consoled himself with the words of St. Thérèse: "Of itself prayer is of more value than work; but it may please God more in a given circumstance to see us working rather than praying."

In order to supervise the building he lived near the site, five miles out of Nassau, in an old house called The Hermitage that had been left to the Prefect Apostolic of the Bahamas by Cardinal O'Connell. It was a beautiful place with spacious paneled rooms, dark oak Jacobean fireplaces and furniture, and grounds that sloped down to the sea.

"We are a very happy little community," wrote Fra Jerome. "There are four Benedictine lay Brothers, and we rise at 5 A.M. for meditation, after which I say Mass. Breakfast is at seven. Then the Brothers go off in a motor lorry to the site. Sometimes I go with them, or else work at my drawing board. . . . I have a big bedroom, 24 feet long and 20 wide, with an 8-foot long table on trestles for my drawing board, and to spread out plans. Then there is a 7- by 5-foot hanging cupboard, too, and even a private bathroom! I have a lovely view over the sea, and just before midday I slip down to the shore and have a swim.

"The Brothers say their office from the shortened Breviary in English (*not* the Little Office of Our Lady), and it is *most* edifying. They recite it slowly and reverently. They return from the site at midday, and we talk at dinner. They keep on their overalls. But supper at six is properly monastic —religious habit, silence and reading.

"When I am beginning my Matins in Latin in a corner of the chapel I like hearing the Brothers say the invitatory with all the lenten 'Proper.' As the Brothers say them, the verses come with quite a new meaning to me. Alone, one has got into the habit, alas, of rushing through the Latin Office without much meditation on what one is saying. I can quite imagine that in the future completed abbey church lay visitors will be more edified by hearing the Brothers reciting their English Office in the crypt than the choir monks chanting or reciting the *Breviarium Monasticum* up above."

A new road up to the site on Fox Hill had been completed, and the summit and slopes of the ridge of hills all cleared. The rocky hill rose about sixty feet above the surrounding level of plain, and its ridge (about thirty to forty feet) twisted east and west. Fra Jerome now realized that there was no room for a quadrangular monastery around a four-sided cloister with a second quadrangle for the college, so he had to scrap his first designs and think out an entirely new conception. He decided to follow the exigencies of the natural site and make use of the varying levels. He knew by experience that something suitable and original would develop out of it.

Father Frederic Frey, representing the Abbot Alcuin Deutsch, was the soul of the operations. Fra Jerome said of him that "no architect would wish to have a more intelligent and efficient co-operator and director than Prior Frederic. He stated his requirements clearly, leaving the architect freedom of action, discussing every detail and making valuable suggestions all along that helped to make useful alterations and practical improvements." They decided that the first section would accommodate twenty-five priests, six lay Brothers, and fifty students. It would be made up of cells, corridors, refectory, kitchen, and would include the choir of the church over a crypt with side chapels. (At the same time Fra Jerome was busy making drawings of a new church at the seaside resort of Koriot in Australia, as well as plans for a new school in the diocese of Ballarat.)

The building was begun almost immediately and had progressed far enough for the cornerstone to be laid on July 11, 1946. Most Reverend Bishop Bernard Kevenhoerster laid the first stone of St. Augustine's Monastery and the sermon was preached by Bishop Stephen J. Donahue, who had come down from New York for the occasion. The venerable architect was requested, or rather commanded, by his Vicar Apostolic to vest in his aged and moth-eaten prelatical robes for the stone-laying function, but there is no evidence that he obeyed the command.

Fra Jerome returned to Cat Island in August to begin painting the big mural of Christ's charge to St. Peter on the interior wall of the south porch at Freetown. But there was no time for any prolonged solitude on Mount Alvernia, for in September he and Oblate William McWeeney, who had been his guest since the hermit got back from Nassau, boarded the mail steamer for Long Island.

Here, at Clarence Town, there was more than enough to do on the unfinished church of Sts. Peter and Paul. Window traceries had to be made, and the stone proved to be very hard and almost impossible to trim. The strength of the arches depended on a good cement mixture. It needed constant supervision to get the local "masons" to fill up the joints properly. But finally the vaulting of the church was completed, along with the central tower over the transepts, and Fra Jerome made a concrete cross to cap the little dome of the lantern. Father Cornelius Osendorf was "a wonderful man," so Fra Jerome wrote. "He has all the people with him, and is making real good Catholics of them, on the foundations laid by Father Arnold before his death. He works like a steam engine, setting out lines, doing mason work, driving and keeping in repair the two trucks, the water pump and electric plant. Over the weekends he is up and down the island visiting his outlying missions, never neglecting the spiritual needs for the ever-present material requirements of building."

One day, early in October, came a telegram that Abbot Edmund of the Cistercian Abbey of Valley Falls, Rhode Island, had arrived by plane at Nassau and wanted to see Fra Jerome immediately. Without delay the hermit left for Nassau, and discovered that Abbot Edmund needed plans for extending the church and for a large new guesthouse. He begged Fra Jerome to fly back with him to the United States to inspect the existing buildings, but this was quite impossible for the hermit because the ground-floor walls of the monastery on Fox Hill were well up by now, and needed his attention.

Throughout November Fra Jerome stayed in the same comfortable Benedictine quarters he had occupied before, and not only worked on the plans for Our Lady of the Valley, Rhode Island, but also completed all the necessary

detailed plans for the rest of the Fox Hill monastery buildings, including the infirmary, refectory, kitchen and the
church with its crypt and the upper and lower sacristies. In
addition to all these drawings he made plans for the college
assembly hall, garages, laundry and gatehouse, as well as
sketches for a future technical school. As if all this was not
enough labor for the seventy-year-old architect, he made scale
plans for the monastery guest hall and the adjoining native
Sisters' convent on the southwest projecting shoulder of the
hill.

Then somehow or other he found time to make and paint
cedarwood images of "Our Lady Queen of Monks" and St.
Augustine of Canterbury, which were to be placed on either
side of the principal altar in the temporary chapel of the
monastery. In odd moments he carved a complete set of crib
figures, twenty inches high, for the Holy Redeemer Church,
Cat Island, and a "black Madonna" for St. Francis', Old
Bight. Then he set to work and made a large rood to hang
above the sanctuary arch of the chapel at the Convent of
Blessed Martin de Porres. Previous to this he had cast the
concrete columns himself for the west gallery of the chapel,
and now he went on to decorate the baroque altar frontal.

How Fra Jerome managed to do all this work in such a
short time is a mystery, but he noted in his diary that very
often he did not leave his drawing board until long after
midnight. "My Guardian Angel helps me," he wrote, "and it
is wonderful what an old man of seventy, with failing eyesight and on all days a splitting headache, can get through."

When in December he returned to Cat Island he did not
take any real rest at the hermitage. Much of his time was
spent in rebuilding the half-ruined cottage and kitchen beside the church at Freetown. "All finished in six weeks" is
his terse comment.

It was remarkable that the job was finished so rapidly, for

according to his letters written at this time the hermit was "head and heels in arduous occupations, spiritual and artistic," here, there and everywhere. He preached an Advent mission down at Freetown, which resulted in the return of a large number of his flock who had joined the "Jumpers' Pentecostal Church of God." He built a new crib, complete with ox, ass, four shepherds, three kings and angels. Crowds came after all the Christmas services to gaze in silent wonder at the black-faced Madonna and her black pickaninny bambino set in an arched stone grotto and illuminated by many candles and votive lamps. After the midnight Mass Fra Jerome re-enacted, so far as he could, that Christmas festival at the hermitage of Greccio when St. Francis greeted the Divine Infant, calling him "Child of Bethlehem" and "Jesus." The old hermit cried out the music of the name as if he were voicing the worship of the sheep on the Judean hillside, bending over the manger caressingly. Then, after a second Mass at 7 A.M., still fasting, the old priest walked eight miles to St. Francis', Old Bight, for a third Mass at 11 A.M.

The wonder was that Fra Jerome was still alive. A few days before Christmas he had sailed over to Old Bight with some food sent him by Bishop Bernard for distribution among the poor out islanders. Just as he was in sight of his haven the wind suddenly shifted. He was alone in the *Rocbird*. Knowing that the people were waiting for the Bishop's gift, he did not like to turn back to Old Bight Creek, since it would have been a long way for them to transport the heavy parcels. So he ran the boat's bow square ashore, lowering the sail and throwing the grapnel out. Then a big wave caught her stern and broached her to, and in a minute she swamped. Until that moment, so he wrote, he had not the strength even to help lift just one end of a bag of flour, "but when you haven't time to think you are too feeble to do a thing it is wonderful what necessity can make you do.

"I was up to my chest in water, but hauled a soaked 100-pound bag of flour out of the boat's well and carried it, wading ashore and up the steep bank of sand, then back for the second one, then a bag of brown sugar. A wooden box of groceries was floating to and fro in the well, and another with tobacco leaf in it, and a box of pork, and then two large bags of cement. One burst as I carried it, and a wave broke over me. There was nobody there to meet me. Just in time I rescued an oar floating away. Then I lost my tin baling can, and tried to use my palm, but—more water came in than any little bit I threw out, and broadside on the boat rolled helplessly from side to side. I prayed hard to my Guardian Angel, and then suddenly a head appeared over the green ·bushes and the sea-grape creepers. Two sturdy women and two good-sized boys. What's more, they had a pail.

" 'You's not gwine ter sail back in dis weather, your lone self?' one of the women asked.

" 'Yes, I am,' I replied, 'if I can get the boat off.'

"The women kept the boat heeled over toward the shore by hauling on the halyard, and the boys held the lee gunwale down while I baled with the pail. Finally, after a terrific struggle, we pushed the boat's bow off the sand and out seawards, and up to my neck in water I managed to hang the rudder. We all shoved, and I threw myself over the gunwale, seized the oars and got beyond the play of the breakers. I stood on the forepeak and hoisted the sail (well reefed down), and waved 'Good-by.' The wind had now backed still more —due north and dead ahead against me, and a terrible-looking sky overhead, with great, rolling, heavy black clouds. The boat so often missed stays in the choppy sea that I found it was no good taking short tacks near shore, so I ran right out to sea in one long beat. Sudden squalls hit me, torrents of rain fell. I was just shivering and shaking with cold. I held the tiller with one hand, the main sheet given a hitch around the tiller, and stooping down baled with the other. It took all my vigilance and a bit of seamanship to meet each sudden puff—luffing right up and letting the sheet run out.

"It was now nearly dark. Far away I saw a big sailboat, the *Eurydice*, running before the wind, hugging the shore, making for Old Bight Creek. This was my third long tack, and I said to myself if I don't weather Cottage Point on this tack I must give up and turn around and run to Old Bight Creek, too. I could hardly see the shore, because night had fallen. At last it loomed up close ahead. I ran in and to my joy and wonder found I was now about a quarter of a mile to windward of the rocky promontory of Cottage Point. From then on I was in more sheltered water, and took short tacks hugging the shore, and eventually sailed into the smooth, protected water off Freetown, and came comfortably to my anchorage at 9 P.M. The rain had stopped and a bit of moon lighted up the shore."

Adventures like this one took their toll of the old man. By the middle of January 1947 Fra Jerome was back again in Nassau, and, considering the mental and physical strain of all he had gone through, it was not surprising that Bishop Bernard was alarmed at the state of his health and insisted that he must see a doctor. The diagnosis was an enlarged heart, and complete rest was prescribed. The aged invalid merely remarked, "Well, to be big-hearted is no detriment, even if the same pumping engine has shifted a bit over to port, showing the red light! But the doctor said I was quite sound otherwise, and I need no drugs for the old heart."

It is hardly necessary to add that Fra Jerome did not obey the doctor's orders. He had not been at Nassau very long before Bishop Donahue arrived from New York, chartered a large special plane, and flew with a party of eighteen priests and nuns to Long Island for the blessing of the new Church of Sts. Peter and Paul on January 27. Of course Fra Jerome could not be left behind. This pleasure jaunt was followed by more work: the carving of two large gargoyles to carry off rain water from part of the roof of the rapidly rising monastery. In more than one letter he said that he was "very tired and suffering from an almost perpetual headache."

On March 11 Abbot Alcuin Deutsch blessed the completed sections of the monastery and college, in the presence of Bishop Bernard, His Excellency the Governor of the Bahamas, and a large, enthusiastic crowd.

Headache or no headache, Fra Jerome kept on working. He busied himself with the concrete traceried windows for the chapter hall, and the pre-cast ornamental buttress scrolls for the stair turret top. With Prior Frederic he decorated the three bays of the quadripartite vault of the chapter hall. The hermit found it "rather nerve-racking" to stand all day on a shaky scaffolding, straining his neck to do overhead painting. Among other projects he produced a cardboard scale model of the future monastery church, complete even to the interior details.

He noted in his diary that he was "doing too much work, and, often having to break off to lie down flat on my back, I could not keep up any proper observance of my Rule. It was no good joining the Benedictines in choir, as I say a different Office from theirs, and it would only be a distraction. I could not rise for my regular midnight meditation and Matins, although I was very often working away under the electric light until the early hours of the morning. As to meals, I adapt the immediate circumstances to the Franciscan Rule of 'eat such things as are set before you.' With so few teeth I am a very slow eater, but have to put down all I can to keep up strength and energy for the work to be done. My manner of living may be temperate and frugal, but that is not mortification in the true sense. . . . Alas! May God forgive me, the poor undisciplined vagrant hermit. I throw myself into all this architectural work with zeal and much labor because it is so congenial to me—art first, prayer second, alas! I am what St. Benedict terms 'the worst sort of monk—a vagrant.' What advance in the spiritual life have I made?"

Life had become something utterly different from what he dreamed of before he left Australia for the Bahamas. He had built a lovely hermitage, but now he seldom had time to occupy it, and even when he did, his life was not that of a true solitary.

It was not until June 10, 1947, that Fra Jerome returned to Cat Island. The chapter-house wing of the monastery had been completed, and the southwest tower of the church was rising, so all the rest was plain sailing for the builders. But no sooner had he arrived at Freetown than he set to work on the three remaining nave arches and gables of the church. By the time he was able to retire to his hermitage he was so exhausted that he "let everything go anyhow for two months —no rule or horarium—just rest and eat and sleep and pray." But he could not bear the sight of solid food, and subsisted mainly on Ovaltine and condensed milk mixed up cold with "lots of Eno's fruit salt." What worried him more than his lack of appetite was that he believed that this diet was "very extravagant and luxurious."

But Fra Jerome was incapable of really resting completely. His assurances to worried friends in England were offset by accounts of weekend sails in the *Rocbird* to and from Old Bight, where he energetically heard confessions, baptized, preached and instructed converts. One Sunday during his period of "rest" he rose from his board bed to celebrate Mass at 6:30 A.M., then walked nearly two miles to the beach, pulled in the trip line on the anchor, hoisted sail and, after a fifty-minute run with a fair breeze, landed at Freetown for a second Mass at ten-thirty. It was not until after midday that he at last lit a fire to prepare his breakfast. "Not a bad

Sunday morning's work for an old man of seventy-one with a weak heart and perpetual pain in his stomach!"

Not a bad morning's work indeed, but Fra Jerome's devotion to his people was only exceeded by theirs for him. He noted lovingly that, "Hermit as I am, and going in and out so little among the island people, I never got to know those in Australia or in London so intimately as I know my little Catholic flock here. They seem bone of my bone and flesh [of my flesh], I feel such intimate sympathy with them and pity for them; and I think I now understand them."

Such sentiments were tempered, however, by an occasional caustic remark on church ceremonials. To Charles Selby-Hall, who had written him of his visit to Einsiedeln Abbey in Switzerland, he remarked, "How I should love the Einsiedeln Gregorian chant, frills and all, because I have a big corner in my artistic heart for everything baroque! I should revel in the orchestral Gounod High Mass on festivals—what a nice change it would be! The Westminster 'wail' can become too monotonous. I suppose that's why the Cathedral authorities removed Eric Gill's carving of St. Thomas More's poor little monkey? The wail would have been too much for it—cruelty to animals!"

Fra Jerome needed his sense of humor when on July 20 the sacristy of the church at Freetown caught fire and, along with all its contents, was reduced to ashes. Somehow or other he found the strength to take this setback serenely and to begin at once the rebuilding of the sacristy. Further, he designed and painted an eight-foot mural for the church showing Christ giving the keys to St. Peter, with crowds of figures, sheep and a three-masted sailing ship in the background. By September he had completed the plans for the Cistercian monastery in Rhode Island and had made perspective sketches for the exterior and interior of the abbey church at Fox Hill.

"If you have four missions to serve and no curates, and

the people still have souls, you can't lie on your back all day," he wrote. "So I do everything that an old man of seventy-one who is supposed to have a weak heart ought not to do. I sail my boat across the Bight alone in squally weather, get soaked through and chilled—and *mirabile!* I feel ever so much better for it the next morning. All this past week I've been climbing up and down ladders on the scaffolding of the church roof and any time I get giddy and feel my heart acting too evidently as an internal-combustion engine, then I obey the doctor's orders at once, and retire into the house to 'take things easy.' Up at the hermitage I live my Franciscan life as a solitary, but when I've said my Office and other religious exercises, not having gifts of the Higher Contemplation and not being favored with ecstasies, bilocations and levitations to pass my spare time away—what am I to do? I can't sit down and twiddle my thumbs; hence I drift into the aforesaid manual labors for the good of my neighbors and for the love of God."

At the end of one letter he remarked with an almost audible chuckle, "P.S. I am realizing the *blessings* of old age—packing up for the last journey when you can take nothing with you. So the blessings of *loss* are that I am gradually losing everything in turn.

"Loss of *teeth*—protection against gluttony.
" " " *hearing*—freedom from idle talk.
" " " *speech*—can't be asked to preach in Nassau since I've only an inaudible cracked whisper.
" " " *memory*—absolves you from keeping appointments!
"etc., etc., *et reliqua.*"

Toward the end of September 1947 the backwash of a great hurricane passed over Mount Alvernia with such strong winds that Fra Jerome dared not open his door for a whole day and night. But the hurricane had the rather odd effect of restoring his appetite, so he said, and he found himself able to eat quite substantial meals again. His voice, however, had not improved, and he was able only to reprove and exhort his flock in whispers: "My little children love one another; live a *new* life in Christ, forgiving one another. Don't go to law with another. Flee fornication, drunkenness, revelings and such like; bridle the tongue."

The hermit continued to drive himself, but his strength was not what it had been. He confessed that he had no energy, that his exertions tired him dreadfully, that even a small amount of correspondence was a great burden. Poor Fra Jerome. What wore him out more than anything else was the responsibility he felt for the souls of the islanders. He could not put their troubles out of his mind and brooded over them continually. His people and their problems were a perpetual distraction to the old man and no matter how hard he tried to leave everything in the hands of God, he found it far from easy.

His Sunday sermons which he now found so difficult to preach haunted him beforehand. If only he had the "gift of gab" like the Negro preachers! Even teen-age boys, he remarked, reveled in preaching at the "Jumper" meetings. His discouragement was so intense that he was glad to shake the dust of Freetown from his sandals on a Sunday evening. As he toiled up the slope of Mount Alvernia he felt as if he never wanted to descend again.

"All in Freetown is lies, duplicity, cunning, ignorance and covetousness," he wrote. "To me the place is Pergamos where the devil's seat is. Where Satan dwelleth, he staggers me with one blow after another. . . . All this past Lent and Eastertide . . . I have constantly denounced the real idolatry of covetousness and fornication, perjury and 'Obeah' superstitions, and my words are carried far beyond the churchyard and merely raise hatred and jealousy."

The truth was that Fra Jerome was tired out. "I find even writing a letter is a terrible effort. I have to break off continually and lie down flat on my back. My stomach gives pain if I go on too long without food at regular hours, so I have put forward *prandium* to twelve noon, then I take a light supper at 6 P.M. of bread, tea (with milk). I sleep such a lot, not holding with the doctrine and practice of the Egyptian hermit Macarius who slept for only one hour out of the twenty-four. I am ashamed to say that I lie down and doze in the morning and take a siesta every afternoon. Bishop O'Collins writes to me: 'Thousands in these days of upheaval and turmoil would envy you the peace of your hermitage,' but I find that a hermit's vocation is not, in the Holy Ghost, all joy and peace, but rather a participation in the sorrow of the cross."

So the hermit ended his diary on a "scorching hot August day," as he sat gazing over the ocean, empty now of the big ships that had passed before him in the war years. Once again he reiterated his concern for his people. "But when, when will I be able to visit my out missions? Old Bight, Port Howe and Baintown? I worry over them all the time. When I was younger and stronger I used to sail—sixty-four miles round trip there and back by sea, or forty miles round-trip walking. Now it's impossible, but the Bishop has no priest he can spare, so what can I do but pray?"

The same note of weariness is apparent in a letter written to Bishop O'Collins on May 7, 1948, in which Fra Jerome says, "But don't think that Cat Island is an earthly Paradise however lovely the colors of the sea and the waving coconut palms! Millions might fancy envying my peaceful retreat on the top of Mount Alvernia, but they would soon find it none too far away a refuge from Freetown and other settlements of the Bight where the devil goes about as a roaring lion amidst cunning thieves and liars, religious hypocrites and false prophets, rejoicing in fornication, drunkenness, wife-beating, witchcraft, knifings and killings. The world flood of unbelief and materialism is breaking its waves even on the shores of these faraway isles of the sea."

12.

The Artist at Work

WRITING in *Liturgical Arts* (August 1954), Maurice Lavanoux remarked: "It would be easy and, I feel, futile to evaluate Fra Jerome's architectural work in the light of rigid critical norms; this would falsify the value of his work, for it contains elements architects too often lack when working for the Church—humility, a deep love for and an understanding of the liturgy, a feeling for proportion. And when one realizes the poverty and economy of means with which Fra Jerome had to cope, it must be admitted that his achievements are really fine. It is on the level of what is called 'liturgical correctness' that Fra Jerome gives us all an object lesson. It is more than mere *correctness;* it is the substance of the liturgy in visual form that emerges from his planning and designs of sanctuaries and altars."

What Mr. Lavanoux writes is perfectly true: it *is* "futile to evaluate Fra Jerome's architectural work in the light of rigid critical norms," because most of it is so far removed from the work of any of his contemporary professional architects. Somehow or other what strikes one when studying his churches and other buildings is that almost all of them possess a subtle yet indefinable Franciscan quality of joyous spontaneity and simplicity of heart. Designing churches was "great fun" even if they were intended for the worship of God. One can picture Fra Jerome, even before he became a hermit, standing at his drawing board or laboring with his own hands, mixing cement or building a wall, saying to himself in the words of St. Francis to Brother Leo when explaining to him what is perfect joy: "Above all the graces and gifts of the Holy Ghost which Christ grants to His friends, there is that of overcoming themselves and gladly for the love of Christ bearing pain, insults, disgrace, and discomfort, because we cannot glory in any of the other gifts of God—they are not ours, but God's. Therefore the Apostle says: 'What have you received that you have not received from God, and why do you glory as if you have received it?' "[1]

Fra Jerome found the "perfect joy" in his architectural work, not alone from artistic satisfaction, but because it was one of the means by which he could take with good cheer the punishments which he knew he deserved for his human frailties. He gave himself to the work of building or rebuilding churches because it was one of the obvious ways in which he could fulfill his Franciscan vocation. He had to make use of the talents given him by God and practice his particular craft for the good of his soul. St. Francis told him that he would be blessed if he labored with his hands, and that was enough for him.

His architectural work can be divided into four main groups:

(1) 1897–1908: Anglican churches and other buildings in England.

(2) 1909–1911: Anglican churches in the Bahamas.

(3) 1915–1939: Cathedrals, churches, convents, etc., in Australia.

(4) 1940–1956: Churches and other buildings designed for the Bahamas and elsewhere.

[1] James Meyer, O.F.M., *The Words of St. Francis* (Chicago, 1952), p. 15.

Fra Jerome's architectural opinions in his latter years can be found in a long article he contributed to *Liturgical Arts* (November 1950) entitled "Scratchings of a Cat Islander: An Attempt to Rediscover Reality in Architecture." Here are some of his statements:

"What is my theory of building? Well! just to follow nature, and the nature of a thing, and not to coerce it. The hermit's eyrie lair where I dwell just grows naturally out of the rock. You can hardly distinguish where God's rock begins. The chapel and the little rooms are all on different levels so you have to step up and down. Old and infirm as I am, that does not bother me; I can find my way in the dark and know exactly where to lay my hand on anything I want. The front of the little house shears off at an irregular angle from the chapel.

"Why is all so crooked and irregular? Is it fancy or a dilettante craze to be picturesque? Not at all! Firstly, it is because it is fitted on to the rocky summit of the hill, just where it would go. Secondly, because the effective operating reason is that I was my own master and had no client to boss and tell me, 'Build it straight and keep your rectangles or I'll get another architect.' "

So he would laugh, and say that had any sensible architect such as one who sun bathes in huge oblongs of plate glass as the base for his reinforced concrete walls, designed the hermitage, he would have leveled the whole area of the hill's summit with plenty of dynamite, so as to create a sensible flat plateau. Then with his T-square and right-angle triangle he would have built a house on any sort of convenient plan, and would have made it look like a suburban villa in a civilized city.

" 'Your hermitage is all right to gape at, but not to live in,' you say, 'it's so inconvenient!' Maybe. But here's my defense, which goes back scores of years to the debunked Victorian era. In my cradle I was taught that 'Britains never will be slaves' (except, of course, to a socialist state in 1950). Now in my second childhood I rebel against the trumpeted march of progress: I won't be a slave to modern conveniences."

To understand Fra Jerome's theories of building it is essential to remember that when he was a student of architecture in the eighteen nineties there had been a violent reaction from formal classicism. John Hawes, like all other young men of his day, was caught up on the fast-running tide of simplicity and naturalness in building. Architects who learned their trade in that decade, or who started to practice it early in the twentieth century, invariably kept one eye on the picturesque. "The little rooms on different levels" of his hermitage on Cat Island, its "irregular angles," and the feeling that it had grown up out of the natural rock are just the sort of qualities which the disciples of Philip Webb (1831–1915) were striving after more than sixty years ago. As H. S. Goodhart-Rendel remarks, "They had built cottages most primitively planned with rooms reached only one out of the other, and with ladders instead of staircases . . . unconventional little whitewashed houses, bashfully virgin in their simplicity, that were beginning to be illustrated in the pages of *The Studio*. . . . The charm of their innocent unsophistication cannot be denied." [2]

The earliest buildings designed by John Hawes were a deliberate imitation of the domestic architecture of Charles Voysey (1857–1941). He records that he greatly admired their picturesque, low, white, rough-cast walls, low windows, leaded-light casements, and green slated roofs. At Bognor, Sussex, Hawes emulated Voysey's work in the seaside cottages

---

[2] H. S. Goodhart-Rendel, *English Architecture since the Regency* (London, 1953), pp. 193, 196.

and houses he designed, but for others he adopted a Queen Anne treatment of red sanded bricks, white-sashed windows, and wide, dentelated roof cornices. His most original house was The White Tower, with four rooms one above the other, a side staircase and a flat roof giving a view over the sea. This house was made the subject of a drawing by Raffles Davison in *The British Architect,* with a most flattering account of "the promising young architect." It was in keeping with Hawes's temperament that he put a few bits of ornamental or grotesque carving of his own into most of his houses and cottages. For two of them he and one of his brothers painted overmantel panels, with knights in armor or Spanish galleons in full sail.

Faithful to the teaching of his former teachers, Professor Lethaby and Professor Prior, young Hawes abhorred the copying of medieval Gothic details. Late in his life he maintained that the village church he had designed in 1899 at Gunnerton, Northumberland, was as good as anything he had done since, and wrote: "The steep-pitched hipped roof of the chancel sheers above that of the nave, the wide, round-arched windows welcome the southern sunshine while the north wall is a blank. The dark blue-gray tint of the hammer-dressed whinstone from the local quarry gives the rough walls an ageless look that blends with the rocky slope dropping steeply to an ever rushing 'burn' (stream). Entering, you would mistake it for a Catholic church, with its stone altar, tapering tabernacle, and six tall candlesticks, its rood beam and twin ambones."

Next came the Gothic gatehouse and adjoining small chapel at Alton Abbey, Hampshire, which hardly does credit to the architect. The large cruciform church which he designed here for the Anglican Order of St. Paul was never built, or, more correctly, Hawes's designs were greatly modified by another architect.

The brick chapel added to Painsthorpe Hall, Yorkshire, in 1902, which then served as a monastery for the Anglican Benedictine monks, was quite unpretentious. Yet, like the little church at Gunnerton, it possesses that particular Hawes quality of looking as if it had grown up spontaneously.

Just as at Gunnerton, so, too, in the guesthouse on Caldey Island, built in 1906, the hammer-dressed blue-gray lime-stone gives the rough walls of this curious castellated structure an ageless look. It is a part of the cliff on which it stands. All the details were inspired by those of medieval buildings on the mainland of South Wales. The unimaginative gate-house, often referred to as The House of Retreat, which was never built, was planned with Cistercian simplicity, even if Hawes allowed the Anglican Benedictines a tall bell tower and a massive entrance tower the Romanesque details of which look as if they had been copied from any history of English medieval architecture.

The great abbey, planned to accommodate more than a hundred monks, never got further than paper and a cardboard model. Here the young architect arranged the domestic buildings around a large cloister garth, with the church on the north side of the enclosure. The drawings show a nave of ten bays, two transepts, an apsidal chancel, ambulatory, and five projective apsidal chapels. There are two western towers, and another much loftier tower with a broach spire over the south transept. It is obvious that Hawes found most of his ideas in the English cathedrals of the eleventh and twelfth centuries, or in some of the Romanesque churches he had studied in France. Had Dom Aelred Carlyle ever found the money to erect this abbey, it would have been the largest group of modern monastic buildings in Britain.

When John Hawes arrived in the Bahamas early in 1909 he realized at once that the only hope for any permanent immunity from hurricane damage lay in stone or concrete roofs. But, as he remarked, "the latter were out of the question because the salt-laden air soon penetrated through to any metal reinforcement, cracking and disintegrating the cement." He saw that some of the reinforced concrete buildings in Nassau had failed to stand up to the force of the hurricane of the previous year, so he decided that the only course was to get back to the simplicity of primitive building methods.

His first experiment with "rock roofs" was on the big Lady chapel of the ruined church at Deadman's Cay, Long Island. The whole of this Anglican church had to be rebuilt. Now, for the first time, he fell under the spell of Spanish baroque, or rather the form it took when transplanted to Central and South America. Over the high altar at Deadman's Cay arose a baldachino with four Doric columns. The chancel and nave were divided by a rood screen. The whole scheme was eclectic and exotic. The new and fascinating tropical environment provided an inspiration which the architect had never found in England. Even more splendid and ambitious was the replanned church of St. Paul, Clarence Town, which was Spanish baroque in style with twin towers at its western end. Besides restoring four Anglican churches on Long Island, Brother Jerome designed a baldachino for St. Matthew's, Nassau, and an altar for the Holy Souls' Chapel in St. Mary's in the same town.

The drawing of St. Francis' Chapel, Graymoor, New York, which Hawes made in March 1911, shows a simple little roughcast building raised, by reason of the ground level, over open brick arches. The curiously planned squat tower looks as if it might have been inspired by some of the eighteenth-century Franciscan mission churches in California, just as those of St. Paul's, Clarence Town, appear to have been taken from the mission at Santa Barbara (1786). The odd-looking curved-stepped buttress on one side of the tower is reminiscent of the pediment details of the façade in the Mission of San Luis Rey (1798).

On his return from Canada in 1912, Hawes added a sanctuary, north aisle and bell tower to the Catholic Church of the Holy Rosary, Sutton, Surrey. The tall, narrow Gothic windows, and above all the steep-pitched roof over the lofty apsidal sanctuary, are obviously German Gothic in inspiration, evoking memories of the Frauenkirche, Nuremberg, or Erfurt Cathedral. There is a vague German flavor about the bell tower.

Western Australia was both the best and the worst field for the practice of architecture when John Hawes arrived there in 1915. To all intents and purposes it was virgin soil. Most of the Catholic churches resembled those which he caricatured for the amusement of his friends at home. Very few of the priests shared the enlightened ideas of Bishop Kelly, who had already asked Father Hawes to prepare designs for a cathedral at Geraldton, which was to be round, with the seats converging on the high altar. After eight years of struggling against prevailing ideas, Father Hawes became disillusioned and felt that there was no hope for the improvement of Catholic churches.

"I know perfectly well what the clergy really desire," he wrote critically, "i.e., an imitation Gothic, 'geometrical decorated'—a church with steep-pitched roof and ornamental parapet or buttresses; these three especially, even though they buttress nothing, since there is no vault but the walls securely tied in and secured from thrust by the tie beams of an open-timber roof. But they must have their pet flying buttresses, also their spires, although by the time the towers for them rise to roof level all the building enthusiasm and flow of donations will probably have ebbed away."

Enclosed with this letter were some sketches, entitled "Australian Ecclesiastical Architecture," with the comment, "This is the acceptable type."

To relieve himself of his feeling of frustration he described the "New R. C. Church at Wyldcatchem—a very chaste design in the early Gothic style which reflects great credit on the talented architects. . . .

"N.B. The same design all in tin can be supplied 25 per cent cheaper. Green plate-glass windows, *without the gable* crosses, and it is equally suitable for Church of England, Methodist chapel, Salvation Army hall, Miner's Institute, or Masonic Temple."

Then beneath a sketch we read the ironical words, "This elegant window above the altar resembles those of Cologne Cathedral and St. Peter's, Rome. It is glazed with tinted 'cathedral glass' of variegated colors, and is not surpassed by any of the Gothic masterpieces of the old country. St. Patrick is shown in the center light."

Nevertheless, the great cathedral at Geraldton was being built, and in spite of strong objections raised by Bishop Ryan, who disliked almost every detail of its plan and details, once Dr. O'Collins became Bishop of the see in 1929 it was completed more or less according to the original designs.

St. Francis Xavier's Cathedral is a far cry from the "New R. C. Church at Wyldcatchem." The former is best described as a brilliant *réchauffé*. The sources of almost every one of its contrasting features can be found in the illustrations of Sir Banister Fletcher's monumental *History of Architecture on the Comparative Method*. At the same time, when one examines this cathedral, it is obvious that John Hawes, during those three years spent in Rome, had not confined himself to the study of philosophy and theology. When wandering around Italy during the college vacations he had kept his eyes open, and he remembered later the churches he had seen.

The huge dome looks rather like a flatter version of the

one designed by Brunelleschi for the Cathedral of Florence, and, like it, the Geraldton dome covers an octagonal space between the nave and chancel. The prototype of the round windows in the walls of the octagon can be traced to the Florence cathedral. The twin-domed towers at the west end are a fairly close copy of those at the California Mission of Santa Barbara. The recessed pediment between the towers recalls that of many a baroque church in Mexico or Peru, whereas the great central portal is French Romanesque in detail.

The round arches of the nave are supported on squat, un-fluted columns of excessive bulk—pure English Romanesque of the eleventh century. The zebra striping on the walls and arches reminds one of the interior of the Siena cathedral. The early Renaissance canopied pulpit projecting from one of the walls of the octagon must have been copied from similar ones in Italian churches. The canons' stalls, with neo-Gothic canopies, occupy the apse. The bishop's throne at the side of the sanctuary is ornately baroque, as are the candlesticks of the long, stone high altar. It has no gradin, but behind the large domed tabernacle rises an immense Gothic crucifix, probably inspired by the famous *Volto Santo* in the Lucca cathedral, except that there are statues of Our Lady and St. John beside it.

Father Hawes let his imagination run riot in this striking cathedral. He sought inspiration from all periods of archi-tecture, picking and choosing according to his fancy. There is Byzantine carving on some of the capitals supporting the great arches of the octagon; and the quaint little round tower with its conical roof that juts out at the east end of the build-ing evokes memories of some early French Renaissance château on the banks of the Loire. Yet one is not conscious of a clash of details.

In the early twenties, shortly after his return to Australia

from his first holiday in Europe, Father Hawes found himself
free to design a church without the need to conform to the
opinions of a client. "I am building into these stones at Mullewa," he wrote, "poor little feeble work as it is, my convictions, aspirations and ideals as to what a church should
be—ideas flatly antagonistic to the prevalent notions over
here:

"(1) That a church should be *monumental;* therefore,
dome, stone vaults, thick walls, massive columns—an heir-
loom for the ages, however small and humble. Here we op-
pose 'the adoration of the useful.'

"(2) That where it cannot all be completed at once, *God's*
part should be built first: the altar and the house of the altar
(*ara, et domus ara*). Let the people continue in their temporary tin part—or look in at the windows. The first thing
is to make a permanent resting place for the tabernacle—a
real home for Jesus and Mary.

"(3) That symmetrical arrangement of parts; their mechanical perfection and smoothness of finish are *not* artistic
necessities.

"(4) That a tower *is* a necessity, not an extravagance, and
the music of its bells is A.M.D.G.

"(5) Orientation: the church must lie east and west.

"I am building my heart into these stones and it is as likely
as not (and perhaps to the greater glory of God) a broken
heart at the end! Frustrated, disappointed, disillusioned; but
I hope resigned and more detached from earthly things."

St. Mary's—the Church of Our Lady of Mount Carmel
and Sts. Peter and Paul—was the expression of the baroque
and rococo architecture of Central America which Father
Hawes was immersed in at that time. On this small village
church he really let himself go, indulging his whimsical fan-
cies. He described it as "of a Romanesque type, somewhat
after that of the churches of southern France when the Ro-

manesque was in a state of transition to the Gothic. The exterior . . . reminiscent of the Spanish Franciscan mission churches of California. . . . It can boast no polished marbles or glittering mosaics, but if the visitor finds the building pleasing it is because of its rough stone walls and the complete absence of hard mechanical finish."

He explained that he had attempted "to reflect (however feebly) some of the romance and quaintness of those old, old churches of the past that were full of such marvels as we shall never see again." And, with an eye on ritual, the plan and arrangement of the church had been strictly designed to meet all liturgical requirements.

The entrance door of the west front of St. Mary's was flanked by three "barbaric-looking" spiral fluted columns on either side with one in the center, representing the seven pillars of wisdom. Along the frieze above the columns Father Hawes arranged a series of eleven carved panels portraying the seven sacraments, with the three central panels devoted to the Holy Eucharist as sacrament, sacrifice and Real Presence. The red tiles of the roof supported fierce-looking gargoyles which carried off the rain water, and the tall campanile terminated in a highly original airy octagonal lantern, buttressed with pinnacles at its base. The bell tower had seven bells, the smaller ones hung in the open arches.

Two inverted cup-shaped domes—one over the circular baptistery, the other above the sanctuary—increased the bizarre effect of the exterior of the church. The north porch was a curious mingling of Celtic and Spanish details.

Inside the building the riot of furnishing was almost overwhelming. The nave of five bays was spanned by transverse pointed arches that supported the roof timbering. A small choir gallery had been constructed over the porch, and in the center of the little baptistery the font was surmounted by a baldachino with four columns. Beside the baptistery folding doors shut off a tiny rock grotto for the Christmas Crib. A rood cross hung suspended from the arch above the entrance to the domed sanctuary. The high altar was a stone sarcophagus of a baroque form, and behind the altar was an elaborate baroque reredos. Above the domed tabernacle Father Hawes placed a painting of Our Lady of Mount Carmel, and still higher a lofty exposition throne. Over all hung a gilded tester or baldachin. The dome was painted blue, powdered with gold stars, with a large silver dove with outspread wings. The large stone paschal candlestand of classic design was carved after that in the Basilica of Sts. Nereus and Achilleus on the Appian Way outside Rome. To the north and south of the sanctuary were two chapels, dedicated to St. Michael and St. Joseph respectively; the latter with a stone altar and reredos of Gothic design; the former a type of early Christian altar found in the Roman catacombs.

On either side of the nave, just within the communion rails, were two more altars. The holy rood altar had a retable in flamboyant French Gothic, framing a *Pietà*. There were carved wooden angels, painted and gilded, on the four corner posts of the altar. The Lady altar had a lofty canopy of Romanesque form. The Sacred Heart shrine, against one of the arch piers, contained a wooden statue, carved after the model of the Sacré-Coeur, Paris. There was yet another altar dedicated to St. John the Baptist. Most of the windows were filled with stained glass. One of the most unexpected details of this little church was a "squint" through the thick wall to enable the bell ringer to see the elevation of the Host at the high altar, and to toll the bell accordingly.

Such is St. Mary's, Mullewa, which was the most extraordinary church ever designed by John Cyril Hawes, and which expressed his whole personality and his eclectic taste in matters of art. What he was striving for is summed up in the concluding paragraph of the descriptive souvenir booklet he wrote.

"If a church carries an atmosphere of prayer and induces a religious mood, an uplifting of the soul, so that merely to enter within its portals helps people to pray—if everything around seems to emphasize the fact of the Divine Presence dwelling with the tabernacle upon the altar—then, and then only, can the building be said to fulfill its purpose."

John Hawes, like Ninian Comper, the well-known English ecclesiastical architect, was essentially romantic in temperament. Both architects in their middle age came to see that beauty can be found only by inclusion, not by exclusion. The latter relates that in 1908 he chanced to pick up a copy of George Wyndham's *The Springs of Romance in the Literature of Europe,* and was struck by the fact that, just as in literature, so, too, in architecture unity is achieved best by comprehension. Father Hawes had absorbed primitive Christian architecture in Ireland, as well as the marvels of Spanish Gothic, baroque and rococo. His artistic "conversion" was complete, and from this time he realized the full meaning of the doctrine of beauty by comprehension and put it into practice. He broke away from convention, and from 1933 until his death his buildings showed no trace of pervading insularity; they were truly catholic, in the sense that they were all-embracing and of wide sympathies.

None of the many other churches in Australia designed by Father Hawes were so ornate as St. Mary's. Among the less elaborate was St. Laurence the Martyr, Bluff Point, Geraldton (1937), a simple little cruciform building with a flat dome over the octagonal central tower, with a faint flavor of early Italian Renaissance. Holy Cross Church, Morawa (1933), also evoked memories of Italy, and in particular of San Domenico at Siena, perhaps because of the wide aisleless nave and the zebra stripes around the sanctuary arch. On either side of the arch the architect placed an altar of late-Gothic design, each surmounted by a niche with a Gothic canopy. Father Hawes reverted to neo-Gothic for St. Mary in Ara Coeli, Northampton (1936), adding a round tower with a conical roof at the southwest corner, with a tall narrow flèche above the chancel.

There can be little doubt that when it came to the interior of St. Joseph's, Perenjon, Father Hawes must have been studying the illustrations in Father Benedict Williamson's *How to Build a Church*. Otherwise it is difficult to see where he could have got the idea for the neo-Egyptian stone baldachino, which is almost a literal copy of Father Williamson's design. It is clear enough that after the publication of *How to Build a Church* Father Williamson influenced his penitent's architecture as well as his spiritual life. The church at Perenjon contains a massive stone paschal candlestick with an attached lectern the effect of which is overpowering and barbaric.

The amazing versatility of Father Hawes was apparent in the quaint little rough stone hermitage he built at Morawa in 1933, with a low-pitched roof of heavy tiles and small windows filled with elaborate Gothic tracery. Another so-called hermitage—actually the red-brick chaplain's residence at St. John of God's Hospital, Geraldton—harked back to those seaside houses designed at Bognor nearly forty years earlier. Father Hawes even employed the cut-out hearts in some of the wooden panels of the entrance hall lounge which were so popular with architects of the "Simple Life" school!

From the time of his return to the Bahamas in 1939 until his death in 1956, John Hawes designed four churches for Cat Island and two for Long Island. In addition he drew up the plans for St. Augustine's Monastery and Boys' College, for the Convent of Blessed Martin de Porres at Nassau, and designed the guesthouse and made plans for the enlargement of the Church of the Cistercian Abbey in Rhode Island. His final plans were those for the Nassau cathedral.

The Freetown church—Holy Redeemer—on which Fra Jerome did so much hard manual labor was begun in February 1941 and completed about twelve years later. According to its architect, "it shows what can be done by an old missionary priest with a bit of sweat but very little money and only unskilled local labor." Fra Jerome then went on to describe the church in detail:

"It has been erected to accommodate one hundred worshipers with provisions for a future extension of the nave to seat another hundred. Sturdy buttresses support three transverse arches of masonry that carry the longitudinal beams of the roof (so that the side walls are merely stone screens with plenty of window space). On the purlins is laid inch-thick diagonal boarding covered outside with pine shingles. The windows have no glass in them, but cement grilles inside and wooden shutters without. Of the fourteen windows, each grille has a different design. The altar steps are large gray weathered blocks of stone, quarried and squared some two hundred years ago for one of the old slavery mansions now in ruins. The liturgical arrangement of the church follows that of the ancient Roman basilicas. The altar is at the west end, the celebrant facing the people, while the morning sun streams in behind them from the wide-open double entrance doors.

"The men all sit on the Gospel side and the women on the Epistle side. The altar is a severely plain concrete table, its ten-inch thick mensa resting on eight massive legs. There would be no sense in having the priest face the people if a big tabernacle and a crucifix and altar card came between them to hide all his actions—so the tabernacle is placed on another and smaller altar just a few paces back. The crucifix hangs overhead. The center altar card is always placed *lying flat* on the front center of the wide mensa, where the celebrant can stretch out his hand and hold it raised up if he wants to use it at the *Gloria* and *Credo*. So the chalice and manual actions are always in the people's view at Mass, and out of Mass; from anywhere in the nave, you can look over the high altar to the white domed tabernacle visible beyond in the little chapel of the Blessed Sacrament.

"Another advantage of this plan is the additional security and reverence afforded to the locked safe of the tabernacle by the padlocked iron gates of the grille in the entrance arch to the chapel. The predella platforms of the two altars merge into one level surface so that there is nothing to trip the priest up when he carries the ciborium from one altar to the other. There is a somewhat similar arrangement at Downside Abbey Church in England, the Blessed Sacrament chapel there being immediately behind the high altar.

"For benediction a light wooden throne of four little posts supporting a curved canopy is placed in the center of the high altar. The campanile is built right on one side of the sanctuary so it is handy for the sacristan or one of the altar servers to chime the two large bells hanging in the belfry above at the elevation and at benediction.

"The large crucifix or 'rood' hanging above the altar is fashioned after models of the Greek rite, the figures not being *carved in the round* but cut out of flat boards one inch by twelve inches. The edges are rounded off, and details such as fingers and toes of the corpus are carved in low relief and then painted and gilded; not colored with any wishy-washy 'art tints,' but with the most vivid and brilliant colors possible."

Every detail of this little church is worth careful study, as, for instance, the stone pulpit and the massive twisted stone paschal candlestick. The rough wooden benches help to give the right note of simplicity to the interior. Fra Jerome also arranged the altar of the little church at Port Howe so that the celebrant faced the people.

Fra Jerome spoke of the Freetown church as a "queer-looking building. I dislike symmetrical, new-looking churches with a finish of mechanical perfection. Without any idea of theatrical picturesqueness or posing as 'antique,' it really has the appearance of an ancient building. It just grew—like Topsy in *Uncle Tom's Cabin*. Some bits of the walls are smooth plastered and others are still rough stonework, weathered and stained with the rains. The campanile is now battered and scored where heavy timbers struck the belfry in the tremendous hurricane of 1941."

In May 1945 he wrote that he was "fed up with some of the articles in *Liturgical Arts,* whose authors were putting forth as something quite new the 'True Principles of Architecture' that Pugin taught us years ago." Their "bombast and aesthetic theorizing" finally drove him to a "protest against their beastly concrete match-box churches." It took the form of "a real *baroque* little mission church with all the applied ornament there was time to stick on to it: bulbous swellings, consoles and curliwigs—a touch of playful gaiety in the stone flèche and gable end expresses Franciscan joyfulness." Such was the origin of St. Francis Church, Old Bight. Never before had Fra Jerome got such fun out of designing a church. This is how he described it:

"In cement I modeled in relief St. Francis preaching to the birds. The background of the panel on the façade is green 'art cement' color wash, and the figure and birds are in silver (aluminum paint). A special Bahamian touch is given by the palm-leaf thatch on the nave roof. The thatching is beautifully executed by local men. The altar dossal is green and silver and gilded candlesticks of turned hardwood. The side curtains are a figured green stuff. I carved and painted a large crucifix, ready beforehand. Above is a rose

Proposed Church of
S.ᵗ FRANCIS ᴏꜰ ASSISI
Old Bight, Cat Island
✠ Vicariate Apostolic
of the
BAHAMAS.
B.W.I.

J.C.H.
may
1944

window with brilliant deep-tinted glass, predominantly red and blue. I modeled a pair of big angels on either side above the crucifix—the angels all silver with wings picked out in blue, red and green feathers." Adjacent to this amusing little church Fra Jerome built a tiny domed hermitage—"just an anchorage when traveling around the out missions," was the way he referred to it.

About a year later he was at work on a very different sort of building—the plans for a new choir for the Cistercian Abbey of Our Lady of the Valley, Rhode Island. The existing church was an unexciting neo-Perpendicular Gothic structure with a circular apse. What Fra Jerome proposed to do was to reverse the plan: make the monks' choir into the public nave, use the nave as the lay Brothers' choir, and add a new, very much loftier monks' choir. The design called for eleven side altars, five of them around an ambulatory behind the high altar, but unfortunately these plans never materialized.

From time to time Fra Jerome received copies of architectural magazines, with the result that a hurricane swept over Mount Alvernia! The reproductions of modern churches, and even more the high praise given to them, roused him to satire, and the drawings in which he expressed his opinion of the new liturgical art indicate that he might have made his fortune as a cartoonist.

He captioned one of them the "altar of the new church at Castlemansionville, Oh-hi-oh, Pa." with its "very practicable form of the tabernacle, with no door to open awkwardly over the corporal; the altar cross can be shifted across, so the priest can stand either side of the altar. The mosaics on the wall at the back of the altar were executed by students of the Nightown Art Institute." He draws attention to "the sense of dynamic *movement* in the archangel, and the didactic vigor of the figure of St. John Chrysostom, also the essential underlying naturalness of the lambkin."

Even more amusing is a pencil drawing described as "my chef-d'œuvre pet design for the Abbey Church, Foxey Hill. *Rejected!* because the community has not enough funds to buy the necessary steel reinforcement and all the extra cement for the concrete—not to mention the thousands of feet of lumber (now about four pounds 100 feet) to be cut up for the form work. 'It won't be wasted,' I told them, 'because it will serve the abbey for years to come as firewood to keep the refrigerator working (if the ants aren't first). Then the idiots said the salt sea air will crack it all up in five years' time, and it might fall in when the prior is preaching.' "

He points out the monks' choir, "concentrated entirely on *one* side only behind the altar." Then he calls attention to a staggered iron grille which "will effectually prevent any goats falling into the crypt. Altogether a dynamatic design, truly hydro-rhythmic in its approach, and refreshingly free from the enthropocentricism of retrogressive sentimentalism." As a final note he lettered in: "How dreadful is this place—O come, let us fall down."

In a repentant moment Fra Jerome noted, "I am too fond of writing; too addicted to butting in on matters of art and liturgiology. It is a subtle form of pride—keeping oneself in the public eye. I must stop it, for a hermit must be more detached." In spite of his good resolution he was unable to resist the temptation to "butt in" when he got thoroughly worked up over the design for the so-called "Chapel of Unity" in the new Anglican Cathedral at Coventry, England (1948). The result was one of his most brilliant and most provocative caricatures, entitled "For a new Interdenominational Cathedral." The drawing is explained as follows:

"The new cathedral is to have a centrally placed 'High Altar' in the middle of the crossing of the transepts. Really congregational! The 'Past President of the Sarum Society of Unantiquated Architects' begs to submit this suggestion for still more progressive comprehensiveness, i.e., *a Circular Altar* (Round Table) standing on a circular ferro-concrete predella; this revolves by electric power. The illustration shows a celebration of the Communion service—celebrants

"For a New Interdenominational Cathedral"

right to left: the Bishop's Chaplain; the Lord Bishop (High Church); Canon Wellington Chasuble (Anglo-Catholic); the Right Reverend the Dean of Canterbury (by special invitation) shown with raised fist at the *Sanctus;* the Orthodox Archimandrake Atheniopilopolis and the Most Reverend the Moderator of the United Free Churches stand blow the sanctuary. The Pope of Rome was also invited. A verger (Holy Pokerman) operates the machinery. Thus every worshiper can see the celebrant of his or her own particular party come round facing them every two minutes." It will be noticed that the hanging banner bears the words: "O & A, & I & O. Round she goes while the Merry Organ blows. Old Xmas Carol, No. 483."

These drawings, and many others of a similar nature, express what Fra Jerome felt about much modern ecclesiastical architecture. He summed up his emotions as follows: "Let me tell you at once . . . that I am all that is bad in these days; I am a reactionary, an obscurantist, medieval, and a double-dyed traditionalist. Semicircular churches with sloping floors and radiating seats like a theater I abominate; and I've no time for mural paintings that portray, for instance, the three chosen disciples on Mount Tabor, dressed in sweaters and trousers (baggy and unsailorlike at that!). Pope Pius XI, an enlightened man appreciative of modern ideas, said: 'This so-called modern art in religion must not disfigure the House of God. Sacred art has no foundation or reason for its existence unless it represents spiritual ideas. Works of art that are *foreign to the Christian tradition* must not be admitted into places of prayer.' " [3]

Now it was just because of his own knowledge of Christian tradition that Fra Jerome knew how to inject that elusive thing called "atmosphere" into his churches. There is not one church that does not pray of itself. Each has an atmosphere of prayer and love. His churches may be "bad architecture" from the contemporary point of view, and it is a waste of time to discuss this, but nobody could deny that they convey the impression of having been built with the primary purpose of moving the soul to worship, to bringing a man to his knees, to refreshing his soul in a weary land. They express the note of eternity. They were designed in accordance with the requirements of the liturgy and the particular needs of those who worship in them. A Hawes church is definitely the product of one mind—a mind so steeped in Christian

[3] "Scratchings of a Cat Islander," *Liturgical Arts*, November 1950, p. 18.

tradition that it could receive the inspiration to apply it to the needs it had to meet. For as we are told in St. Matthew's Gospel: "Every scholar, then, whose learning is of the Kingdom of Heaven must be like a rich man, who knows how to bring both new and old things out of his treasure house."

There were many new and old things stored away in Fra Jerome's treasure house, and he knew how and where to make use of them for the greater glory of God and for the benefit of His Church.

Fra Jerome completed the drawings of the interior and exterior of the new cathedral at Ballarat in 1943 and sent them to Australia from the Bahamas. Fra Jerome explained the problems he had to solve on this big job.

"Bishop O'Collins has decided not to complete the existing cathedral, but to begin an entirely new one. The present 'Victorian Gothic' building is much too small; it seats only 800. So he has asked me to plan a new one. He proposes to build the choir and transepts first, and sent me a plan of the site and measurements, so I planned out the biggest the site would hold. That makes a cathedral to seat 1,800 to 2,000 in emergency (with extra seats). You may wonder from the sketch why I have made the dome elliptical in plan instead of circular? Because there is only 84 feet from the end of the existing church to the fence, and I have to leave 14 feet for a procession path outside, so I had only 70 feet to work on. I wanted to get a very wide nave—40 feet clear. I had a letter from the Bishop a few weeks ago. He is very pleased with the design. On the other side there is a circular baptistery and a sacristy, 50 feet by 20.

"In form and construction I have aimed at the utmost simplicity so that it will be an economical structure. All useless (or merely pretty) ornament and decoration are avoided, in favor of spaciousness and bigness. It will be a big barn of a church, but massive and strong, and I hope dignified. You may think the apse of Ballarat Cathedral resembles the bridge and gun turrets of a battleship! We are all so 'war-minded' these days that even the hermit engaged in the peaceful planning of a church can't help but give it a fortress look. It is to be faced outside with hammer-dressed bluestone that will give it a very rugged appearance."

In this cathedral the influence of Father Benedict Williamson on Fra Jerome's work is most obvious. The factory chimneylike twin towers at the west end of the cathedral are strongly reminiscent of those of a church in the Via Mazzini, Rome, shown in Father Williamson's *How to Build a Church*, as well as those shown in a frontispiece drawing by the author. The prototype of the dumpy columns dividing the wide nave from the narrow aisles can be found in other illustrations in the book. The planning of the sanctuary, however, is highly original and well worth study. The high altar is a double one; the upper being the pontifical altar facing the people as in many of the Roman basilicas. The bishop's throne and the canons' stalls are placed in the apse. Behind the apse are four circular chapels with three curious little shrines between them. In the designs for Ballarat Cathedral (designs which are still in abeyance) Fra Jerome quite broke away from the antiquarianism which characterized Geraldton Cathedral. Taken as a whole, the former is definitely a "modern" church. The extraordinary thing is that he should have worked out all these ideas in solitude with no assistants to help him. It is impossible to calculate the number of hours he must have spent on these plans.

In an article in *Liturgical Arts* in November 1950, Fra Jerome wrote: "Any buildings in my long life which people have praised, I find, when I analyze it, that I did not subjectively *design*. It was not a question of cleverness (and I have seen plenty of buildings much *too* clever). I did not design, but I *discovered*. I got a vision, a hunch of my imagination, and I had to marshal all the practical requirements of purpose and use and to study obediently the exigencies of site, levels, surroundings and materials until I got some misty vision of fleeting beauty. Then sketch followed sketch of every variation, pruning and eliminating until I could catch the rhythm of a poem in stone. Humanly to take a similitude from the sublime master, Michelangelo, who, facing a huge block of shapeless marble saw, with prophet's eye, an angel in it and started with furious blows of mallet and chisel to liberate the angel, so I discovered my churches. Perfection in any sort of work comes not from ourselves but from the Divine beauty; so if a man excels in anything it is *something Divine in* him, not from himself, but given to him for the world's good. I like to live in a reality that is opposed to super-realism." [4]

Ten years before his death, at seventy years of age, he started on his *magnum opus*—St. Augustine's Benedictine monastery and school at Nassau. He wrote: "The fashion of building my hermitage, small and poor (like the *Carceri* at Assisi), would have pleased my holy father, St. Francis, but is hardly suitable to the Benedictine tradition of spacious and stately monasteries. The spirit of their holy founder, St. Benedict, would have everything in order and to make use of every available convenience. Could this old Franciscan maniac rise to that? Sure! The very reason I threw myself, as a young man, so wholeheartedly and exclusively into ecclesiastical architecture was the fact that in the London architects' office where I was an 'articled pupil' we did little else but banks and 'pubs.' For relief I fled every evening to night schools of art and handicraft. In a spirit of revulsion and rank rebellion, as soon as my time was up, I deserted the temples of money and beer for the Gothic temples of true Jerusalem. Since I had perforce learned to plan out every

4 *Ibid.,* p. 18.

corner and detail of a bank or 'pub,' I was quite familiar in my slavery with all the extremes of modern convenience in the building trade." [5]

Fra Jerome's theory of following the exigencies of nature in building was the basis of the plan of St. Augustine's Monastery and College. Realizing that his site was a long, narrow, rocky ridge of serpentine ground, he evolved a quite novel and interesting monastic plan, about six hundred feet in length, winding in and out, up and down, of monastery, church and college.

This layout had the great advantage that both ground and upper floors had but a single line of rooms opening out onto a spacious corridor or cloister. Thus they were cool and airy. Every room, upper and lower, had an arched stone roof, and the exterior of the upper vaults was asphalted. The whole building was hurricane-proof and immune to termites and fire. The floors were cement or tiled. Wooden doorframes were eliminated by fixing the door hinges onto hardwood plugs in cement-rabbeted reveals, and the same was true of most of the glazed casements for the windows.

The "old Franciscan maniac" got down to the most practical details. He provided a concrete tank up in the southwest tower of the church, so as to ensure a good pressure of water in every room. The water was pumped up from wells in the monastery garden. Underground, stone-vaulted rainwater tanks added to the supply. He took infinite pains over the plumbing, and was very pleased with the cement pipes built into the triangular buttresses that drained the water from the roofs.

Since he was not tied to any contract, it was easy for Fra Jerome to ponder over and revise his plans and, as the work progressed, he made many alterations. By November 1949 he was preoccupied with the planning of the church. He

[5] *Ibid.,* p. 19.

felt that he had managed to provide something "quite novel in sacristy accommodation" for the twenty altars. There were to be four sacristies, each with a separate approach to five altars. The details of the architecture were nothing if not eclectic. The massive round columns of the nave were meant to be reminiscent of those at Tewkesbury Abbey, England, and St. Nazaire, Carcassonne, France. The high altar in the center of the church, well raised up above the crypt (the lay Brother's choir), was to be planned like the altars of most of the Roman basilicas, with the celebrant facing the people, and with large baroque candlesticks. Above it would be a suspended crucifix. One of the drawings showed an early Christian ciborium over the Blessed Sacrament altar in the western transept.

About a year later Fra Jerome wrote, "The choir being loftier, to increase a soaring effect, I have designed pointed arches over the internal buttresses for the recesses that carry the upper range of stalls. I purr over these pointed arches out of defiance of super-modernists who regard anything Gothic as heresy!" In the same defiant mood he inserted three tall, narrow lancets in the east wall of the choir, with a rose window above them. When he began to work on the spacious crypt, he designed an altar almost as Egyptian in inspiration as the one at Perenjon, Western Australia. The walls and piers of the crypt were three feet thick in places to take the thrust of the arched stone vaults above.

Fra Jerome's efforts to achieve beauty by comprehension puzzled many visitors. Some remarked: "It's Moorish, isn't it? Or Saracenic, or Gothic, or Byzantine, or isn't it rather Egyptian?"

He would reply: "Well, the Egyptians were great people —they used stone and lime, and so do we, and that's all there is in it, but of course we are the heirs of all the ages." [6]

6 *Ibid.,* p. 20.

Fra Jerome confessed that he could not make "scientific geometrical perspective drawings," and that he had forgotten all that he had ever learned about them as a student. "I just draw the thing as I see it in my head," he wrote, "and then hold it back to front (looking-glass way) and upside down to detect the biggest errors in drawing. The revised design of the church conveys a truthful impression of the *idea* of the building, with the dim, shadowy, mysterious effect of the low, wide-spreading nave, with its massive Egyptian-like columns, and the sunlit upstanding choir beyond with its pointed arches. Yes! *Joie de vivre*—better *Venite exsultemus Domino*."

From the time the hermit started work on the plans of the Nassau monastery and its church he was always comparing St. Augustine's in his mind with other modern monasteries both in Europe and America. In November 1945 he pointed out that, comparatively, the church would be quite small: only 30 feet high inside with a central span of but 15 feet and an over-all length of about 130 feet. It was only natural that he should think of his monastery church at Nassau in relation to the proposed abbey church at Prinknash in England, and it amused him to discover, after rough calculations based on the human figures in the photographs sent him, that the total height of the Prinknash Abbey church, inclusive of its crypt and subcrypt, would be not far short of the 175 feet of Beauvais Cathedral, the loftiest in Europe. How modest was his church when compared with the monster which was to be erected on the slopes of the Cotswold hills. The latter, he worked out, would be even longer than Winchester Cathedral, which has the greatest total length (560 feet) of any other medieval cathedral in Europe.

The long-drawn-out nave roused the hermit-architect to fury. "If there *must* be a nave," he wrote, "then three bays would be quite enough instead of seven. The view of the new

Prinknash Abbey from the west is just a dreadful and appalling conglomeration of discordant features, a jumble culminating in a front of pure bathos! I have always said that the nave was far too long, and now with the extension of the narthex it makes the building look like a snake crawling down the hill, and the main entrance, the serpent's mouth —or, at best, the entrance to an air-raid shelter! I notice that, like the Basilica of San Francesco, Assisi, it is to have *three* churches superimposed; yet in spite of all modern appliances and facilities I doubt if the good monks will get the job through so expeditiously as Brother Elias did!

"Some bishops, abbots and architects are certainly men of far-seeing vision. But it is a gamble with the future. For myself, while designing a church [it should be] not so small and mean that it can be built right off the bat, but that the first novices of the new abbey may have a sure hope of seeing it completed in their lifetime. So at Nassau a start will be made right off by worshiping in a portion of the permanent church, i.e., the crypt under the future monastic choir."

Fra Jerome's opinions were not necessarily right or wrong, but they indicated how strongly he felt about architecture, and how much it meant to him. The English churches which he had admired in his youth never lost their hold on his imagination, and in 1942 he could still write, "Anglican clergy of the early 'Ritualistic' movement and their architects often got the right idea. Look at St. Bartholomew's, Brighton: a great brick barn, 120 feet high, but what a fane of awe and dignity! James Brooks's churches, too—St. Columba's and St. Chad's, Haggerston, and the Ascension, Lavender Hill Clapham. When I was an articled pupil in the early nineties, how I used to love my Saturday afternoons of exploration and discovery of fresh architectural triumphs, such as St. Agnes', Kennington (Gilbert Scott the Second),

Holy Trinity, Sloane Street (J. D. Sedding)—what a genius!
A. W. Pugin and J. D. Sedding were the morning and evening stars of the Gothic Revival."

On the other hand, illustrations of the designs for the
new Catholic cathedral at Liverpool aroused in him a strong
and scornful reaction. "Prinknash Abbey reminds me of
Liverpool Cathedral," he wrote. "I said to the Bishop of
Geraldton once, 'Let's build a new and even bigger cathedral; Downey's is only second in size to St. Peter's, Rome.
We will advertise ours by making it bigger than St. Peter's.
I think we could get enough money in a few years to build
the toilets and an oval macadamized track for motorcars to
view and encircle the seven-acre site! We could charge the
cars one shilling admittance and put the proceeds to pay for
the weekend cleanup of our existing cathedral.' "

When Fra Jerome became serious about designs for the
Nassau cathedral, however, his facetiousness vanished and
a concept both romantic and harmonious took its place. He
spoke of his dissatisfaction with his original plans for this
building and in 1947 indicated that "now I have a far better
inspiration. The harbor and ships were in my mind, and the
Mauretania lying at anchor just outside. The passengers leaning over the toprail gazing at 'lovely Nassau' ought to be
made to say, 'And what's that tall tower right opposite?
Oh! the Roman Catholic cathedral. . . . And what's that great
round tower? Is that the pirate Blackbird's tower? . . . Oh!
it's a water tower. And what are those two tall blue spires
far away behind out there to the east? . . . St. Augustine's
Abbey—more Roman Catholic, eh! They get there, don't
they?' "

That dream tower facing the main entrance of the harbor
at Nassau must stand up like an Egyptian pharos, so he felt.
He wanted this cathedral—which would probably be his last

building—to be "of the soil of early Catholic Spanish America." He put his whole heart, soul, mind—and even his body —into designing this proposed cathedral.

The Convent of Blessed Martin de Porres, begun about the same time as St. Augustine's Monastery, was similar in construction, but the lower and upper floors were planned with rows of rooms off both sides of the central corridors. The spacious chapel was designed with a central stone vault of parabolic curve. In the new church at Bimini the vaulted roof was built of conch shells, found in abundance on this island. Fra Jerome's design for the church at San Salvador, conceived as a memorial to Columbus, was frankly a period piece, built in the sixteenth-century Spanish colonial style.

Sts. Peter and Paul, Clarence Town, Long Island, is the largest of the churches which Fra Jerome designed for the out islands in the Bahamas. It stands on a hilltop overlooking the lovely harbor and has three towers. He records how Fra Cornelius, "who worked on it himself all the time, devised a clever and economical method of freeing the timber centering under the main stone vault and moving it on rollers from one section to the next. These stone vaults are splendid for sound-singing. The twin towers on the main entrance façade are circular, like marine lighthouses, and rise to fifty-five feet, with a central turret opening into a little gallery guarded with a safely high parapet, whence a superb view is obtainable."

It was a great joy to Fra Jerome that most of the few decorative features of St. Augustine's Monastery were "monastic handmade handicraft." He wrote with pride of the six medallions, carved by Father Alban, O.S.B., over the upper air vents of the chapter room. Three of the medallions represented monks engaged in manual labor: agriculture, building and scriptorium. The fish portrayed Friday fare from Bahamian blue waters. These medallions particularly pleased the hermit for all his life he loved carving and especially the carving and painting of crucifixes. The first of his crucifixes seems to have been the large rood with figures of Our Lady and St. John which he painted in tempera colors above the round chancel arch of the ancient village church on Caldey Island in 1906. He designed other roods for Anglican churches on Long Island in the Bahamas. Several of his Australian churches were provided with suspended crucifixes, which he himself carved, painted and gilded. When he returned to the Bahamas in 1939 he executed many more crucifixes, some of them with negroid features and coloring. On the hanging rood at Clarence Town, Cat Island, the *corpus* of the Christ was painted with white enamel, whereas in the large rood in the chapel of the Convent of Blessed Martin de Porres at Nassau all the body parts were left unpainted, showing the natural cedarwood waxed, contrasting with the silver drapery and the robes of Our Lady and St. John. The cross and haloes were gold, picked out with vermilion borders. The features were outlined in plain, broad lines of black enamel.

Fra Jerome wrote, "The figures are certainly not the type of Nordic white Europeans. The good dark-skinned Sisters when they look at Our Lady can naturally feel 'she's truly *our* Mother,' and 'St. John, he's no conchy Joe!' The pale pink flesh of the conch shell is the colored native slang term of attribute for the white Bahamian." The altar built by the boys of the Nassau prison had another large crucifix painted by Fra Jerome which stressed that Our Lord himself was "no conchy Joe."

How much he enjoyed not only designing, but making and decorating the furnishings of his churches, was clearly indicated in a letter written while he was at work on some of the altars at St. Augustine's Monastery. "Every day I get into my overalls after breakfast. I've already built two altars myself, one of St. Benedict with Sts. Maurus and Placid. After the modeling and carving are complete I put on a coat of 'Dusseal' and can use oil paints—silver and gold—right away. St. Benedict has a black cowl, gold halo, dark olive face and patriarchal gray beard. At his feet are the raven (eyes turned up at him) and a broken cup with a snake coming out, colored green, silver and gold. . . . Some of my work may be a bit hurried and rough, but all my saints have, I think I may say, character and individuality, and cause much interest from the uncultured and ignorant. The little picka-ninnies love to come in and point a finger at every detail. They love the realistic snake, the raven, fishes and birds, and my triumphal zoological piece, the gray wolf of Gubbio with snarling teeth and red tongue on St. Francis' altar. What specially tickled the Apostolic Delegate, and he pointed his finger at it laughing, was a rat praying for a bit of bread below the basket of Blessed Martin de Porres as he distributes 'pannioti' to the little Negro waifs—a side wing to Our Lady of Guadelupe's altar."

That Fra Jerome derived great fun from painting the big mural at Freetown can be seen from the long and detailed description he wrote of it. It was deliberately "primitive and crude, but outright and vivid, planned as a didactic catechism instruction." The painter himself did not care whether critics would regard it as "high" or "low" art. His reward would be that his own people, adults and children, would linger, discussing every detail: the fish, the net, the cork floats on it, the woolly sheep—the rigging ("in that I was *very* particular as to every stay, rope and pulley") of the big schooner at anchor on the calm waters of the lake.

One pope was depicted in a flowing paenula and omo-phorion, another in a fiddleback chasuble. An altar boy re-marked, "Look! Farder's even drawn de lace jus' like life!" St. Peter, garbed in blue jeans, was surrounded by carefully drawn species of all the fish most common in the Bahamas. But it was a "high-pooped (fore and aft) schooner, flying the papal flag," which seems to have given the painter the greatest satisfaction. "It took me one whole day from breakfast after Mass to sunset (with a ten minutes' rest for a biscuit and cheese lunch) just to paint the schooner's rigging," he wrote. "Our island sailormen are very pleased with the schooner and haven't been able to find any fault in her details—not even the rigging!"

As has been noted already, it is easy to trace the influence of some of the late nineteenth-century English architects in Fra Jerome's earlier work, but it must be stressed that he never belonged to any particular school or clique. His work is *sui generis*. A romantic by temperament, in many ways he was more in touch with the past than the present. He belonged to the end of an epoch rather than to the start of a new one, but it would be utterly wrong to describe him as a diehard, although he enjoyed using the expression himself. Rather is there an ageless quality about almost all his architecture, bound up so closely as it was with nature. Like a true Franciscan he remained a child at heart, and continued to get as much amusement out of designing churches and monasteries as he did in playing with his fifth birthday present box of toy bricks.

In his seventy-fifth year he wrote, "And now I am definitely making my final retirement from the practice of architecture and the handling of a stone ax and trowel. This is my 'swan song.' I am too tired to make any more wildcat pen scratchings." [7]

[7] *Ibid.*, p. 20.

13.

Toward Evening

FRA Jerome's health, undermined by overwork and peculiar diet, began to decline steadily, and from the autumn of 1948 he wrote again and again of his weakness and lack of energy, complaining that he seemed to get nothing done. Yet he could say, "Where I would break down if I attempted any further enterprise on my own volition, when it is clear God is calling me to do something, He gives me sufficient strength for it, often when it looks impossible."

This was put to the test when in October the hermit decided that the Port Howe people could be neglected no longer, and that he must set out to take care of them. He had asked the Bishop to send someone to these people, but no priest could be spared from Nassau. There was nothing for it but to make the long journey himself. On a moonlit Friday night Fra Jerome rose a half hour before midnight, made his preparations, and started down the hill for the shore and the road to Port Howe. After a two-hour walk he reached Old Bight Creek where he girded his habit about his neck and waded into the sea to revive himself. Then, barefoot, he covered the remainder of the seven miles to St. Francis' Church where he said Mass in solitude at 2:30 A.M.

After a rest on a palm mat he awoke at dawn to rain and

a breakfast of dry bread and raisins. He was so thirsty that he picked up a bottle lying on the floor of the sacristy and drained a long draught from it. Instantly he spat it out—it was surface spray for mosquitoes and bugs. Poor Fra Jerome. He had forgotten that he had brought the bottle along on his last journey and he wrote ruefully: "Moral: always stick a *label* on your bottles!"

Ignoring the bad taste in his mouth, the hermit set off in the direction of Port Howe and by midday he was among his people there. He said Mass for them on Sunday, then discovered that because of hurricane reports the mail boat would not be sailing. For two days he waited in Port Howe until, bored and impatient, he decided to walk back to the hermitage. It was not surprising that this tramp of seventeen miles each way exhausted the seventy-two-year-old pedestrian. He was too tired to eat or sleep, and was laid up during the following week with a sore throat and a bad cold. He wrote later, "Well, it shows one if God wills you to do an impossible thing, He will give you all the necessary physical strength and grace for it."

Three days after this long journey on foot a man arrived at the hermitage with a message from Devil's Point, twenty-six miles away by road, that seventy-eight persons—all Baptists—wanted to be received into the Catholic Church. "So I wrote to the Bishop," Fra Jerome records, "asking him to send a priest to visit them; explaining that he could land from the mail boat at Port Howe and walk the remaining ten miles, and then take a motor bicycle with him to return here from Port Howe. I pointed out that if we do nothing for these people the 'Jumpers' or Adventists will hop in. If the Bishop cannot do anything to help, then I'll have to struggle to do the job myself. If this Devil's Point 'corporate reunion' comes off, it will bring the Catholic population of Cat Island up to more than 300, i.e., nine years' growth out of a population of about 4,000. What a lot a zealous and active young priest might do with a motor bike or jeep to cover the main road through the island; it is so *very* little that I have been able to do."

It was a bitter disappointment to Fra Jerome to receive a reply from Bishop Bernard informing him that he just could not spare a priest at that moment; and that no more monks could be sent to the Bahamas from St. John's Abbey, Collegeville, until 1950. "Well, I am not going to worry or shed any unnecessary tears," was Fra Jerome's comment. "The Lord and the Abbot must provide. I shall have to do the walking!" But in the end the aged hermit did not have to walk to Devil's Point, for in November Bishop Bernard managed to send Father Herman to care for the more than a hundred catechumens.

Relieved of these onerous journeys, Fra Jerome by April 1949 was feeling "much better," although he claimed it was from a strict observance of Lent rather than the lessening of duties. He admitted, however, that he still had "a more or less perpetual headache." And he was also "stony broke" because there had been so many calls on his charity, owing to a long drought which resulted in a food shortage on the island. He had banished the straw mattress in his narrow bunk, and found that a palm mat was sufficient to allow him to sleep "very well and comfortably. I often think how luxurious is my life compared with the poor prisoners and slaves behind the Iron Curtain."

How kind and devoted were the people of Cat Island to their hermit! Despite their poverty they brought him a steady stream of corn grits, potatoes, breadfruit and bananas; sometimes even a little money dribbled in from partial repayment of outstanding loans. This was enough to provide Fra Jerome with coffee beans, sugar and cooking fat. He had given up butter, cheese and tinned milk long ago. His spirits were high, too, since all was going well after the "corporate reunion" at Devil's Point. The ex-Baptists had already learned to sing the *Missa de Angelis.*

It was inevitable at his advanced age that Fra Jerome should begin to give serious consideration to the precise nature of eternity. The resurrection of the dead occupied his thoughts and he laid bare his ideas in several letters. For example, "Since we shall not be metamorphized into angels at the Resurrection but remain *Homo,* where would be the congruity of our souls being *joined* again to our bodies if those bodies do not bring in pleasure, the substance of bodily things? They are indeed no longer 'sensual' but changed and glorified bodies, but still *bodies*—recognizable by varying traits. As St. Augustine says, with all deficiencies corrected. Thus the over-fat St. Thomas Aquinas will be not too fat; the lean no longer too thin; the lame equalized; and the babe grown to man's stature.

"See our Blessed Lord Himself—the glorious constellation of five stars, those scars of five wounds in His hands, feet, and side, in His visible, tangible body. Mankind will there no longer marry nor be given in marriage in the union of souls. This union of souls will be perfected as one of the joys of Heaven—union of (souls of) husbands, wives, parents and children. All Heaven is one great marriage: that of all the redeemed—the mystical body, the spouse of the Lamb. In the Beatific Vision we shall gaze on God. God *is* Beauty —the All Beautiful. Art is Beauty, and Beauty *is* God. . . . So we shall find and enjoy in the Beatific Vision the essence of all the beauty of mountain scenery, of architecture, of sculpture and painting, and of music. Such will correspond to the yearnings of our *glorified human nature,* else *why* a resurrection *body?* Since human nature loves what God has made so lovely and dear in animal creation (a creation also reflecting His limitless beauty with infinite variety) there will be animals, e.g., horses and dogs, to fulfill the scope of our human nature in our risen bodies. Rejoicing in these things, we rejoice in God and in His beauty. There are many mansions, and some saints of a differing and more surpassing glory, who attained to God by pure abstract contemplation here below, will need nothing else in the Beatific Vision but the same pure contemplation. One star differeth from another in glory.

"St. Paul, St. John of the Cross, St. Teresa, and other high mystics will be looking at and satisfied with the pure essence of the Blessed Trinity in the Beatific Vision. You and I, and many other art and animal lovers, will rest (D.V.) in the same Beatific Vision, in the love of beauty, of God our Creator, but will see the same reflected in such humbler things as we understand and love of what God created in our *human* nature; for we are still *Homo* in Heaven—else why a resurrected *body?*

"My (resurrection) eyes will not be good enough to be able to ascend to live in a mansion which is pure essence of light and glory (perfect contemplation); but, rather, to bask in God's love and beauty in an architectural mansion of form, shape and measurement. And after all, the apocalyptic seer St. John and the Angel went up and down the heavenly city with a measuring rod. An orchestra played on *harps,* and others who preferred riding to music came forth (attending their king) *riding* on white *horses.* 'Without are dogs!' But those are the *bad* dogs. Holy Scripture has it worth while to recount how Tobias's dog wagged his tail and ran in front of the Angel, and ran forward joyously announcing their return home. And then there were the good dogs that charitably licked the sores of Lazarus (applying anti-toxin). Into some species of animals God puts such beauty of individual character. I think of my little fox terrier Dominie—such love, trust and faithfulness—one cannot but mourn the separation from and loss of such a one.

> "All which I took from thee, I did but take,
>   Not for thy harms,
> But just that thou might'st seek it in
>   My arms."

Then, without a break, Fra Jerome switched off from speculating on the after life and hurled himself into a discussion of a proposed baldachino or a reredos for St. Paul's Cathedral, London. Curiously enough, his letters seldom dealt with theology. This example suggests that he was becoming more conscious that his time on earth was nearing an end.

A month or two later, however, he could write that he was feeling wonderfully rejuvenated. Stimulated by the carving and painting of the altars in the crypt of St. Augustine's Monastery, every morning he donned his overalls, and worked hard most of the day. "It's just fascinating," he wrote. "God is very gracious to me that at my age I have enough strength left to do it. The more I work, the less I eat, but drink a lot of iced goat's milk, and plenty of Eno's Fruit Salt. 'Tell yer, I punish plenty!' as poor sick Bahamians exclaim, and I thank God for 'the thorn in my flesh' (hernia) that I may have some part with Christ in our suffering brethren behind the Iron Curtain who are ever in my thoughts and prayers. After supper I fall asleep sitting in my cell saying my Office, and don't get finished and in bed until usually eleven o'clock, and then up at 3 or 4 A.M. Alone in the dark chapel until the holy old contemplative lay Brother [Anselm] . . . joins me soon after four until the bell rings for the Angelus at five. Prime and Terce are at five-twenty, then Conventual Mass, then private Masses. I get the special grace of suffering most of all during my Mass. Often I can't genuflect and can hardly stand. Then I lie down for a quarter of an hour before break-fast at seven, and when I've had my coffee I'm a different man. When I've changed and work begins at eight on the church, I feel just like a young man of thirty!"

Certainly Fra Jerome's mind was as young and lively as it had ever been. His letters were filled with trenchant opinions on art, architecture, monasticism, liturgy, ceremonial and even politics and economics. His interests ranged the globe from Europe to Asia, Africa, Australia and back to America and the Bahamas. It was hard to believe that now, in 1949, he was seventy-four years old. Although he was de-prived of his solitude by his prolonged stay at Nassau he was contented and happy, "luxuriating in the monastery," as he put it.

He described the "grand Requiem (five absolutions) and funeral" of the Vicar Apostolic of the Bahamas. "Such a crowd that Mass had to be in the open air; thousands of people." He was delighted by the monastic community, so regular and fervent; by the food, "very wholesome and simple, with plenty of vegetables, goat's milk and honey, all from the monastery land." In the evening he liked to walk up and down the long upper cloister, enjoying the view of sea and green land spread out before him on one hand, or, on the other side of the cloister, a glimpse of a "silent, indus-trious monk sitting at his desk reading or writing."

"What happy creatures they are!" he wrote. "At recreation after supper they seem to me just like little children, so merry and laughing, and still plenty of elevating and cultured dis-cussion; and such a nice family spirit. . . . A visiting Bene-dictine from New York said this is the 'most monastic monas-tery' he had ever seen—nothing like it in the U.S.A. 'Inter-esting, austere and delightful,' so said another much-traveled abbot.

"It is a pleasure to me as the architect to see how really delighted they are with the building. One monk remarked the other day, 'I never thought it would be anything like this!' The Prior, Father Frederic Frey, is really an outstanding man, and to him is due the whole initiation and conception of the monastery, both spiritual and material; adding, of course, the wholehearted approval and financial backing given by Abbot Alcuin of St. John's Abbey, Minnesota.

"These monks are the most zealous and devoted apostles. Sometimes they nearly work themselves to death, what with sports, brass bands, and tearing about all the time in cars and on motor bicycles! They make lots of converts, and are most exemplary and assiduous in visiting the hospitals, prison camps and leper settlement. The colored people love them. 'Lift up your eyes: the harvest is ripe'—'Pray ye the Lord of the harvest to send forth more laborers'—'Feed my lambs, feed my sheep.' The religious orders must adapt themselves to the needs of the age we live in, and also be ready for persecution and confiscation of all their possessions. . . . But how I wander on!"

It was not often that Fra Jerome's letters contained references to his friends, apart from the Bahama Benedictines or his own island people, but on December 19, 1949, he wrote a long epistolary appreciation of Father Benedict Williamson whose death had occurred in Rome a year earlier. Father Williamson during World War I, in which he had been gassed and wounded, had been sought out as a confessor and had made many converts. Three of his earlier converts had become monastic priors, one of them the Carthusian prior of Parkminster. Fra Jerome always referred to Father Williamson as his spiritual director, but actually they met only three times between 1913 and 1939. Their relationship consisted in a constant exchange of letters and an admiration of each other's character and architectural work.

Summing up Father Williamson's career, Fra Jerome said, "Here was a man who had given himself absolutely to God. He lived in another world and to him were shown things hidden from lesser souls. A man utterly impervious to the world and unconscious of ridicule. His works live after him."

An avalanche of unwelcome publicity now began to descend upon Fra Jerome. During the summer of 1949 *Collier's* magazine had sent Bill Davidson, one of its writers, to the Bahamas to prepare an illustrated article on the "Hermit of Cat Island." Fra Jerome, innocent of the interviewing techniques of professional journalists, proved to be spectacularly good "copy," and made no objections to being photographed in color in several picturesque poses. The old hermit was horrified when a copy of the magazine reached him, and bitterly regretted his folly in talking so freely to Davidson.

Fra Jerome explained that "all his information he just wormed out of me in affable conversation—he just *mesmerized* me! He got me talking on this or that experience of my past life; and an old man loves to go over the memories of his past just for the fun of remembering it, and will talk it all out (led on by judicious queries) quite oblivious of the fact that 'everything you say will be used in evidence against you.'

"Then he had heard from someone of *Soliloquies of a Solitary* and he referred to that as 'Father Jerome's published Diary.' In the hermitage he scanned through a Ms. scrapbook in my little shelf and found a memorandum of dates and places in my life. Then he interviewed the Cat Island Bight commissioner for two hours one evening, and culled legends of an African and Obeah nature from the talk of his 'native' escort. 'Highly detailed,' you say; but 'accurate' biography? There is certainly nothing omitted that vivid journalistic imagination and artistic license could supply to make good reading for *Collier's*. But Bill is a charming fellow, and I wrote to him: '*I forgive you!*' with a little sketch of a cat and kittens playing under a palm tree on an islet with hermitage atop. . . . ''

After the publication of this article in July 1950, the hermit was never left in peace. *The Catholic Digest* reprinted the *Collier's* story, publishers besieged him for an autobiography or biography, authors offered their services and proposed financial terms, "fan mail" poured in. Distracted and annoyed, Fra Jerome wrote, "Oh, why, oh, *why* did I foolishly babble out so freely to Bill Davidson? Yet natural kindliness and courtesy could not brutally turn down a man who had traveled all that distance, at such expense, to get to Nassau and Cat Island from New York. The Fathers tell me some people say that Fra Jerome must have got a big check from *Collier's* for that article! Yes—sleepless nights and a string of annoying 'fan letters,' many of them from scheming phonies begging, gathering from *Collier's* that Fra Jerome must be a philanthropic millionaire and a perfect mug."

All this unwanted publicity worried him terribly. When he wrote *Soliloquies of a Solitary* he did so first under the safeguard and protection of anonymity, not minding very much what he said in print. These articles, when they appeared in *Pax,* were addressed primarily to those few souls who are "fed up" with so-called modernity and progress and seek after real solitude. But after their republication in the Capuchin Annual, the identity of the author was revealed, and he realized too late that the general public did not want to read about the eremitical life; it wanted only an imaginative fairy tale "smeared in high lights about some 'wonderful worldwide *curiosity*,' " as the miserable author remarked to a friend. After 1950 it is not untrue to say that Fra Jerome almost regretted that he had ever built that romantic hermitage on the highest hill in the Bahamas, much as he loved it. Instead of enabling him to lead a solitary and hidden life, it had brought him right into the full glare of the limelight. He found himself a "star," and regarded as a public entertainer!

"I've lived too long!" Fra Jerome realized that he did not belong to the "brave new world" which had arisen after World War II. About the only thing left that he still enjoyed was architecture, his first love. He seems, however, to have found time for a considerable amount of reading, in spite of failing eyesight. His comments on new books were pointed and critical.

For instance, Père Regamey's treatise, *Poverty,* was dismissed as "an insult to Franciscans and our holy founder. . . . I become more and more impatient with this modernistic world of cranks! Nowadays some people will compass heaven and earth to have Mass in a bedroom on a scullery table when there is a proper church only three minutes' walk down the street. The next thing we shall hear of is a vernacular dialogue Mass in Notre Dame, Paris, celebrated by a 'guy' sitting at a little three-legged table in front of the high altar (that being too 'bourgeois' to use!) dressed in a warm bell-shaped paenula only over his blue jeans; and the 'workmen' congregation (mostly?)—how many of them are but fervent student Catholic Actionists? But I *do* admire the work of those Paris Benedictines out in a communist suburb. I've forgotten their name, but they wear their habit and say their Office in church and have converted most of the Communists in the parish.

"Thank God! I see *Liturgical Arts* no longer. It's not worth the present rate of dollar exchange for the purpose of receiving sickening illustrations of steel and reinforced workshops and factories masquerading as churches. As to those headless trunks and ruptured intestines daubed on the wall or hacked out of stone—Painting? Sculpture? Art?—Tripe and onions!"

This letter was accompanied by some particularly malicious caricatures of contemporary church architecture.

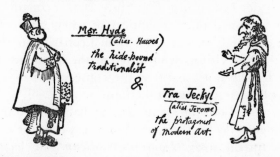

Solitude, now that it had become so hard to capture, was more dear to the hermit than ever. On his periodic visits to the Nassau Benedictines he could admit that he enjoyed the "roomy cell, comfortable bed, water and electric light," but such externals only helped to convince him of his Franciscan vocation. He wrote, "The *Opus Dei* is all right for Benedictines and very edifying to outsiders, but on feast days and many solemn Offices and Masses for the dead, when it is stentoriously chanted with rhythmic roar, it gets on my nerves. I don't mind a little of it, but not too much. And the more perfect it is, according to the up-to-date, most approved Solesmes method of plain chant, the more it irks me, with its up and down twenty to thirty notes on one syllable, as in the introits, graduals, tracts, offertories and alleluias—a-a-a-a- Aa Aa Aa, aaa, ad infinitum! More *acrobatics* than in a soprano's warbling of any of the florid operatic Masses! Give me the jolly old hearty (and I suppose incorrect) Mechlin or Ratisbon chant!"

It was a great joy to Fra Jerome when Dom Paul Leonard Hagarty, O.S.B., was appointed to succeed Bishop Bernard as Vicar Apostolic of the Bahamas on June 25, 1950. The new Bishop, whom Fra Jerome described as "a most lovable man and the most popular priest among the natives," had been working in the Bahamas since 1937. The aged hermit had been devoted to him ever since Dom Leonard had cut open and cleaned out his septic foot when giving his first mission on Cat Island in 1940. Dom Leonard had also been one of the first visitors who stayed at the hermitage. So Fra Jerome felt he must assist at the consecration ceremonies, much as he detested such functions.

He described how he sat in his gray habit in a retired corner among the lay Brothers, and how every time the Apostolic Delegate turned to say *"Dominus vobiscum"* an electric flash bulb caught him blinking! There were two other archbishops, six bishops, five abbots, four masters of ceremonies and monsignori "like the sands of the sea"; but Monsignor John Cyril Hawes was thankful that moths had long since eaten his purple robes, and thus he was able to hide himself. "I looked back and sighed for the good old days," he wrote, "when it was strictly forbidden even to photograph an empty church interior if the Blessed Sacrament was in the tabernacle. But Yankees love publicity and advertising, including the clergy, and an American archbishop will stop in the middle of a procession, grin and pose for any photographer there!"

More and more did the old hermit find it difficult to understand the world in which he was forced to linger—it was so different from that of the days of his youth. There were moments now when even the observances of the good and kind Benedictine monks at Nassau puzzled him. Yet what fine and utterly devoted mission priests they were, he stressed again and again, even if he regretted that they did not go about in their habits and were usually disguised as clergymen, tearing around on motor bicycles or driving automobiles! Poor Fra Jerome wished he could get back to the thirteenth century and forget all the inventions of the twentieth century. He felt like a square peg in a round hole.

His publicity had brought him at least half-a-dozen correspondents who begged to be allowed to come and lead an eremitical life on Cat Island under Fra Jerome's direction, but he managed to "choke them off," saying: "I could not run a community, however small, even of hermits, and I am not called to do so. How could I dictate to other people how to live? I am more and more alone now, my daily prayer is 'Give us to see Thy Will and power to walk in its path,' striving after more interior detachment, expiation and penance like a Cistercian or Carthusian." Fra Jerome insisted that "proper hermits" do not found orders or communities.

He admitted that he could never have endured the Carthusian life because of the terribly long-drawn-out Office, with the added burden of the Little Office of Our Lady, the Office for the Dead, and the "extra *dry* Mass" every morning. He had always been more attracted to the Camaldolesi hermit-monks, who do not add on extra Offices, but who spend much time in silent mental prayer. He felt that people ought to realize that a *hermit* is not the same thing as an *anchorite*. In the Middle Ages most hermits, although living alone, *"had jobs*—looking after lighthouses, bridges, chapels, leper houses, hospitals, even schools. Richard Rolle went in and out of the people's houses. Only the anchorites (when walled in) were *ipso facto* solitaries, and their anchorage always had a window where the people (often of their own town or village) came to pour out their troubles. The sorrows of the world must have sorrowed the anchorites, however much their inmost soul was fixed in union with God. The very early solitaries of the Egyptian desert were the only real hermit crabs! I don't see that the missionary and solitary elements of my poor character war with each other, any more so than in the Celtic, Anglo-Saxon and medieval hermits (*not* anchorites) who loved plenty of cold-water baths, long walking pilgrimages, and yet lived in close contact with the people. 'Surely He hath borne our afflictions,' and the medieval hermit was close to Him, in taking to heart the afflictions of the people even more intimately and sensitively than any Trappist monk."

It pleased Fra Jerome to discover that Thomas Merton in *The Seven Storey Mountain* and *The Waters of Siloe* "fights all the time to show that the mortification and isolation (contemplation) of the Cistercians and other 'purely contemplative' orders is *for* the salvation of souls. . . . Real love of God can find its expression only in the salvation of other souls— in mission work or propitiation. *God calls* chosen souls apart into the desert; and some of these solitary souls *He sends out again* into the haunts of men."

By 1952 the old hermit had to struggle hard against interior temptations, which he revealed in letters to his more intimate friends. A vigorous young Benedictine priest was sent to Cat Island whose ideas of mission work differed strongly from those of Fra Jerome, and who made many changes.

There were complaints, and Fra Jerome tried to pour oil on the troubled waters and to rally the people to their new pastor, trying hard not to interfere in any way and to do nothing without being asked. He wrote, "I am sure that God lets all this come to teach me detachment, and to purge me of pride, self-satisfaction and self-preoccupation. I try not to brood and grumble. No doubt, if I could only see it so, God is leading this priest to do things in a much better and more efficient way than I could ever have done."

On March 5, 1953, he was feeling depressed with everything and almost everybody. "I suppose that a hermit even more than a monk is an outmoded anachronism even to many Catholics, and that *I* am still quite wrong, even in my architecture." This mood persisted, and on September 7 he wrote, "Today is my seventy-seventh birthday—seven years too long beyond the allotted span. I'm getting more and more 'stripped' of everything, and detached. Even architecture interests me very little now. I sleep very badly and have fearful nights. The new mission priest is away in the U.S.A. on a three months' vacation, and no help has been sent me except *one* visit of another priest to the outlying southern stations. So all the burden is on my shoulders. Yesterday at dawn I started for Sunday Mass and slipped on the wet rock and fell down twice on my back on the way down the hill. If there is any bad behavior or laughter in church I miss seeing or hearing it. I can't intone anything or make myself heard."

It was not quite true when Fra Jerome said that even architecture interested him very little now. He expressed at this time some very strong opinions about the new Catholic cathedral at Liverpool, doubting if it would ever be built. He made two sketches showing his ideas of a simple and far less costly reinforced concrete cathedral, which could be completed in a few years, saying that Lutyens' designs, in these days, were "quite impracticable."

A few months later he wrote, "I *look* well (so everybody tells me), sunburned, but I am full of infirmities—weak and dizzy. I have no taste, no smell, and hardly any voice, only a croaking, hoarse whisper with great effort. Three hours' sleep at night is my best. St. Teresa of Avila in her old age complained of noises and weaknesses in the head, and of the continuous roaring like waves of the sea in her ears. I have just the same, a continual buzzing and hissing sound. God goes on stripping me of everything. I am in the dark night of the senses. My constant prayer is to have unreserved surrender and conformity to His holy will."

Like many another old man Fra Jerome was living more in the past than in the present; spending long hours dozing or dreaming of his boyhood, youth and early manhood. He jotted down reminiscences that were still fresh in his mind.

"In earlier years I once felt that I could make a readable

book on 'Places where I have slept'—not meaning such respectable spots as my baby cot, a back form in the school classroom, a high-paneled box pew in an old-fashioned Protestant church, an armchair in the front row of a convent college concert during a recitation, or even a straight-backed seat during a midday meditation delivered at a priests' retreat. No—I was thinking of myself as a barefooted tramp under a haystack in the English countryside, or in a ditch under a hawthorn hedge in the open fields. Under an overturned railway trolley with a hostile dog of large dimensions sniffing and growling outside. In a farmer's barn entered stealthily after dark. In a twopenny 'doss house' of a town slum. In the jail-like cell of an old-style British 'workhouse.' In a cold North Sea breeze, a coil of rope for my pillow, on the deck of a coastal tramp steamer. Under the tropical stars below the flapping sails of a trading schooner. In a tool shed amidst the graves of the dead in an untidy churchyard. Below decks in a stuffy six-berthed cabin of an emigrant ship, where the rats and mice ran over us. In one of the shelflike tiers of bunks of a Salvation Army shelter in Montreal. In a cattle van on a Canadian freight train, reposing in the hayrack just above the horned heads of the animals. As a tired-out mule driver in a tent beside a rushing mountain torrent in a Canadian railroad construction camp. In a snow-covered settler's log cabin beside the rail track high up over the Great Divide into British Columbia.

"In such places it was rather where I did *not* sleep but shivered through the long night watches till dawn. I have sat out the night with intermittent dozing, stiff and cramped, in the corner of a third-class carriage in Spain, crowded with peasantry getting in and out at every little station, but feasting my eyes in the morning on the Alhambra of Granada. One night I spent with the mosquitoes, trying to sleep on a stone bench against the wall of Our Lady's pilgrimage chapel on the height overlooking Matanzas in Cuba. A succession of five weary nights I endured on the heaving bare boards in the hold of a West Indian trading sloop, the bilge water gushing through the seams of the inner lining boards at every lurch and plunge, with swarms of cockroaches scuttling to and fro.

"While I was a sub-deacon I slept once in a quaintly perched little room over a transept of an Italian mountain church; it was wedged in between the vaulting and the outer tiled roof, and reached by walking along the giddy top of a cornice inside the church, crossing the end wall of the transept. The window opened on to a little balcony from whence you gazed down on a sheer drop of hundreds of feet on to the treetops of a pine-clad ravine.

"Of places where I have slept I could count up many happy recollections of Western Australia. As a 'bushwhacker' priest, with a parish of 40,000 square miles, how often have I camped the night out under the moonbeams or the brilliant stars. One must scoop a little hollow in the ground for one's hip-bone, and then lying down beside the red embers of the campfire, with saddle for pillow, one can restfully study the wonderful constellations in the clear heavens above. A soft, warm breeze wafts aft the healthful scent of eucalyptus from the gum trees, and the tinkle of the horse's back bell, as hobbled he feeds contentedly in the long grass and wild flowers, affords a comforting sense of companionship.

"And once on a pitch-black night lit up by blinding flashes and with peals of thunder, in a deluge of rain I crouched under the belly of my tall seventeen-hands saddle horse, standing against the roofless mud-brick walls of a lonely old bush hostelry, known as 'Shadow of Death.' A change of scene to a bed, improvised on bags of cement within the rising stone walls of a new church, to be awakened abruptly from solid slumber by a fight between my dog and the carpenter's. Not to speak of nights broken by sick calls necessitating a motorcar drive of sixty miles or more, carrying the Blessed Sacrament and holy oils, with many bumps and shakings, along those deeply rutted tracks. I call to mind a night spent in my stable, nursing a deadly sick foal, a prize thoroughbred who made a wonderful recovery from tetanus and grew up to achieve some honor on the race track and to become an outstanding stallion.

"Then there was another sleepless night when 'Florinda' had a litter of six pups in my bedroom at the priest's house, at 12.30 A.M. on a Sunday morning—and to choose a Sunday of all days! In railroad journeys, between the four little 'bush towns' of my Australian parish, many a night I have traveled sleeping on the floor boards in the swaying, rattling guard's van of a stock train; getting home earlier this way than waiting for the daytime slower passenger express. Well! Here I must put on the grinding brakes for a station."

These were the things Fra Jerome recalled as he lay on his palm mat, more often than not unable to sleep and often racked with pain. Few laymen, and even fewer priests, could look back on such a strange and varied past as that which filled the recollections of the Hermit of Cat Island.

14.

The Last Journey [1954–1956]

DURING July of 1954, Fra Jerome's last year on his Cat Island hilltop, Maurice Lavanoux, Secretary of the Liturgical Arts Society, flew to the Bahamas and climbed the narrow path to Mount Alvernia—"the last word in roughing it for a city man"—to visit the old hermit. These two men, both so enthusiastic about Christian art but seeing it from different angles, had often fought on paper, yet for an hour or two past battles were forgotten. This is how Mr. Lavanoux recorded his impressions:

"As we came near the top of the hill, there was Fra Jerome standing near the little tower of his stone hermitage. I had seen the fine color photograph illustrating Bill Davidson's article in *Collier's* . . . but on first meeting Fra Jerome in the flesh, a flood of memories crowded on me and I could not say much. We often hear of completely dedicated persons whose life of devotion to the will of God and to the precepts of holy poverty is an uncomfortable reminder of our own daily indifference, but then our modern mind goes back to the days of St. Francis of Assisi to St. Benedict. We complacently isolate such thoughts in that shadowy past and unconsciously forget them. The life of a hermit today is difficult for many

267

of us to understand. In Fra Jerome's case we have a hermit whose life has been a productive one."

The immediate result of Mr. Lavanoux's visit to the Bahamas was the inclusion of some very appreciative remarks about Fra Jerome's architecture, carving and painting in the following issue of *Liturgical Arts,* some of which already have been quoted. But the seventy-eight-year-old hermit was too weary now to entertain distinguished visitors even when they shared his interests.

By November Fra Jerome confessed that his hand was so unsteady that it was difficult for him to hold a pen, and said, "When a man has become a useless encumbrance it is futile to prolong old age by making all sorts of efforts. God works in different people in so many different and opposite ways. One must be content to look upon one's missionary work as a failure. I accept all that He sends. I criticize (still less condemn) nothing. When I built this hermitage I thought nothing of the rough steps to climb. *Now* all is different, and it has become a most awkward and dangerous place—a real prison. Even the very Bahamas, which I once thought a 'Paradise,' I now regard as most unpleasant, what with the hurricanes, storms, winds, extreme heat and cold, insects, impenetrable bush, thunder and lightning. I suffer from nervous breakdown—'the jitterbugs'—and a sort of St. Vitus's dance. I cannot lie down or sit still. I am all jerks! Usually I have three bad nights, sometimes no sleep at all, followed by one good night. During the day I have a perpetual headache and feel ever so tired.

"In September one night I fell down in the kitchen and caught my head against the rough stone jamb of a doorway, badly cutting and bruising the top of my cranium, the blood streaming down my face, but I felt no pain; it bled for ten hours. I lay down on the bed. I could not say Mass that morning. Not a soul came near the place, so after three days I stumbled down the hill to seek some help. I was hauled and pushed home, and then I did not leave the hermitage for eight weeks. . . . I long to put off this tabernacle and to cry 'Welcome! Sister Death,' but I have to tarry till she comes. *Fiat Voluntas Tua* in universal surrender and conformity to God's will. The kind Bishop heard of my accident and begged me to stay at Nassau. But I want to be alone, and left *quiet* here in the hermitage."

In a letter dated February 7, 1955, he admitted that he might be an "obstinate old man," but that he was determined to remain on by himself, maintaining that his vocation was that of a hermit and that he could not face the idea of living in a monastery and having everything done for him. He had some consolation in the appointment of a good new priest at Cat Island, Father Nicholas Kremer, O.S.B. He felt so tired that it was difficult even to say the rosary without falling asleep. The Bishop had sent him vitamin pills, but in spite of everything he often found it impossible to stand or walk straight. The writing in pencil had become a scrawl and difficult to decipher. But he could still draw a rough Franciscan *tau* cross, and around it the words: *"Deus meus et omnia."*

The hermit was now in his eightieth year. Reports of his rapidly failing health alarmed Bishop Leonard, who eventually insisted that Fra Jerome must go to Nassau, where he could be cared for by the monks. After a few weeks in the monastery he moved to the Bishop's house, but he did not remain there for long. His condition became worse and there was nothing to do except care for him in the infirmary of St. Augustine's Monastery. In the late autumn of 1955 a typed letter was sent to several of his friends, to which he scrawled his signature. He said: "I am unable to write or to do any sort of mission work or to dispense any charities because I am a very sick man. So please do not write to me any more. I suffer from all the weakness and infirmities of old age. I am very giddy and can scarcely walk at all. My memory fails me and I have lost my voice. I can only offer my infirmities in union with Our Lord's watching in Gethsemane. His holy will be done in all things. I pray for you and for all those who have commended themselves to my prayers. Let us all practice penance and pray for a sick world. God bless you and yours."

Now he knew that the end was not far off, even if Sister Death lingered on her way. He wanted her to come boldly, for like the Little Poor Man he knew that she was the gate of life. Maybe, just as Francis sent for his beloved disciples Leo and Angelo and said to them, "Sing to me; sing to me my song of the creatures," Fra Jerome may have wished to ask some of the monks to do the same for him. No matter—there can be little doubt that as he lay in bed in the monastery at Nassau he remembered that new verse of the Canticle of the Sun, composed by Francis as he lay sick in the bishop's palace at Assisi.

> Be praised, my Lord, for Sister Death,
> From whom no man living can escape,
> Alas for those who die in mortal sin,
> But happy they who find themselves within Thy will,
> On them the second death can work no harm.

On March 28, 1956, the hermit sent out a similar typed letter containing further details. He had now lost all sense of taste and remarked that this was "a good safeguard against gluttony," and that "onions taste just like carrots; cheese is like soap or sawdust." So, unlike St. Francis, who asked the Lady Giacoma to bring him some marzipan when he lay dying in the isolated cell beside the chapel of the Portiuncula near Assisi, Fra Jerome would not have been able to taste candy if any rich lady of Nassau had visited him in the monastic infirmary. He could hear a little with one ear, but even with glasses could hardly read at all. His constant prayer was that he would be able to return to his beloved hermitage. In literal imitation of the Little Poor Man, he wanted to be laid upon the bare ground and there to die. However, the state of his health, both physical and mental, made this impossible.

What happened during the last two months of his life was recorded by the Prior of St. Augustine's Monastery, the Very Reverend Frederic Frey, who was in close touch with Fra Jerome during this time.

"On the evening of April 19, 1956, he sustained a broken femur as the result of a fall in his room. Due to excessive pain he was taken to the local hospital for care and treatment but the X ray indicated that the break was of such a kind that he could not be treated at Nassau and required attention in the United States. At the doctor's suggestion he was flown the following day to St. Francis Hospital, Miami Beach, Florida. He consented to this very reluctantly and only when we told him that he would be in the care of Franciscan Sisters and a Franciscan priest at the hospital. On his arrival at the hospital it was discovered that he had contracted pneumonia. This delayed for one week the surgical treatment of the broken femur.

"I might add as a side remark that the doctors and nurses at first had great difficulty in understanding Fra Jerome's eremitical mode of life, especially as regards his abstinence in food. But they developed a great attachment to him during his weeks with them as the result of his extraordinary degree of patience and humility which he showed at all times. His cheerfulness captivated them. I mention this as I was with him for almost three weeks on his arrival and again during his last two days.

"His recovery after surgery had been performed was quite normal. At the time the doctors were treating him for several of his infirmities. He had progressed so well that on the morning of June 23 the Sisters at the hospital wrote that Fra Jerome was well enough to be taken back to the monastery. That same afternoon he suddenly had a relapse, in all probability owing to the extreme heat and humidity. His breathing became very labored and he was immediately put into an oxygen tent. However, the congestion which had developed in his lungs and throat weakened him extremely, and we were notified that he had been anointed that evening, and that I should come to him. This I did at the first opportunity on the following morning. On my arrival I found that he was still very weak and unable to speak but apparently not in pain. He was most cheerful and greeted me with a big smile. He made an effort to talk but was unable to do so. He was perfectly contented and willing to answer the summons of his Master. These three last days were days of prayer and resignation to the will of God, and he quietly breathed forth his soul at 2.07 A.M. on June 26."

In one of his notebooks Fra Jerome had left the following instructions:

"In the event of my death please notify the Bishop, The Priory, Nassau. Please bury me *immediately* in the *Burial Crypt* (little cave) just below the chapel. (This presupposes that I'm not drowned at sea and disposed of by a shark.)

"NO COFFIN or *wooden shell*.

"Place the body clothed in the Franciscan habit and rope girdle, barefooted; no flowers. Place it lying flat (on back) on the bare rock at the extreme east end of the cave with feet toward the east and arms outstretched in the form of a cross. Then wall up the low arch of natural rock at A.B. with stones and some lime mortar.

"*J. C. Hawes*
Fra Jerome"

In accordance with these instructions the hermit's body was taken by boat to Nassau where it arrived on the afternoon of June 28. The following morning the Office for the Dead was chanted in the cathedral by Bishop Paul Leonard Hagarty, the monks and the clergy; then the Bishop sang the pontifical Requiem Mass. Fra Jerome's body was flown to Cat Island, where it was placed in the cave on Mount Alvernia, just as he had always desired. The Hermit of Cat Island had at last found the solitude for which so many years he had struggled in vain.

LAST WILL & TESTAMENT OF

Joannes Cyrillus Hawes, Sacerdos
Antistites Urbanus idest Praelatus Papae Domesticus

Feast of Our Lady of the Angels
(Portiuncula)

I BROTHER JEROME of the Third Order of Saint Francis, hermit, die in the Faith of the One True Holy Catholic and Apostolic Roman Church of Our Lord Jesus Christ. I commend my soul to God, to Our Blessed Lady, to my Holy Father Saint Francis and to the charitable prayers of my friends and especially of my brother priests. I have left no legally attested will, because there is no need of one: In loving response to the call and counsel of my dear Lord and Saviour Jesus Christ I have already disposed of such earthly goods as I had, and given to the poor. I carry on by a small yearly annuity which I cannot alienate and which expires with my death; and until then, of the said annuity I pray I may be found a faithful steward to share it with Christ's poor in my neighbors here.

The Hermitage of Mount Alvernia, together with the eight acres of land surrounding it, is not my property: after purchase of the land in 1940 (February) I legally transferred it, with everything at any time thereon, to "The Roman Catholic Prefect [now "Vicar"] Apostolic of the Bahamas." I have nothing else to leave and thank God that I die a poor man.

This is my hand and seal
Brother Jerome
John C. Hawes   [SEAL]
2 August 1942

Witness
       My Guardian Angel   [SEAL]
Witness
       Blessed Bernard of Quintavalle (Assisi)   [SEAL]

Signed, sealed and delivered at the Hermitage, Mount Alvernia, The Bight, Cat Island, Bahamas.

THE LITANY OF THE HERMITS

*Drawn up by Fra Jerome and
recited by him every night*

St. Mary, Queen of Hermits, pray for us
St. Mary of Mount Carmel . . .
All ye holy hermits and solitaries . . .
St. John the Baptist, "Prince of Hermits" . . .
St. Mary Magdalene . . .
St. Paul the first hermit . . .
St. Anthony . . .
St. Mary of Egypt . . .
St. Jerome . . .
St. Martin . . .
St. Romuald . . .
St. Celestine . . .
Holy Father St. Francis . . .
All ye holy Franciscan hermits and solitaries . . .
Brother John of Alvernia . . .
Brother Giles . . .
St. Clare . . .
Bl. John of Parma . . .
Bl. Paolo Giustiniano . . .
St. Bruno . . .
St. Benedict Joseph Labre . . .
St. Cuthbert . . .
St. Godric of Finchale . . .
St. Neot . . .
St. Roman . . .
St. Guthlac of Crowland . . .
St. Petroc . . .
Bl. Richard Rolle . . .
Bl. Juliana of Norwich . . .
Bl. Charles de Foucauld . . .
Holy Hermits of Tintagel . . .

Appendix

BUILDINGS DESIGNED BY JOHN C. HAWES

1897–1908

Bognor, Sussex: The White Tower and three other seaside cottages

Gunnerton, Northumberland: St. Christopher's Church

Painsthorpe Abbey, Yorkshire: Chapel for Anglican Benedictines

Alton Abbey, Hampshire: Gatehouse, and church,* for Order of St. Paul

Coltishall, Norfolk: Billiard room and additions to The Grove

Caldey Island, South Wales: Monastic guesthouse; restorations of medieval priory church, village church and round tower oratory; "gatehouse" monastery*; and new abbey and church* (for Anglican Benedictine monks)

Saltley, Birmingham: Alteration and refurnishing of three churches

1908–1911

Bahama Islands, B.W.I. Four Anglican churches on Long Island; (Nassau) baldachino in St. Matthew's, and Holy Souls' Chapel in St. Mary's

Graymoor, Garrison, New York (1911): St. Francis' Chapel

Surrey, Sutton, England: New chancel, Our Lady of the Rosary Church

1915–1939

Geraldton, Western Australia: Cathedral; St. Lawrence Church, Bluff Point; cemetery chapel; Nazareth House; St. John of God Convent; Christian Brothers' school; "The Hermitage."

Churches: *Mullewa, Perenjori, Morawa, Northampton, Carnarvon, Nanson, Willina, Three Springs.* Convents: *Yalgoo, Tar-*

¹ Those designs marked (*) were not executed.

276

dun, Nanson. Christian Brothers farm school, *Tardun;* P.S.M.
Monastery, *Tardun;* priest's house, *Mullewa*
Ballarat: New cathedral * and two churches *
Perth: New cathedral *
Melbourne: Chapel for diocesan seminary *
New Norcia: Abbey church *
Costa Rica: Additions to sanctuary and chapels of church at
Port Limón

1940–1956
Cat Island: (1940–1) Hermitage and Chapel of the Holy Spirit,
Mount Alvernia; (1941–7) Holy Redeemer, *Freetown;* (1942)
Our Lady of Sion, *Port Howe;* (1943) St. John the Baptist,
Bain Town; (1945) St. Francis of Assisi, *Old Bight*
Long Island: (1947) Sts. Peter and Paul, *Clarence Town;* (1946)
Dunmore
New Providence Island: (1946) St. Augustine's College, Fox
Hill, *Nassau* (enlarged by R. V. McCann, 1953–4); St. Augus-
tine's Monastery, Fox Hill, *Nassau* (first unit, 1947; crypt and
foundation of church, 1949–50) ; (1948–9) convent and chapel
of Blessed Martin de Porres, *Nassau;* new cathedral,* *Nassau*
Bimini Islands: Holy Name
Rhode Island, U.S.A.: Cistercian Abbey of Our Lady of the Val-
ley, designs for guest house and enlargement of church *

Index